PRINCESSES
ON THE WARDS

PRINCESSES
ON THE WARDS

ROYAL WOMEN IN
NURSING THROUGH
WARS AND REVOLUTIONS

CORYNE HALL

To the memory of my parents, Peggy and Ernie Bawcombe.

First published 2014

The History Press
The Mill, Brimscombe Port
Stroud, Gloucestershire, GL5 2QG
www.thehistorypress.co.uk

© Coryne Hall, 2014

The right of Coryne Hall to be identified as the Author
of this work has been asserted in accordance with the
Copyright, Designs and Patents Act 1988.

British Library Cataloguing in Publication Data.
A catalogue record for this book is available from the British Library.

ISBN 978 0 7524 8859 2

Typeset in Bembo 11/13 pt by Thomas Bohm, User design
Printed in Great Britain

Contents

Acknowledgements

I would like to acknowledge the permission of Her Majesty Queen Elizabeth II to quote from material in the Royal Archives at Windsor; and the permission of His Royal Highness The Duke of Edinburgh to quote from published letters of Princess Alice (Princess Andrew of Greece) of which he owns the copyright. My thanks also to Pamela Clark, Laura Hobbs and the staff of the Royal Archives, and Dame Anne Griffiths DCVO, archivist to His Royal Highness The Duke of Edinburgh, for their invaluable assistance.

The original idea for a book about royal women and nursing came from Robin Piguet, who some years ago suggested it as a feature for *Majesty* magazine. So my thanks go to Robin, and also to Joe Little, managing editor of *Majesty*, for encouraging me to expand the original article into a book.

I am immensely grateful to Doña Beatriz de Orleans-Borbón, granddaughter of Infanta Beatrice, who provided information about her grandmother's work and permitted use of photographs from the Archivo Orleans-Borbón, Fundación Infantes Duques de Montpensier. In this respect a very big thank you must go to Ricardo Mateos Sainz de Medrano, who not only provided me with material, but read and commented on the chapter about Queen Ena and her cousin Infanta Beatrice. Any mistakes, of course, remain my own.

Countess Mountbatten of Burma and Lady Brabourne kindly granted access to the Broadlands Archives and Sandy McGuire made us most welcome. The family of the late Princess Margarita of Baden permitted use of her photograph; Archduke Dominic provided a picture of his mother Princess Ileana of Romania; and Her Royal Highness Princess Marie-Astrid of Luxembourg, Archduchess Carl Christian of Austria, allowed me to use her photograph. I am grateful to them all.

A big thank you also goes to Arturo Beéche of Eurohistory for providing images from the vast eurohistory.com royal photo archive.

A large number of friends have lent me their books and photographs, copied research material, identified pictures, translated text and been ready with useful suggestions. I am also grateful to all the archivists who granted me access to their collections. To everyone listed below I therefore extend my thanks. Your help was really appreciated, and without it the book would have been all the poorer.

In Britain: Janet Ashton; Robert Baker, archives officer of Blind Veterans UK (formerly St Dunstan's); Nicholas Baldwin, archivist at Great Ormond Street Hospital; Harold Brown; Sarah Cox, museum and archives assistant of the British Red Cross; Richard Davies, archivist at Leeds Russian Archive; Nicola Dyke at the Pump Room Museum, Harrogate; Stewart Gillies at The British Newspaper Library Colindale; His Royal Highness The Duke of Kent; His Royal Highness Prince Michael of Kent; Ann Kent at Tyne & Wear Archives; Sue Light of the Scarletfinders website; Diana Manipud and Lianne Smith at King's College London Archives; Marion Roberts and the staff of Bordon Library; Karen Robson and the staff of the Hartley Library, University of Southampton; Ian Shapiro; John Van der Kiste; Hugo Vickers; Katrina Warne; John Wimbles; Stella Wiseman; Sue Woolmans; Marion Wynn; Charlotte Zeepvat.

In Belgium: Olivier Defrance; Professor Dr Gustaaf Janssens, director of The Royal Archives, Brussels; Christophe Vachaudez; Professor Robert Van Hee, M.D., PhD., emeritus professor of surgical and medical history at the University of Antwerp.

In Brazil: Alberto Penna Rodrigues.

In Denmark: Jesper Lillelund at The Royal Danish Arsenal Museum, Copenhagen; Stig Nielsen.

In Germany: Florien Heitzmann at the Press Office, Insel Mainau; Gunna Wendt.

In Italy: Luciano Regolo.

In Luxembourg: Pierre Bley, Maréchal de la Cour; Josette Neiertz-Mehling; Liviana Pannacci of the Archives Grand-Ducales, Berg.

In the Netherlands: Mrs H.G. Eerkes, Private Secretary to Her Royal Highness Princess Margriet of the Netherlands and Professor Pieter van Vollenhoven; Netty Leistra; Marianne Teerink-Kouwenhoven.

In Russia: Galina Korneva; Yuri Shelayev of Liki Rossii publishers, St Petersburg.

In Spain: Don Miguel Ruiz Cabrera at Archivo General de Palacio, Palacio Real, Madrid; Don Javier Gonzáles de Vega.

In Sweden: Ted Rosvall, of Rosvall Royal Books.

In Switzerland: Her Royal Highness Princess Marie-Gabrielle of Savoy; Karen Roth-Nicholls.

In the United States of America: Mark Andersen; Marlene Eilers Koenig; Mary Ann Fogarty; Professor Joseph T. Fuhrmann; Griffith Henniger III; Dr William Lee; Ilana D. Miller.

My thanks also go to everyone at The History Press, particularly my commissioning editor Lindsey Smith for having faith in the project from the beginning, and Mark Beynon and Lauren Newby who saw it through to completion.

Every effort has been made to trace all copyright holders. We will be happy to correct any errors and make suitable acknowledgement in a future edition.

Last, but by no means least, thanks to my husband Colin, who never expected someone as squeamish as me to write a book about nurses. He helped with the research, kept things running smoothly while I was busy on the computer and read numerous drafts of the text. Without his constant support and encouragement the book would never have been possible.

Introduction

Royal ladies have always aided the sick. In 1148, Queen Matilda founded the Royal Hospital and Collegiate Church of St Katharine by the Tower and reserved the choice of master to all the queens of England who would follow her. Since then, royal women have patronised, endowed and founded – but their place was certainly not caring for the sick and wounded in a hospital ward. In peacetime it was not considered appropriate for them to nurse. However, war was instrumental in changing that perspective.

As the men flocked to war, European queens and princesses wanted to 'do their bit' for their country. Towards the end of the nineteenth century, as conflicts broke out all over the continent, they volunteered as Red Cross nurses. This they believed was an entirely appropriate activity in which they could contribute. Through wars and revolutions they were not afraid to roll up their sleeves, work in the wards and help in the operating theatre. These experiences were similar to those of thousands of others and yet they were shared by a group of dedicated royal ladies who wanted to go that extra mile.

It was not always as easy as they had expected, as one young woman recalled:

I can remember well the half-sick feeling which I at first experienced from the horror of the wounds and the smell of the blood ... This became a constant sensation during the hours when the men were first received and their wounds dressed; but it was always offset by excitement, by intense interest in the poor fellows themselves, and by the natural desire to relieve their suffering.[1]

This sensation was probably felt even more acutely by women brought up in a palace, although I suspect that few princesses went as far as the Duke of Rutland's daughter Lady Diana Manners, who before volunteering went down to the kitchen of her parents' London home and saw an animal gutted, 'to prepare me for operations'.[2]

For princesses accustomed to a life of luxury and privilege, nursing was a revelation. It gave them a sense of freedom and liberation which in ordinary circumstances, when they were strictly chaperoned, they could never experience. Most of them had hardly ever travelled overnight without a maid to help them undress. Nevertheless they did not hesitate to volunteer for work in front-line hospitals.

In Russia, Greece, Spain, Romania, Belgium and Britain, Empress Alexandra of Russia; Queen Marie of Romania; Princess Marina, Duchess of Kent; and Princess Alice of Greece (mother of the Duke of Edinburgh) were among the many royal women who set an example of service and duty well beyond that considered necessary at the time. None requested any privileges, they wanted to be treated the same as everyone else. They became the human face of royalty.

For some, donning a nurse's uniform was simply good propaganda. For others it was more than a symbolic gesture, it involved real hospital work, unaccustomed physical effort and mental activity. In most cases they were unable to devote all their time to nursing – they had other duties to perform, especially in the case of the higher-ranking ladies, but whatever time they could spare was used to the best of their ability.

Many of these ladies were awarded the Royal Red Cross. The medal was instituted by Queen Victoria in 1883 for women of the Military Nursing Service who had shown exceptional devotion and competency in the performance of their nursing duties, or for exceptional acts of bravery and devotion while on duty. The gold cross is edged with red enamel and had the words 'Faith, Hope, Charity' engraved on the arms with the date, 1883. The queen's head appeared in relief in the centre with the Imperial crown and cipher on the reverse. The dark blue ribbon, edged in red, was worn tied in a bow on the left shoulder. Among the early recipients were the queen's daughters: the Crown Princess of Prussia, Princess Christian and Princess Beatrice; her daughters-in-law the Princess of Wales and the Duchess of Connaught; and her cousin the Duchess of Teck (mother of the future Queen Mary). Others were awarded a Red Cross Medal from their own, or another foreign country.

The Red Cross was at the heart of nursing work. The International Committee for the Relief of Military Wounded was formed in 1863 and owed its existence to Swiss-born Henri Dunant. His book *A Memory of Solferino*, published at his own expense the previous year, gave a vivid description of the 1859 battle and the suffering he witnessed on the battlefield afterwards. His account shocked Europe: 'At the beginning of the century,' wrote *The Times*, 'the hospitals which followed armies in the field, or which remained to mark the site of some battlefield after the armies had passed on, were little better than charnel houses.' Dunant called for: 'some sacred international principles, sanctioned by convention, which, once signed and ratified would serve as the basis for the creation of societies for the aid of the wounded in the different European countries.'[3]

The result was the Geneva International Conference, which discussed measures to help the wounded on the battlefield and to protect neutral medical services and field hospitals. The Geneva Convention for the Amelioration of the Condition of the Wounded in Armies in the Field was drafted and approved, and in 1867 the First International Conference of the Red Cross was held. Their emblem, a red cross against a white background (the reverse of the Swiss flag), 'was to be accepted as the universal emblem for all medical people and places, whether on a flag or as an armband'.[4]

This is not a history of nursing, nor of the Red Cross, but the story of several queens and princesses who volunteered to help their fellow human beings. There were many royal nurses, particularly among the German royal families. I have therefore concentrated, with a couple of notable exceptions, on those with British links or with links to Queen Victoria.

Beginning with two of the queen's daughters, Princess Alice and Princess Helena, this book will show the difficulties they faced and the successes they achieved while carving out a worthwhile role. They were all born royal and not all of them were fully trained nurses, but each of them made a positive contribution to alleviating suffering.

Notes

1. Mary Allsebrook, *Born to Rebel: The Life of Harriet Boyd Hawes* (Oxbow Books, 1992) p.47.
2. Quoted in Pamela Horn, Ladies of the Manor (Alan Sutton, 1991), p.209.
3. *The Times*, 28 April 1883.
4. Caroline Moorehead, Dunant's Dream (Harper Collins, 1998), p.45.

'The Calling I Should Have Most Liked to Follow'

Florence Nightingale returned from the Crimean War in 1856 as a national heroine. 'I envy her being able to do so much good and look after the noble heroes,' Queen Victoria wrote, full of admiration.[1] Inviting Miss Nightingale to dine at Balmoral, the queen was surprised to find her quiet, ladylike and extremely modest. She so enjoyed their discussion on the defects of the military hospital system that she later drove over to Birkhall unattended to continue the conversation. Yet even if Victoria had really wished 'to lead a private life, tending the poor and sick', as she wrote ten years later, it would have been impossible.[2]

Miss Nightingale made a profound impression on the royal family and, for some of the queen's descendants, tending the poor and sick became almost a way of life. Well to the forefront was Victoria's second daughter, Princess Alice. Born on 25 April 1843, Alice had a strong desire to help others and was sensitive to suffering. In 1855, she and her eldest sister Vicky accompanied the queen on a tour of the London Hospital to visit soldiers wounded in the Crimea. On the Balmoral estate, Alice visited the cottagers to learn about their lives and see what could be done to help. Her health was never strong but in 1861, with Vicky now married to Crown Prince Frederick of Prussia, it fell to Alice to comfort the queen after the death of her mother, the Duchess of Kent. Later that year, during the final illness of the prince consort, Alice showed a maturity and presence of mind which belied her 17 years and the young princess was transformed by the experience. Despite her own grief she looked after her mother, sleeping in her room at night and displaying the care and compassion of a trained nurse. She had, said her grandson, 'without suspecting it, passed her first exam in nursing which was to become her destiny'.[3] She also had to act as an intermediary between the queen and the ministers, whom Victoria was too upset to see. In later years, Alice wondered how she and her mother came through these weeks without losing their minds.

At the time of her father's death, Alice was already engaged to Prince Louis of Hesse-Darmstadt. Alice's wedding at Osborne House on 1 July 1862 was more like a funeral, with the queen in deepest black, barely able to restrain her tears and the few female guests wearing grey or violet mourning dress.

Alice arrived in the provincial, old-fashioned town of Darmstadt on 12 July 1862. She and Louis had no proper home and spent their early years of marriage in a tiny house on the Wilhelminenstrasse – it was all vastly different from the palaces of Alice's youth. By the following spring when Alice and Louis arrived at Windsor for the wedding of the Prince of Wales and Princess Alexandra of Denmark, Alice was heavily pregnant. The queen had already decreed that the child would be born in England, so it was at Windsor Castle that Princess Victoria of Hesse was born on 5 April 1863. Barely a month after the birth, Alice accompanied her mother on a visit to the wounded just back from India.

Princess Victoria's birth was followed by that of Elisabeth (Ella) on 1 November 1864. To the disgust of the queen, who thought it unseemly for a princess, Alice breast-fed Ella herself. Comparing Alice's behaviour to that of a cow, the queen named one of her heifers at Balmoral 'Princess Alice'. Ella's birth was a turning point. Alice became interested in all aspects of childcare and the workings of the human body and began to investigate how she could contribute.

In conservative Darmstadt, where it was not appropriate for women to take up social causes, Alice had to move carefully. She began by visiting the hospital in the town. 'I want to be able to do something for it and hope to succeed, for the people have plenty of money but not the will', she told her mother.[4] The place was clean and fresh, the air in the wards was good and Alice arranged for a supply of linen to be lent to poor women for their confinements.

Alice then became patron of Wöchnerinnen ('women in childbed'), whose members helped those in need by bringing linen and food. Accompanied by a lady-in-waiting, Alice visited the poorer parts of town to see conditions for herself. Hearing about a poor woman who had just given birth, she helped the husband to cook a meal, arranged his wife's bed, bathed her eyes and did some other small jobs while the lady-in-waiting kept an eye on the children. Alice found it good to get away from court circles and help those less fortunate, although she was careful to keep these visits secret from the disapproving members of Darmstadt society. 'If one never sees any poverty, and always lives in that cold circle of Court people, one's good feelings dry up, and I felt the want of going about and doing the little good that is in my power,' she explained to Queen Victoria.[5]

Alice and Louis finally moved into their own home, the newly completed Neues Palais in Darmstadt, in 1866. Although it put a severe drain on their limited financial reserves, the princess now had a permanent base for her philanthropic activities. She attended lectures, cultivated the right contacts and founded a home for the mentally handicapped. Shortly afterwards the Seven Weeks' War broke out.

By now the Prussian Minister-President Count Otto von Bismarck was set on his policy of 'blood and iron' and in the summer of 1866, Prussia declared war on Austria in a bid to establish supremacy in the German confederation. Saxony, Hanover and Hesse sided with Austria and Louis was given command of the Hessian Cavalry Brigade. To Alice's despair, she was now on the opposing side to her elder sister Vicky, the Crown Princess of Prussia. As the Prussian Army crossed Hesse's frontier Alice sent her daughters to their grandmother in England.

Hesse was unprepared for war. Alice was expecting her third child shortly, but espite feeling tired and suffering the last uncomfortable stages of pregnancy she made bandages and stockings for the soldiers and corresponded with Florence Nightingale about the state of Hesse's ill-equipped field hospitals. 'Collections are already being made for the hospitals in the field and the necessary things to be got for the soldiers,' she told Queen Victoria. 'Illness and wounds will be dreadful in this heat.' She was busy gathering rags, shirts and sheets and begged the queen to send some old linen. 'Lint I have ordered from England by wish of the doctors; and bandages also they wished for. If you could, through Doctor Jenner, procure me some of these things I should be so grateful ...'[6]

On 3 July, the Austrians suffered a heavy defeat at the battle of Königgrätz with 45,000 casualties. Vicky's husband Fritz had played a decisive part in Prussia's victory. There was now no longer a question of whether Prussia would emerge victorious from the war, it was just a question of how severely Bismarck would deal with the opposing side.

Louis was back in Darmstadt on a few days' leave when Alice's baby was born on 11 July. The town was full of Prussians, there was fighting in the streets and from her palace Alice could hear the guns firing – they named the baby Irene ('Peace').

A few days later the Bavarians were defeated at Aschaffenburg and as the wounded flooded into Darmstadt the military gymnasium (school) was quickly converted into an emergency hospital. On 21 July the Prussian Army marched into Darmstadt, looting the barracks and the arsenal before occupying the town.

Despite constant anxiety for Louis, who had returned to the front, as soon as she was up and about Alice became a familiar sight in the hospitals, visiting the wounded to give what comfort she could. One man had died since her last visit; another was feeling very low after an operation and 'crying like a child. I could scarcely comfort him, he held my hand and always moaned out "it burns so",' she told her mother.[7]

When Austria was defeated, all the small German states who had sided with her were annexed by Prussia and their rulers dispossessed. Hesse-Darmstadt was one of only four German states to remain independent of Prussia, although with the loss of some territory and an enormous bill for reparations. The armistice was signed on 3 September.

In the aftermath of the war, Alice's interest in both nursing and biological knowledge increased as the need for more humanitarian organisations became tragically clear. The next four years saw an immense amount of activity as she began to help those in greatest need by setting up societies to help pregnant women, the blind and the mentally ill. She attended lectures, often on subjects that Queen Victoria thought indelicate and far outside the scope of activities which should be undertaken by someone of Alice's rank. Florence Nightingale now became both a friend and a major influence on Alice, who used Miss Nightingale's *Notes on Nursing*, published in 1860, as a guide. Alice became vigilant in ensuring that 'cleanliness, ventilation and water supply' were well maintained in all the hospitals. When Miss Nightingale forwarded some money sent by English supporters of the princess, Alice added it to a fund to help those seriously injured or maimed in the war.[8]

The war had highlighted the need for efficient aid to the wounded on the battlefield. Nursing had previously been done by deaconesses or Sisters of Mercy from the religious orders but it was now felt that a committee should be formed to organise the training of specially qualified nurses.

With the example of Florence Nightingale before her, on 1 June 1867 Princess Alice founded the Alice-Frauenverein (Women's Societies) to train Red Cross nurses in case of another conflict and to assist the Geneva International Convention in nursing and giving support to the troops in wartime. This would avoid the situation where untrained nurses were sent to a war zone. In Darmstadt, Alice headed a committee of six ladies and four doctors, under which was a network of local committees who would collect all the necessary things for both the wounded and the troops on the march, ensuring that everything was sent to the correct place. To recruit members, lectures were given all over the country by eminent medical men. By 1869, the number of ladies involved had risen to 2,500.[9]

Alice was greatly interested in the advancement of women so that they could earn their own living. In 1872, she chaired the 'Frauentag' (Ladies' Assembly) in Darmstadt, which discussed 'the further employment of women, the sale of women's handiwork, nursing, better schools for girls and how all these issues had been handled in England'. The princess also founded an orphanage, a girls' school to train girls as clerks or to make handicrafts, a home for unmarried mothers and an asylum for the insane.[10] Bazaars – a novelty in Germany at the time – were held in the palace grounds to raise money by selling needlework and handicrafts made by women. They became known as the Alice Bazaars.

Yet Alice's main interest remained nursing. Florence Nightingale had waged an epic struggle to establish nursing as a respectable profession, 'no longer associated in people's minds with drunkenness and prostitution',[11] but these changes were slow to be recognised in Germany. Nevertheless, the first two nurses completed their training in January 1868 and soon ten nurses were working either in private or military hospitals supervised by experienced doctors. 'There is a great deal to be done, and in the hospitals I have been able to get some very necessary changes made,' Alice told Queen Victoria.[12]

★★★

In 1869, Alice spent a holiday with Vicky at the Grand Hotel in Cannes. Vicky had long been concerned with improving the care of the wounded but her life in Berlin was not easy. Her 'English' ways were disliked and her liberal and Anglophile views put her into conflict with Bismarck.

During Prussia's war with Denmark in 1864, Vicky started an army nursing corps. She later gave active support to the International Congress in Aid of the Wounded, attending the Congress in 1869 and urging her mother and the British government to give their support as well. She was desperately anxious to be of use to her new country, remembering meetings with Florence Nightingale in England during the Crimean War. From her husband she had also heard about the lack of proper medical attention for soldiers at the front.

In Cannes, Alice and Vicky discussed subjects of interest to them which would have appalled their mother. One of these was anatomy, which they had been learning a little about to help with their interest in hospitals and the training of nurses. Queen Victoria thought such a subject disgusting. Alice told her that the ingenious structure and various bodily functions filled her with wonder. Furthermore, if a sudden illness occurred in her family she found it useful to know what should be done before the doctor arrived. For the queen, of course, such knowledge was unnecessary, as she was surrounded by eminent physicians. Alice's concern was borne out when in January 1870 she nursed Louis, Victoria and baby Ernest Louis through scarlet fever.

In July 1870 both sisters found their skills needed when the Franco–Prussian War broke out. Louis was again sent to the front with his division, while Alice helped the sick and wounded as well as those left destitute by the fighting. She turned her palace into a Red Cross depot and drove there every morning from their summer residence, Kranichstein. ' … so much rests on me,' she told her mother, 'and there are so many to help – the poor forsaken soldiers' families amongst others! I have seen that all is ready to receive the wounded, and to send out help. I sent out fourteen nurses for the Field Hospitals.'[13]

Darmstadt was very near the seat of war and there were still only sixteen trained nurses ready to work in the Hilfsverein, a voluntary organisation which worked in Alice's palace to help servicemen. As huge numbers of wounded poured into Darmstadt more nurses were urgently needed. Alice now worked hard to get nursing accepted, so that women could be seen handing out refreshments to the troops at railway stations, working in hospital trains and hospital steamers, as well as in hospital wards, which would not formerly have been tolerated. Thanks to Alice's encouragement, some of the best medical men held classes at various locations for women who wanted to nurse during the war. More women volunteered and there were soon 164 nurses available to work in reserve hospitals, field hospitals or the Hilfsverein.

Alice was soon sending nurses to the front. Conditions in the field hospitals were often primitive; with little understanding of germs, many of the wounded died of infections picked up during surgery. Doctors wandered around the battlefields wearing aprons smothered in blood and buckets of sand were used to mop up the blood on the floor of the operating room. Chloroform did not reach the battlefields until later in the century, although it was used in the main civilian hospitals (as was ether) and in some field dressing stations. The surgeon Joseph Lister's findings on antiseptics were only published in 1867. Battlefield surgery was more or less restricted to whether, and how soon, to operate and only recently had the number of amputations decreased. The term 'ambulance' could be used for anything from a rickety cart carrying wounded from the battlefield, 'to field hospitals, first aid stations', temporary hospitals in schools or old barracks, and 'entire self-sufficient medical units with surgeons, priests, nurses, carriages, horses and all food and medical supplies'.[14]

At Pont-à-Mousson in north-east France a church had been converted into a hospital and an appeal went out for 250 iron bedsteads. Thanks to the efforts of another of Alice's sisters, Princess Helena, these arrived within forty-eight hours, conveyed by a young doctor, as Alice told Queen Victoria:

> This morning we got two large wagons ready and sent off for Pont-à-Mousson, where they telegraph from the battlefield of the 16th [regiment] that they are in great want. My best nurses are out there; the others are in three hospitals: two of them – military ones – were not ready or organised when 150 wounded arrived a week ago.[15]

The following day Alice sent off two more wagons loaded with provisions, bandages, medicines and mattresses to bring back as many as possible of the wounded by rail. 'My nurses reached the battlefield in time and were of great use,' she added proudly.[16] Despite the risk of infection, she then went round the hospitals and had any able-bodied men sent back to their homes in order to make room for the next batch of wounded. One day she helped lift a wounded man and it was then discovered that he had smallpox.

During the war the Alice-Frauenverein took over the running and administration of Darmstadt's three reserve military hospitals – the Riedeselstrasse, the Pioneer Barracks and the military hospital erected by the English National Society for Aid to the Sick and Wounded, which was staffed with English surgeons. This 120-bed hospital was given the name of the Alice Hospital. Soon the military authorities built a further four barracks with 450 beds staffed by medical officers from England. The nurses for this, and the other military hospitals, were supplied by the Alice-Frauenverein.

Alice spent her days visiting hospitals and dressing stations, and building up a storeroom to accumulate the supplies necessary to nurse and transport the injured. The French needle gun, the Chassepot, was more capable of shattering bones than any previous gun, even though it left comparatively small wounds; nearly every hour trains brought in more wounded, who soon included many French prisoners. The state of many of them shocked Alice and she complained to Louis that it was a '*terrible*, bloody war'.[17]

The princess soon discovered the War Department's inefficiency. Nothing was ready and the hospitals did not have the things they desperately needed. Two field hospitals went off without instruments and Alice could do nothing to rectify the situation. One old doctor and two of Alice's nurses had to cope in a badly ventilated, overcrowded clinic overflowing with the sick and seriously wounded because all the young doctors had gone to the front. Alice sent much-needed supplies, more staff and partitions so a new hut could be built.

Alice lived in constant anxiety for the safety of Louis and worried about her children. When they drove out they were escorted by gendarmes to protect them from the gypsies and undesirables who followed the army. French prisoners were housed in huts on the drill ground and there was nowhere the children could walk safely without fear of infection from the sick troops who wandered around the town. At the foot of Alice's garden was another barrack containing 1,200 French prisoners, many of whom were also sick. 'We have over 500 wounded; as soon as they are better they will be sent north and worse ones will fill the beds,' she explained to the queen.[18] Sometimes, Alice took her eldest daughter to visit the German and French casualties, and little Victoria later recalled visiting huts in the Orangery Garden. Two wounded officers were being nursed in the Neues Palais – one had typhoid and was very ill; the other liked to show the little princess the pieces of bone from his shattered leg that he kept in a pillbox.

In Berlin, Alice's sister was equally active. 'A wounded man,' Vicky said, 'has ceased to be an enemy', and she sent her mother a long list of requirements, begging for help. England was officially neutral but the queen agreed to provide 'some old linen and oilcloth' on condition that her name did not appear anywhere on the packages. Vicky was busy forming a separate staff of doctors and nurses and, although delighted that some were being sent from England, she wished they could be sent direct to her where they were very much needed. 'I have borrowed money and given some of my jewels in trust to be able to do this,' she added.[19] Vicky's work in Potsdam and Berlin was not appreciated by her mother-in-law Queen Augusta of Prussia, who was organising hospital services in Berlin, or by Prussian society. Her efforts were 'contemptuously rejected, presumably on account of the anti-British feeling,' Crown Prince Frederick recorded in his diary on 23 August, so Vicky decided to establish a model hospital in Homburg in the Taunus mountains, near the border with France.[20]

In early September, Vicky and Alice arrived in Homburg, where the crown princess moved into the old castle which had once been the home of George III's daughter Landgravine Elisabeth. A large barracks had been put at Vicky's disposal for a military hospital but it was in a disgraceful state, so was being renovated to her own requirement at her own expense. She was also having a new 'hut' built. The Victoria Barrack had twenty-four beds for special cases and all the latest medical equipment. 'To overcome the prejudice of doctors and patients against fresh air is really almost impossible,' she told her mother. 'We have not one nurse or dresser here yet, only people from the town, who are dirty, ignorant and useless in the extreme, but we have sent for some better help …'[21] Florence Nightingale sent out her friend Florence Lees to assist and soon fresh air breezed through the wards and vases of flowers were placed by the beds. Miss Lees warmly praised the crown princess's model hospital.

Vicky also undertook several tiring journeys to inspect hospitals along the Rhine. The weather was beautiful, the scenery superb but most of the hospitals were 'wretched, dirty and ill managed'. A few were good but the remainder were merely tolerable. Although she found that the people were 'touchingly kind' to the wounded, they 'do not understand how to take care of them and are dirty beyond description,' she explained.[22] Queen Victoria, pressed to send even more supplies, provided some 'splendid cases of old linen'. When they arrived in Homburg they were made into 'handkerchiefs, compresses and pillowcases', and Vicky ensured people knew that these things came from the Queen of England.[23]

On 6 October Alice gave birth to Frederick William (Frittie). She was so weak that Vicky, who had given birth to her seventh child Sophie in June, helped to nurse him.

By now Crown Prince Frederick had heard that his wife's efforts were being properly appreciated, and that she was held in high esteem by the doctors, who were 'astonished at the wide range of her knowledge'.[24] He informed his father King William but the result was not what he had anticipated. After barely a month in Homburg, Vicky was informed that Queen Augusta was arriving imminently. Augusta was 'very kind and amiable' but a few days later the king ordered Vicky back to Berlin; it appears that her energetic efforts did not show Queen Augusta in a good light.[25]

Although Vicky's actions were not appreciated in Berlin, a model of the Victoria Ward at Homburg was exhibited in Washington DC for many years, 'as an example of the latest methods in nursing and hygiene'.[26]

★★★

The war ended in early spring but its effects lasted much longer, especially on the wounded. During January and February 1871 Alice was working in the hospital every day, as well as looking after the two patients in the Neues Palais and visiting the wives and widows of the soldiers. She was especially upset by the fate of one young man whose heartbroken father sat by the bed holding his hand. She told her mother sadly:

> I would give anything to save his life; but all efforts will, I fear, be in vain. Though I have seen so many lately die hard deaths, and heard and seen the grief of many heartbroken widows and mothers, it makes my heart bleed anew in each fresh case, and curse the wickedness of war again and again.[27]

The queen sent a cape which Alice gave to a dying soldier, telling him it was from the Queen of England. He held it tight, refusing to part with it and died with it wrapped around him. His mother kept it as a precious relic, as it had given her son so much pleasure.

When men recovered, Alice rejoiced. In December, she reported that her patients in the palace were much better, 'and the one who during six weeks lay at death's door is recovering. I have seldom experienced so great a satisfaction as seeing this young man recover, and the doctors say I have been the means of saving his life.'[28]

Louis returned home in June 1871. He and Alice went for a holiday on the Belgian coast and by September were at Balmoral, where they found the queen suffering from a throat infection and a 6in abscess on her arm. When doctors lanced the abscess, Alice took on the duties of a nurse. 'Dear Alice was in and out constantly, and very affectionate and kind, helping my maids in moving me,' the queen wrote.[29]

Alice and Louis then went to stay with Bertie and Alexandra, the Prince and Princess of Wales, at Sandringham. Just as they were about to leave, Bertie was stricken by typhoid. 'Papa's dreadful illness, which I know so well,' Alice lamented.[30] Alexandra summoned Dr Gull, also accepting the queen's suggestion of sending for Dr Jenner. Louis returned home but Alice used the experience she had gained in wartime hospitals to serve as a self-trained nurse.

On 29 November Bertie's fever was so violent that Alexandra sent for the queen. This was her first visit to Sandringham. Led into the darkened sickroom, she could see little but could hear the rasping sound of her eldest son gasping for breath.

As the press descended on Norfolk, in order to allay public anxiety the queen returned to Windsor. She was joined by Louis, who had raced back from Darmstadt. On 8 December a telegram arrived saying the queen should come immediately. Victoria, together with other members of the royal family, reached Sandringham that evening in deep snow to find Alice and Alexandra sitting by the prince's bed. The queen retired for the night, Alice and Alexandra remained.

Throughout this time Alexandra only left the sickroom to snatch some sleep or pray in the little church nearby. As the prince's ravings became more wild, with all sorts of revelations bandied about, Alice ministered to him, while Alexandra was kept away to save her embarrassment. In a letter to her husband, Alexandra's lady-in-waiting Lady Macclesfield accused Alice of being 'meddling, jealous and mischief-making'.[31] The prince hurled objects around the sickroom and explicit expressions, never uttered in royal homes, were heard. Alice took it all in her stride but Alexandra, desperate to see her husband, crawled in on all fours and Bertie felled her with a pillow.

When the crisis began Alice was probably among the first to realise that the turning point would come on 14 December, the tenth anniversary of the prince consort's death. As the dreaded anniversary approached the country held its breath. On Friday, 13 December, the prince was weaker and Alice, white faced, told the queen there could surely be no hope. Victoria sat vigilantly by the bedside as Alice and Alexandra snatched what sleep they could. The following morning the Prince of Wales awoke and asked for a glass of ale. The crisis had passed.

The press immediately credited Princess Alice with his recovery. However, to the queen's reaction of overwhelming relief was added the anxiety that Alexandra, rather than Alice, should be given the credit for nursing the prince through his illness. Alice returned home in the New Year, exhausted both in mind and body. 'I still do not like leaving England before Bertie's convalescence is more firmly established,' she told Louis. 'But his condition improves so slowly that I shall just have to go ...'[32]

★★★

In Darmstadt, Alice's achievements were reaching their climax, although some of her ideas did not meet with approval. During a meeting regarding the building of a block of flats for workers, Alice expressed the view that there should be a communal bathroom on each floor. This notion of maintaining personal cleanliness was looked upon as very English and was therefore unwanted in Hesse. One irate elderly man said that he had never had a bath in his life.

Alice's own hospital was nearing completion and would function as a nurses' training school and a home for probationers who had completed their training. After the Franco-Prussian War, the small provisional Alice Hospital erected and run by the English National Society for Aid to the Sick and Wounded was taken over by the Hessian authorities. All the furniture and equipment was left to the Alice-Frauenverein for its own small hospital, which was staffed by a small body of doctors in Darmstadt. This new Alice Hospital had begun modestly in a small house at 17 Mauer-Strasse and was now completely reorganised by the Alice-Frauenverein, with additional buildings and a total reorganisation of the interior. Later, it was separated from the Frauenverein and supplementary funds were made available. In their correspondence, Florence Nightingale gave Alice her opinion on subjects such as discipline and the length of training required for nurses, saying that the Nightingale Committee would be willing to train probationers for Alice's hospital in Darmstadt, 'if satisfied that a really useful result would be attained'.[33] The women would, of course, need to understand English. Alice paid for the training of the first matron of the new hospital, Charlotte Helmsdorfer, in Leipzig and Liverpool, where she studied at Miss Merryweather's institution to gain experience in district nursing. Alice also arranged with Miss Nightingale that Miss Helmsdorfer would train at the Nightingale School at St Thomas's Hospital, London, from January 1873. The Alice Hospital remained a project very dear to the princess's heart.

★★★

Alice had given birth to her sixth child Alix on 6 June 1872. The family now suffered a series of tragedies which would ultimately lead to Alice's own early death. On 29 May 1873 her 3-year-old son Frittie slipped and fell through an open window while playing with his elder brother Ernest Louis. He landed on a stone balustrade on the terrace 20ft below, where he was picked up unconscious and bleeding. Frittie suffered from haemophilia and by the evening he was dead. Queen Victoria's youngest son Leopold also suffered from this malady and two of her daughters – Alice and Beatrice – were carriers. In later years when their own daughters carried haemophilia into the royal families of Russia and Spain there would be disastrous consequences. Alice never recovered from the loss of her son and even the birth of Marie ('May') the following year did not heal the gaping wound.

In March 1877, Louis' father Prince Charles of Hesse died, followed three months later by the Grand Duke of Hesse. Alice's husband now succeeded his uncle as Grand Duke Louis IV of Hesse and by Rhine. As the Grand Duchess of Hesse, Alice's official duties increased and this, together with the good works that she was already involved in, proved tiring. 'Too much is demanded of one; and I have to do with so many things,' she told Queen Victoria. 'It is more than my strength can stand.'[34]

By the following year Alice's health was causing concern and Queen Victoria sent the whole family to Eastbourne for the summer at her own expense so that she could recuperate. Even here Alice could not relax. She visited the sick in the fishermen's cottages, called at many homes and penitentiaries for poor women and girls, inspected the hospitals and opened charity bazaars. She also visited the Albion Home for Girls (many of them reformed prostitutes) in Brighton and agreed to become its patron. Alice was slowly wearing herself out.

Back in Darmstadt she devoted herself to her various charitable causes with renewed energy, but by the beginning of November she was again weary and incapacitated. Alice told the queen she was still 'leading a very quiet life, which is an absolute necessity. It is so depressing to be like this ...'[35]

On 8 November, 15-year-old Princess Victoria complained of a sore throat. The next day doctors diagnosed diphtheria, a highly contagious disease of which Alice had a particular dread. Helped by Miss Macbean (who was standing in for the lady-in-waiting, who was on leave) and the nurses and lady superintendent of her hospital, Alice immediately took charge of the nursing arrangements.

Although Victoria was immediately isolated from the family, by the following week 6-year-old Alix had the disease. 'I ... looked into her throat, and there were not only spots, but a thick covering on each side of her throat of that horrid white membrane,' Alice told the queen. 'I got the steam inhaler, with chlorate of potash for her at once, but she was very unhappy, poor little thing.'[36] Dr Eigenbrodt immediately had Alix moved upstairs near Victoria. Meanwhile, Alice fumigated the nursery to stop the disease spreading and the queen sent her personal physician Sir William Jenner to Darmstadt.

During the next few days 4-year-old May, Irene, Ernie and even Louis all went down with diphtheria. Only Ella escaped. She was sent to her paternal grandmother Princess Charles of Hesse, away from the risk of infection. 'Well Katie,' Alice said to Miss Macbean, 'you and I are the only ones who are not ill, and we must not be ill, there is so much to be done and seen to.'[37] As the doctors tried to keep up with her demanding schedule, Alice went from room to room, soothing, comforting and doing everything she could for her family.

In between nursing her husband and children, Alice sent regular updates to Queen Victoria. Gradually they began to recover, except for May whose fever remained very high. Early on 16 November Alice was woken by the doctors, who reported that a piece of membrane had crossed May's throat. Alice rushed to her daughter's side but it was too late. Her beloved, adored little May had choked to death.

With Louis sufficiently recovered to be told the tragic news, Alice now had the difficult task of concealing May's death from the other children, who constantly asked after her and wanted to send her their books and toys. Even the funeral was held in secret so as not to alert them. Although Victoria and Alix were out of danger, Ernie's life was still in peril. A few days later Ernie was out of danger and he gave Alice a book, asking her to give it to May. The effort of concealing the truth was almost too much for the poor mother.

At the beginning of December Alice steeled herself to tell Ernie that his sister was dead. He at first refused to believe it and as the tears streamed down his face Alice now did the worst possible thing. Breaking the doctors' instructions that there should be no contact between her and the patients, she bent over and kissed him. It was the kiss of death.

On 7 December she wrote her last letter to Queen Victoria, saying they would go to Heidelberg for a few days while the sickrooms were aired and repapered. A few days later she complained of feeling ill and on the following day the dreaded symptoms appeared.

From the beginning her fever was high and Alice, worn out from the recent strain of nursing her family, was unable to fight it. On Saturday, 14 December 1878, the exact anniversary of the prince consort's death seventeen years earlier, Alice died. She was 35 years old. Her last words were 'Dear Papa ...'[38]

Her death was an irreparable loss, not only to her husband and children but to the people of Darmstadt where she was greatly mourned. 'She had a warm heart for all necessity', wrote Louis' cousin Princess Marie of Erbach-Schönberg. 'She knew how to initiate schemes for the general welfare in the most practical fashion.'[39]

The people of Eastbourne, where Alice had gone to recover her strength in the autumn of 1878, wanted to raise a memorial. So much money poured in that they decided to build a small hospital. The foundation stone was laid by Princess Helena in 1882 and the Princess Alice Memorial Hospital was opened by the Prince and Princess of Wales in June 1883.

Princess Alice achieved so much for nurses and nursing during her short life. Writing to Florence Nightingale in 1872, the princess said that if she had remained single, then nursing 'is the calling I should have most liked to follow'.[40]

For the moment the flame would continue to burn brightly in the actions of her sister Helena, but in the years to come Alice's daughters and granddaughters would be among the many other royal ladies who made their own contribution to nursing.

Notes

1. Frances Dimond & Roger Taylor, *Crown & Camera* (Penguin Books, 1987), p.38.
2. Elizabeth Longford, Victoria R.I. (Weidenfeld & Nicolson, 1964), p.436.
3. Prince Louis of Hesse, 'The Alice Hospital', lecture 1953. Quoted in Gerard Noel, *Princess Alice: Queen Victoria's Forgotten Daughter* (Constable, 1974), p.79.
4. Alice, Grand Duchess of Hesse, *Biographical Sketch and Letters*, 21 September 1863, p.61.
5. Alice, *Biographical Sketch*, 5 March 1864, p.69.
6. Alice, *Biographical Sketch*, 24 June 1866, p.134.
7. Alice, *Biographical Sketch*, 17 August 1866, p.144.
8. Noel, Gerard, *Princess Alice: Queen Victoria's Forgotten Daughter* (Constable, 1974) p.133.
9. The Alice-Frauenverein merged with the German Red Cross in 1937.
10. Miller, Ilana D., *The Four Graces: Queen Victoria's Hessian Granddaughters* (Kensington House Books, California, 2011), p.14.
11. Noel, *Alice*, p.142.
12. Alice, *Biographical Sketch*, 25 June 1870, p.241.
13. Alice, *Biographical Sketch*, 26 July 1870, p.243.
14. Moorehead, *Dunant's Dream*, p.67.
15. Alice, *Biographical Sketch*, 19 August 1870, p.245.
16. Alice, *Biographical Sketch*, 25 August 1870, p.248.
17. Noel, *Alice*, p.162.
18. Nina Epton, Victoria and her Daughters (Weidenfeld & Nicolson, 1971), p.128.
19. Hannah Pakula, *An Uncommon Woman: The Empress Frederick*, (Weidenfeld & Nicolson, 1996), p.283.
20. Sir Frederick Ponsonby, *Letters of the Empress Frederick* (Macmillan, 1929), p.89.
21. Ponsonby, *Letters*, p.94.
22. Ponsonby, *Letters*, pp.96, 91.
23. Pakula, *Uncommon Woman*, p.284.
24. Ponsonby, *Letters*, p.94.
25. Pakula, *Uncommon Woman*, p.285. In January 1871 the German Empire was proclaimed and King William I of Prussia became Emperor William I of Germany.
26. Roger Fulford, *Your Dear Letter* (Evans Brothers, 1971), p.286.
27. Alice, *Biographical Sketch*, 12 November 1870, p.252.
28. Alice, *Biographical Sketch*, 19 December 1870, p.255.
29. Epton, *Victoria*, p.137
30. Noel, *Alice*, p.171.

31. Noel, *Alice*, p.173.
32. Noel, *Alice*, p.174.
33. Noel, *Alice*, p.254. Memo of 23 March 1872.
34. Alice, *Biographical Sketch*, 30 October 1877, p.359.
35. Alice, *Biographical Sketch*, 6 November 1878, p.367.
36. Alice, *Biographical Sketch*, 12 November 1878, p.368.
37. Noel, *Alice*, p.236.
38. Alice, *Biographical Sketch*, p.276.
39. Princess of Battenburg, Marie zu Erbach-Schönberg, *Reminiscences* (The Ipswich Book Company, 1925. Reprinted by Royalty Digest, 1996), p.178.
40. Noel, p.249.

2

'My One Great Object and Desire'

Following Prince Albert's death in 1861, the queen began to see the folly of marrying her two eldest daughters to princes living in Germany. She was determined that this should not happen again.

Princess Helena had been acting as both companion and assistant to her mother and with Alice unable, or unwilling, to spend more time in England the queen insisted that she must have a daughter permanently around. Helena had proved dutiful and reliable, so Victoria resolved to keep this most useful daughter nearby – but where to find Helena a husband? 'Poor dear Lenchen', as the queen called her, using the German diminutive, 'does not improve in looks and has great difficulties with her figure and her want of calm, quiet, graceful manners'.[1] The queen wanted a son-in-law who would not object to living in England and she soon found the ideal candidate.

On 5 July 1866, 20-year-old Helena married Prince Christian of Schleswig-Holstein-Sonderburg-Augustenburg, a penniless, balding, 34-year-old German whose family were dispossessed in 1864 when Denmark and Prussia went to war over the duchies of Schleswig and Holstein. For political reasons (and because of the age difference) most of the queen's children were against the marriage – the war had divided the family. Christian IX of Denmark was the father of the Princess of Wales; Vicky was the Crown Princess of Prussia. However, Helena did not argue, perhaps realising that her matrimonial prospects were as limited as those of Christian, now a homeless exile who Bismarck had deprived of his army commission. Despite this inauspicious beginning the marriage lasted for over fifty years.

Prince and Princess Christian made their home at Frogmore House near Windsor Castle. The prince was created a Royal Highness and given the hardly onerous position of ranger of Windsor Park. Helena was now officially known as Princess Christian, the title by which she is more widely remembered. During the first few years of their marriage the princess gave birth to three children: Christian Victor in 1867; Albert in 1869; and Helena Victoria in 1870. By the time her fourth child Marie Louise was born in 1872 they had moved to Cumberland Lodge in Windsor Park, from where the princess danced attendance on the queen and concentrated on her philanthropic interests.

Stories about the experiences of the nurses in the Crimean War made a great impression on the princess, as she learnt how Florence Nightingale had brought order and cleanliness into the wards in Scutari. Miss Nightingale had introduced women nurses into military hospitals, set up diet kitchens to prepare invalid food, introduced recreational facilities, looked after the welfare of convalescents and methodically distributed the vast consignments of goods sent by the British public.

The Franco-Prussian War in 1870 gave Princess Christian a chance to put her own good intentions to use. As England was not at war, it was not considered appropriate for her to become a nurse like Alice, instead she acted in an organisational capacity.

On 22 July Colonel Robert Loyd-Lindsay (later Baron Wantage) wrote to *The Times* calling for a National Society for Aid to the Sick and Wounded in War to be founded in Britain, as had been done in other European countries. A committee of twenty-two members was formed, chaired by Colonel Loyd-Lindsay with the queen as patron and the Prince of Wales as president. Greatly distressed at 'the fearful loss of life and sufferings of so many thousands,'[2] Princess Christian became chairman of the Ladies' Committee, which also included her sister Princess Louise and the queen's cousin Princess Mary Adelaide, Duchess of Teck.

At No. 7 St Martin's Place the Ladies' Committee received donations of money and gifts. Appeals went out for items ranging from smelling salts to concentrated meat essence and the 250 iron bedsteads needed at Pont-à-Mousson. Princess Christian urged the Duchess of Sutherland to send 'any old linen',[3] while other contributions included eighteen flannel bandages and six pillowcases from Queen Victoria; twelve pairs of socks and two invalid coats from Princess Louise; and a cheque for £1,000 from Mr Balfour (the later prime minister). As offerings flooded in, the Ladies' Committee overflowed to a wing of the disused St Martin's Workhouse, the large vaults under St Martin-in-the-Fields church, and even a tent in the churchyard. While men packed and labelled bales for France, Princess Christian fired off letters to friends, collected lint and bandages, and supervised the women who washed old clothes and turned them into charpie (a kind of lint). Eleven surgeons and five nurses had already been sent to the front. By September 1870, the committee had collected nearly £200,000 and it was decided to give £20,000 each to France and Prussia for the benefit of their sick and wounded. For her work in the Franco-Prussian War, Princess Christian was awarded the Bronze Cross of the French Red Cross Society.

Fired with enthusiasm, the princess attended the ladies' classes of the St John Ambulance Association in Windsor, receiving a framed certificate for proficiency, and she also did some practical nursing training in the 1880s. She made a 'close personal study of English, French and German hospitals'[4] and in 1882 translated the German Professor Friedrich von Esmarch's book *First Aid to the Injured* into English. Von Esmarch (who had married Prince Christian's sister) was a distinguished authority on hospital management and military surgery, and as surgeon general in the German Army during the Franco-Prussian War he was the first person to introduce antisepsis.

Princess Christian founded many nursing and hospital facilities for the poor, especially in Windsor. The name 'Princess Christian's' in the title bore witness to the enormity of her efforts. At committee meetings she exercised her authority firmly. 'Then we all agree on that, don't we?' the princess would say resolutely, before adding quickly, 'Then let us pass on.' Nobody dared to contradict the queen's daughter.[5]

At a public meeting in February 1888 the princess accepted the presidency of the British Nurses' Association. Its founder Ethel Manson had resigned as matron of St Bartholomew's Hospital the previous year and married the well-known physician Dr Bedford Fenwick. Mrs Bedford Fenwick, as she then became known, promptly began a campaign for the registration of nurses. She called a meeting of matrons to discuss the future of nursing as a profession and it was decided to form the British Nurses' Association, of which Princess Christian became the honorary secretary.

In her acceptance speech Princess Christian stressed that:

> the first object of the Association is to obtain for the calling of nursing the recognised position and legal constitution of a profession … It will follow from this that in future every member of the nursing profession must have been educated up to a definite standard of knowledge and efficiency … [6]

The princess also designed the association's badge, incorporating her father's motto *Steadfast and True*. She worked hard for the British Nurses' Association and took an active interest in all that concerned it. she wrote to the lady superintendent of Sir Patrick Dun's Hospital in Dublin in 1893:

> The Executive Committee have quite determined to establish a Branch of the Association in Dublin, simultaneously with one at Edinburgh, in order that the members of the Association residing in Ireland and Scotland should have some

direct knowledge and be able to take a more direct and active part in the work
of the Association. I venture therefore to ask you if it would be possible for you
to come to London … in order to confer with the Executive Committee? We
are very anxious to discuss matters with you and obtain your help …'[7]

At that time the nursing community was racked by internal conflicts for
and against the state registration of nurses; Princess Christian was a strong
supporter of registration and the British Nurses' Association considered
it a matter of national importance, in order to protect the sick from the
ministrations of unskilled workers. In this she came up against the direct
opposition of Florence Nightingale. In 1889, the princess chaired a meeting
at which a resolution was passed to obtain a royal charter for nurses' legal
registration. She saw two preconditions to the advancement of nursing:
training and increased educational facilities. In a letter to *The Times* she was
adamant that:

> a nurse must attend lectures, and must pass through medical, surgical, and special
> wards before she can be fully capable of doing all which can be required of her.
> In other words, her professional education can only be completed at the cost
> of much time, industry, and expense. Student nurses, or 'probationers', in many
> cases pay to be taught, and even when they do not actually give money, they are
> required to work for a smaller remuneration than they might easily obtain in
> other kinds of employment.

The princess cited the many women who entered nursing but left, or were
dismissed, after only a brief period of instruction and then went on to 'seek
employment in nursing describing themselves as "hospital trained nurses"'.
There was also the problem of private agencies, where some of the managers
'do not always require sufficient security for the fitness of those who they
engage'. The British Nurses' Association, she continued, 'is now seeking
to establish, it is hoped on the secure basis of a Royal charter, a system of
registration which will enable every trained nurse to produce documentary
evidence of her education and attainments.'[8]

As president, she saw her function as 'improving the education and status
of those devoted and self-sacrificing women whose whole lives have been
devoted to tending the sick, the suffering and the dying'[9] and she appealed for
donations towards increased facilities for the education of nurses.

Princess Christian also promoted the establishment of a convalescent and
holiday home for trained nurses, writing that on wages of only £20 to £25
a year, 'very few can afford a short rest now and then which, we contend,
would enable many to work with less detriment to their own health, and

therefore with greater benefit to their patients'. She appealed for donations to buy a suitable house in Brighton which would also provide somewhere for nurses to convalesce after illness, 'as invalids are not always welcome guests' and many others 'can never obtain the advantage of a seaside visit by reason of the incidental expense'.[10]

Princess Christian was 'a prime mover in the establishment of the second British training college for nursery nurses, the Princess Christian College, which opened in Manchester in 1901. This grew from the discussions of the Gentlewomen's Employment Association, which was founded in 1891 with the princess as its patron.'[11] The college still trains children's nurses today.

By the end of the century there was also the beginning of an organised district nursing service. In 1887, Queen Victoria donated £70,000 raised by the women of England for her Golden Jubilee and it was decided to found an institute to promote the training of nurses for the sick poor in their own homes. The Duke of Westminster wrote on behalf of the committee:

> We would recommend that the Nurses should all be duly approved women of excellent personal character, and of good education, including an education similar to that of well trained Nurses in Hospitals and a special training in district nursing, and in Maternity Hospitals so that they may be fit to attend poor women after childbirth.[12]

Queen Victoria's Jubilee Institute for Nurses received a royal charter in 1889 and the following year the queen's private secretary recorded that Princess Christian was to be added to Princess Louise and Princess Beatrice on the council, although the queen thought that the princesses should be honorary or extra members. After the queen's death the patronage was taken over by Queen Alexandra, who devoted much of her life to the work, and later by Queen Mary.

★★★

Princess Christian was keen to add the prefix 'Royal' to the British Nurses' Association. On 3 January 1891, she therefore wrote to the queen's private secretary Sir Henry Ponsonby:

> I am sending you today as President of the British Nurses' Association and on behalf of the Association the Petition to the Queen, craving H[er] Majesty to become its Patron and to allow the word Royal to be prefixed to its name. The Association has been in existence 3 whole years – has done good work – is supported by all the leading Physicians and Surgeons of the country who

aid us by their personal co-operation and advice. In fact, I may honestly say we are a most flourishing Institution in the face of much opposition and misrepresentation.

If the Queen would grant the petition and become the Patron of the Association allowing it to call itself [the] *'Royal* British Nurses Ass[ociation]' *I* and *all* concerned w[oul]d be so deeply grateful.[13]

The Petition, signed 'Helena, Princess Christian, President and on behalf of the Executive Committee of the Association', was duly submitted. Sir Henry told the queen in a memorandum:

It is an excellent Association and most useful and Your Majesty will probably grant the title of 'Royal' when the application comes through the Home Office.

But as to Patronage Sir Henry Ponsonby has written to Princess Christian to ask if Her Royal Highness does not think this Association should not remain at present – as it is now – under her own patronage.

There would then be The Queen Victoria Jubilee Nurses under the Queen
The Pension for Nurses under the Princess of Wales patronage [*sic*]
The British Nurses Association under Princess Christian patronage [*sic*]

The queen concurred. 'Quite agree and approve. VRI' she wrote at the top of the page.[14]

The announcement of the new title, the first Royal Charter granted to an association of professional women, was made on 26 February and pleased the princess immensely. *The Times* reported that the association's 'first and primary object has been the publication of a register of trained nurses. This, the first annual register, is now in course of issue'.[15] Writing in 1895, the princess confidently hoped 'that the time is not far distant when all those who employ nurses ... will decline to repose confidence in any nurses but those whose testimonials undergo the searching scrutiny of the Registration Board of the new incorporated RBNA'.[16]

★★★

Florence Nightingale had been instrumental in establishing an Army Training School for Military Nurses at Netley in 1860, in which the queen and the royal family took enormous interest. In 1881, the Army Nursing Service was formed to provide nurses for the military hospitals, with Princess Christian at its head. In March 1897, Princess Christian's Army Nursing Service Reserve was created under the princess's presidency to supplement the permanent staff of military hospitals both in Britain and overseas.

On 23 November 1898 it was decided to form 'a permanent Central Red Cross Committee for the British Empire and dependencies' under the chairmanship of Baron Wantage and the honorary presidency of the Princess of Wales. The Committee consisted of representatives of the National Society for Aid to the Sick and Wounded in War, the St John Ambulance Association, and the Army Nursing Reserve (represented by Princess Christian and Miss Wedgewood). Its aim was to supplement the Army Medical Service in time of war by providing 'prompt and efficient aid to the sick and wounded',[17] including surgeons, nurses, administrators, ambulances and medical equipment. Princess Christian was actively involved in this joint committee and personally interviewed the nurses to ensure they were suitable for work abroad.

The National Society for Aid to the Sick and Wounded in War was formed just in time. On 11 October 1899 war broke out against the Boers in South Africa. Few in Britain envisaged a serious campaign but the war dragged on until 1902. As the British suffered a series of major defeats Princess Christian began a project to help the wounded soldiers.

At her instigation a seven-carriage hospital train with twenty bunks in each compartment was built and equipped by the Birmingham Carriage and Wagon Company at a cost of £10,000, with money provided by the British Red Cross committee, a donation of £6,100 from the Borough of Windsor and a further £650 from the princess herself. In December, she inspected the lavishly equipped train, the first of its kind built in England, which included gifts from Queen Victoria and other members of the royal family. The *Princess Christian Hospital Train* was shipped to South Africa in sections and reassembled in Durban in February 1900. Painted white so that it would be easily recognised and not fired upon, it steamed into Ladysmith three days after Sir Redvers Buller had raised the siege. During the South African War the train carried 7,548 sick and wounded, the majority very seriously injured, and made 108 journeys covering over 12,000 miles. It was handed to the military in June 1901 but retained its name. At Pinetown Bridge, near Durban, the Princess Christian Hospital received its first patients in April 1900. Donated by Mr Alfred Moseley, the hospital had expanded to 200 beds by July. It was later presented to the government and continued to work as No. 13 Stationary Hospital.[18]

In July the same year, the princess opened Princess Christians's Homes of Rest for Discharged Soldiers at Bisley. She and her daughters each endowed a bed, as did Queen Victoria and the Duke and Duchess of York (later King George V and Queen Mary).

Princess Christian's eldest son Christian Victor was serving in South Africa and on 29 October 1900 he died of enteric fever in Pretoria. Once the family had recovered from the enormous shock the princess planned a memorial. In 1894 she had purchased two houses in Trinity Place, Windsor to accommodate her recently started Princess Christian District Nurses. After her son's death she bought numbers 3 and 4 Clarence Villas, which were converted into a medical and surgical nursing home in his memory. The Princess Christian Nursing Home opened in 1904.

In the middle of the war, on 22 January 1901, Queen Victoria died. Upon the accession of Edward VII, Princess Christian became involved in a battle royal with her sister-in-law Queen Alexandra over the Army Nursing Service Reserve.

★★★

As Princess of Wales, Danish-born Alexandra had already taken a great interest in nursing, even doing a St John Ambulance first aid course at Sandringham. Although profoundly deaf, Alexandra was able to convey her sympathy and understanding to those who suffered. People felt that she was personally interested in their problems and that this feeling was sincere.

In February 1885, with fighting going on in Egypt and the Sudan, she formed The Princess of Wales's Branch of the National Society for Aid to the Sick and Wounded in War. With typical insouciance, Alexandra ignored the fact that she was restricted by the Red Cross to aiding only the wounded. Worried about the welfare of the fighting men as well, she raised funds to send medical aid, books and comforts to the British, Indian and Australian servicemen. A steam launch, *The Alexandria*, was deployed to evacuate up to forty-eight wounded at a time from the lower reaches of the Nile.

Danish Döeker huts[19] were to be given to the troops for recreational purposes but there was a delay, as she informed Sydney Holland, chairman of the London Hospital. 'Then about the Döekers Houses I am still waiting for the answer from Copenhagen,' Alexandra told him, 'but if they no longer as you say are found there nothing will induce me to get them from Germany.'[20] Alexandra's anti-German feelings, dating back to the war of 1864, were well known. Nevertheless, she was 'delighted with all the magnificent gifts we have received for Our precious Ships'.[21]

During the Boer War the princess sent £9,000 (the balance of the fund collected by her branch for the Egyptian campaign) towards the cost of converting a yachting cruiser into *The Princess of Wales Hospital Ship* for 200 patients. Alexandra ordered special mattresses, enquired whether there would be a chaplain on board and was delighted when several cases of champagne arrived for the wounded officers. The ship took a large quantity of stores to Cape Town and then treated over 700 wounded men outside Durban.

As Honorary President of the Central British Red Cross Committee she also sent twelve nurses to South Africa. 'I am writing in a desperate hurry to thank you first of all for the trouble you have so kindly taken about everything finding the nurses and arranging with the War Office etc.,' she wrote to Sydney Holland. 'I am delighted with all you settled and that all Y[ou]r first rate nurses [*sic*].'

It was arranged that the War Office would pay for their travelling expenses and their uniforms. 'I will call these My Military Nurses,' Alexandra added proudly.[22] Later, at her own expense, Alexandra sent a further twenty military nurses although, to her regret, she was not allowed to select any of these women herself.

As queen she made nursing her special concern. One of her first acts was to receive over 700 Queen's Nurses at Marlborough House, where many of them were presented with badges and certificates. 'I'm so glad it all went off so well (including my reading the Speech!! which I did "quaking and shaking") and that all the Nurses enjoyed their tea and garden party here,' she wrote to Sydney Holland, thanking him for his help with the arrangements.[23]

Soon after King Edward's accession Queen Alexandra wrote to William Brodrick, Secretary of State for War, about the reorganisation of the Army Nursing Service Reserve:

> As you will have heard from Lord Roberts my great wish [is] to reorganise the whole system of our Army nurses. I write to ask you to kindly give official sanction and support our new scheme which will in fact be a national benefit to the entire Army and Navy – hoping therefore to have a favourable reply.[24]

Queen Alexandra had already discussed the matter with Sydney Holland, as she naturally wished to head the new organisation herself. This brought her into conflict with Princess Christian and King Edward now found himself in the difficult position of witnessing friction between his wife and sister. Eventually, Princess Christian was persuaded to resign as head of the Army Nursing Service Reserve and on 27 March 1902 the queen became president of the newly established Queen Alexandra's Imperial Military Nursing Service (QAIMNS), which operated under the control of a nursing board. (A permanent reserve was formed in 1908. However, Princess Christian remained as head of Princess Christian's Army Nursing Service Reserve.) The queen personally devised their badge: 'a cross as borne on the Royal Arms of Denmark, surmounted by an Imperial Crown, and the cipher "A" within the cross.'[25] She intervened to obtain better accommodation for them and took an interest in their uniforms, writing to Sydney Holland in 1915: 'You will be glad to hear that I have now at last succeeded in getting a new sketch done for our Army Nurses with their Red Capes (at an enormous price though!!)'[26]

In 1902, the queen paid a surprise visit to the military hospital at Netley. William Brodrick later told King Edward that the queen's acute observations had confirmed his suspicions that 'the system there is capable of great improvement; and Mr Brodrick is convinced', he continued, writing in the first person, 'that the knowledge and interest displayed by Her Majesty in Hospital questions will greatly strengthen his hands'.[27]

It had long been on the queen's mind to reorganise the Red Cross. In July 1905 King Edward announced the amalgamation of all the societies connected with Red Cross work into one association under the queen's presidency, to be called The British Red Cross Society. Alexandra presided at the first council meeting, which was held at Buckingham Palace on 17 July. In June 1907, the 8th International Red Cross Conference was held in London. The king and queen gave a reception in the Picture Gallery at Buckingham Palace, where the Japanese delegate praised Queen Alexandra's 'great humanitarian work'. The following year she played a crucial role in the granting of a royal charter to the society and in 1914 Alexandra appealed for money and gifts to help the Red Cross cope with the increased numbers of sick and wounded during the war.

King Edward died in 1910. Two years later, to mark the fiftieth anniversary of her arrival in England in 1863, the queen founded Alexandra Rose Day. Every year ladies sold artificial wild roses made by the disabled in aid of the hospitals and charitable institutions in which Queen Alexandra was interested. The event raised the equivalent of millions of pounds and the queen's annual Alexandra Rose Day drive through the streets of London became an institution. She continued these drives until two years before her death in 1925.

Queen Alexandra's 'great humanitarian work' may have been confined to visiting hospitals, writing letters and attending the occasional meeting but, as her biographer points out, 'in her own age and generation … nothing more arduous would have been expected or desired of her.'[28] It was left to other royal ladies to work in the hospital wards.

★★★

In 1916, the College of Nursing, a rival group to the Royal British Nurses' Association, was founded with backing from the medical royal colleges. Its aim was to act as a professional institution for trained nurses, pioneering professional standards of education, practice and working conditions. At first the college was supported by the Royal British Nurse's Association but soon Princess Christian, the college's nominal president, was unhappy about the situation. In a 'private' postscript of a letter to Miss Isabel Macdonald, Secretary of the Royal British Nurses Association, in 1917, the princess complained about her treatment by the college. 'You will understand in what a very difficult position I am placed,' she wrote from Cumberland Lodge:

> Virtually I am the nominal President of the new College, but I am told nothing by the College of what it is doing and am never contacted or asked about anything. I feel therefore doubly troubled about being in any way responsible for the College's actions, promises etc! I wish the College Council could be made to understand this ...[29]

The next day the princess went on the attack again. She strongly resented a statement published in *The Hospital* which suggested that the college would be given a royal charter. She wanted the statement refuted without being involved personally. The college, she said, must understand that it is to merge with the Royal British Nurses' Association, and not vice versa.[30] The princess was also anxious that the Trained Nurses' Auxiliary Fund should be affiliated with the Helena Benevolent Fund and the Settlement Fund.[31]

Mrs Bedford Fenwick was seeking to be nominated to represent at least one of the societies of which she was a member upon its affiliation with the Royal British Nurses' Association. Princess Christian welcomed closer co-operation. 'My one great object and desire has ever been to further the success and prosperity of our Associations, and to strengthen its [sic] position and to widen its sphere of influence,' the princess wrote to Mrs Bedford Fenwick.

> It is for these reasons that I welcome the suggestions ... for closer co-operation between the various Nurses Societies and affiliations with the Royal British Nurses' Association. I feel that to be strong and united is the only way to increase ... the welfare and prosperity of Trained Nurses as a great profession.

Princess Christian added that she would be pleased to accept Mrs Bedford Fenwick's nomination:

> ... as I feel I can rely on your help and co-operation in everything tending to the good and welfare of the cause we have so much at heart. I feel most strongly that if all the affiliated Societies will support and aid our Associations and myself, and be united as one big strong body, we need have little fear as to the ultimate result.[32]

By April there was a problem, as Mrs Bedford Fenwick clearly believed that she would be vice-president of the association. the princess told Miss Macdonald:

> It was on the Council that I did not object to Mrs Bedford Fenwick but I have no recollection of the other suggestions, ... had she become Vice President it would have laid me open to attacks of all kinds and from all sorts of quarters. It would have been absolutely impossible. I am so sorry if I have caused any trouble.[33]

Princess Christian's relations with Mrs Bedford Fenwick seem not always to have been easy. A few days later the princess was delighted to hear that the National Union of Trained Nurses had agreed to affiliate with 'our Association'. She was even more delighted that Mrs Bedford Fenwick had no influence with the nurses' union:

> I sincerely trust that no effort will be made ... to get Mrs Bedford Fenwick on to our Executive Committee. I could never agree to that and would certainly oppose it. I don't for a moment think that anyone has ever thought of such an eventuality but ... I could not agree to any such proposal. I have been rather disturbed at hearing from outside quarters not connected with the RBNA that Mrs Bedford Fenwick is saying that 'she has captured the Association' and 'got ascendancy over it' ... Whatever I may have done ... to make peace with her, has been done in order to help the Nurses and the cause! I am however determined she shall not have any say in the internal management of the Association ...[34]

The Nurses' Registration Act came into force on 23 December 1919 and after this date the College of Nursing (from 1928 the Royal College of Nursing) emerged as, and remains, the dominant professional nursing body.

★★★

After the death of her husband in 1917, Princess Christian continued her charity work and remained devoted to nursing. At committee meetings, the words 'it is my wish, that is sufficient' from her ended any discussion.[35] By the end of her life she had signed and presented proficiency certificates to thousands of women, as well as handing many medallions and certificates to members of the Windsor branch of the St John Ambulance Association. In 1922, when the Red Cross launched a public appeal to provide medical relief to refugees in Greece, many of whom were British subjects, she immediately lent four ambulance coaches.

Princess Christian died on 9 June 1923. She had been patron or president of 123 organisations and had made a lasting contribution to the welfare and training of nurses. Although the role of Queen Alexandra cannot be overlooked, the improvement in the condition of nurses and nursing during the late nineteenth and early twentieth centuries owed a lot to Princess Christian's influence.

Notes

1. Roger Fulford, *Dearest Mama* (Evans Brothers, 1968), p.311.
2. Epton, *Victoria*, p.129.
3. Ibid.
4. Seweryn Chomet, *Helena: A Princess Reclaimed* (Begell House Books, 2000), p.123.
5. John Van der Kiste, *Queen Victoria's Children* (Alan Sutton, 1986), p.77.
6. *The Times*, 14 February 1888.
7. King's College London Archives, RBNA7/PC1, Princess Christian to Miss Huxley, 31 March 1893.
8. *The Times*, 11 July 1888.
9. Speech of June 1893 given to the Scottish branch of the RBNA in Edinburgh. Quoted in Chomet, *Helena*, p.120.
10. *The Times*, 26 June 1890.
11. Charlotte Zeepvat, *From Cradle to Crown* (Sutton Publishing, 2006), p.36.
12. RA VIC/ADDJ/178. From the Duke of Westminster, 26 December 1887.
13. RA PPTO/PP/QV/MAIN/1891/282. 3 January 1891.
14. RA PPTO/PP/QV/MAIN/1891/282. 13 January 1891.
15. *The Times*, 26 February 1891.
16. *Women at Home*, 1895.
17. Letter from Lord Wantage to *The Times*, 30 September 1899.
18. Peter Prime, *The History of the Medical & Hospital Services of the Anglo-Boer War, 1899–1902* (Anglo-Boer War Philatelic Society, 1998), pp.74, 56.
19. Döecker (or Døckerske) tents were invented by the Danish officer Johan G.C. Døcker (1828-1904) and made of canvas and felt. Döecker huts were built from timber and planks and placed in a pit, which was covered by a slanting roof that rested on the sides of the hut. The entrance was on the third, open side and covered with wickerwork to ensure ventilation. Easily transportable, they measured 6–10m long and could house up to twenty men as a barracks or emergency hospital if necessary. Alexandra's huts, intended for recreational purposes, eventually had to be purchased from Germany.
20. RA VIC/ADDA21/233/8, 9 November 1899.
21. RA VIC/ADDA21/233/10, 16 November 1899.
22. RA VIC/ADDA21/233/31, 6 July 1900.
23. RA VIC/ADDA21/233/60, 4 July 1901.
24. 24 April 1901. Ian Shapiro collection.
25. Georgina Battiscombe, *Queen Alexandra* (Constable, 1969), p.233.
26. RA ADDA21/234/23. Christmas 1915.
27. RA VIC/MAIN/W/23/24, 22 August 1902.
28. Battiscombe, *Queen Alexandra*, p.238.
29. King's College London Archives, RBNA7/PC6, 6 July 1917.
30. King's College London Archives, RBNA7/PC1-2, 7 July 1917.
31. King's College London Archives, RBNA7/PC12, Princess Christian to Miss Macdonald, 13 March 1918.

32. King's College London Archives, RBNA7/PC14/1-2, Princess Christian to Mrs Bedford Fenwick, 15 March 1918.
33. King's College London Archives, RBNA7/PC15, Princess Christian to Miss Macdonald, 18 April 1918.
34. King's College London Archives, RBNA7/PC16/1, Princess Christian to Miss Macdonald, 20 April 1918.
35. Battiscombe, *Queen Alexandra*, p.233.

3

'Some Damn Foolish Thing in the Balkans'

The Balkan states of Greece, Romania, Bulgaria, Serbia and Montenegro emerged during the nineteenth century as each won independence from the decaying Ottoman Empire – 'the Sick Man of Europe'. With the growth of nationalism the area remained a powder keg with a fuse likely to explode at any time. When the inevitable wars broke out, royal women took up nursing.

Among the first were Queen Olga of Greece and her daughters-in-law Sophie and Alice. Queen Olga was born in Russia, where her mother Grand Duchess Alexandra Josifovna was for many years patron of the Alexandrovskaya Community of Sisters of the Red Cross. After Olga married King George I of Greece in 1867 she took up similar good works. Among the many charitable institutions she founded was the first Greek hospital, the Evangelismos, which opened in 1884 and was described by the British diplomat Sir Horace Rumbold as 'a hospital worthy of any great Western capital'. Olga encouraged donations towards its upkeep and visited regularly, sending food to poor families until their breadwinner recovered from illness.[1] She also built a hospital for Russian sailors, constructed at Piraeus on land bought with her own money, furnished and maintained out of her personal funds. The queen took a great interest in the welfare of these sailors, always visiting any Russian ships when they came into port, sending them delicacies in the hospital and summoning relatives to see those who were dying. She always had a supply of Russian soil available to be sprinkled on the coffins of Russians who died in Greece.

In 1889, George and Olga's eldest son Crown Prince Constantine married Princess Sophie of Prussia. Sophie was born on 14 June 1870, the seventh child of Queen Victoria's eldest daughter Vicky. Sophie had no real interest in national issues, preferring to concentrate her limited energy on home and family. Although she shared the interest of her mother and mother-in-law in nursing and welfare work, nursing in Greece was in its infancy. A training school was associated with Queen Olga's hospital but nursing was not yet highly regarded by the more intelligent members of Greek society.

Then in February 1897 the people of Crete rebelled against their Turkish overlords and demanded union with Greece. King George sent troops to help them but the Great Powers (Great Britain, France and Russia) would not permit the Ottoman Empire to be dismembered and sent an international force to Crete, ordering the Greeks to withdraw their troops. They refused. Encouraged by their countrymen, the Greeks in Turkish-ruled Macedonia (on the Greek-Turkish border) rebelled. In April, the Sultan of Turkey declared war and the Greeks found they had insufficient trained nurses to cope with the casualties.

The newly formed Union of Greek Women, which dedicated itself to welfare work, owed much to Sophie's inspiration. It trained medical staff, collected funds and organised medical supplies, humanitarian relief and hospitals. Queen Olga visited the barracks at Piraeus to help distribute bedding and food to the refugees who flooded in from Crete and then put the women to work making army uniforms.

As Sophie had discovered, Greece was 'a beautiful undeveloped country which ignored the first principles of hygiene,'[2] so the Red Cross group organised by the Union of Greek Women ran classes under Dr Kalopothakes, an American lady who had trained mainly in Paris. Sophie and Queen Olga attended the lectures, where Dr Kalopothakes explained the position of bones and organs, how to bandage splints and make plaster of Paris, the use of anaesthetics and the principles of basic hygiene. Soon Sophie became involved with nursing care, administrative duties and fund raising.

The queen and princess also sat in on the final examinations of the Red Cross nurses. The women were first called individually to answer questions on anatomy and hygiene, and then given a practical test. It was, said American-born Harriet Boyd, a 'nerve-wracking experience'. Soon volunteer nurses were called for and Queen Olga's influence secured Miss Boyd a place in a Red Cross hospital. Offers of help poured in and Vicky (now the widowed Empress Frederick of Germany) told Sophie that five of her own nurses had volunteered to go to Greece with the Red Cross. 'Doctors and material will go with them', she added.[3]

The Greek Army in Thessaly was commanded by Crown Prince Constantine. There was no plan of campaign, the Turks were superior in numbers and weapons and the Greeks were spread thinly along a long, difficult frontier. Constantine's headquarters were in Larissa, where Sophie arrived on 15 April accompanied by her lady-in-waiting Angeliki Kondostavlou.

They converted a newly completed military school into a hospital and nursed the wounded and dying for the greater part of every day amid the sound of gunfire. The shortage of nurses was acute, so Sophie transmitted an urgent request to her aunt the Princess of Wales, asking her to send some thoroughly trained nurses. Here she struck the right chord. King George of Greece was Alexandra's brother and she was following events anxiously.

Public opinion in Britain was also pro-Greek. Alexandra immediately sent the request to Mrs Bedford Fenwick, who chose four nurses to work under Sophie's direction and teach the nurses in Greece. Wearing 'a blue uniform, lined with red, upon which appeared a Maltese Cross', they left Charing Cross for Athens on 16 April along with a supply of medical stores.[4] Sophie wanted them to go north to Tyrnavos using Harriet Boyd (who spoke Greek) as interpreter but she was told that Miss Boyd was needed at Volos, where some of the wounded from Larissa were being treated. The English nurses eventually went to Epirus.

By 24 April more women and medical supplies were on their way from London in response to Sophie's appeal 'for still further nursing assistance'.[5] The crown princess emphasised the urgency by telegraphing to Mrs Bedford Fenwick, now appointed Honorary Secretary of the Grecian Nursing Committee, three times in twenty-four hours. Donations were pouring in and it was decided that the crown princess would be 'relieved of the expense in the matter of the equipment and sending out of the nurses'. Mrs Bedford Fenwick intimated that both funds *and* nurses could be supplied if required. 'Sincerest thanks; deeply touched. Surgical stores and clothing badly needed,'[6] Sophie telegraphed in response. She also asked her mother to send vaccine to immunise against tetanus.

The Empress Frederick was concerned about how her daughter would manage the wounded, suggesting that if the weather was warm she could stretch canvass overhead and cover it with brushwood to keep out the sun. and was horrified to hear that operations had been performed at Larissa without chloroform. 'If you still need some, telegraph to Aunt Alix, Grandma or me,' she instructed.[7] By the end of April nineteen nurses had left England for Greece and a well-known doctor had ordered £50 of chloroform from Messrs Duncan and Flockhart in Edinburgh for the use of Sophie and her nurses.

Heavy battles near Tyrnavos soon forced the Greeks to withdraw, spreading panic among the population, and by 25 April Larissa had fallen and Sophie was back in Athens. Queen Victoria urged the tsar to mediate and a ship stood by in case the Greek royal family had to be evacuated.

Meanwhile Sophie continued her work in the hospitals with Queen Olga, where they nursed both Greek and Turkish soldiers. One man had an infected leg and the queen ordered it to be amputated to save his life. He reacted so badly that Olga sat and patiently calmed him down. Later she had a house built for him at the king's country estate Tatoi and appointed him church bell-ringer, as well as buying him a knitting machine so that he could work to support himself.[8]

By the middle of May Athens lay open to the Turks and the Great Powers forced Turkey to grant an armistice. Greece had to withdraw her troops from Crete, leaving Turkish troops on Greek territory., which led the people of greece to turn against the royal family. As anti-monarchist feeling rose, German-born Sophie, whose brother the kaiser had sided openly with the Turks, was blamed for the defeat, and she and Constantine were openly spat upon in the streets. The crown prince was forced to relinquish his army command and Sophie's dedication to nursing the wounded was forgotten. Mediation continued throughout the summer, but when the peace treaty was signed Greece was forced to pay a £4 million indemnity.

Once more the Empress Frederick was ready with advice and encouragement:

> Do you think that the way the English nurses worked in your war hospitals opened the eyes of the Greek ladies about nursing? *There* is a great field for good work! Could not some young women of good family go through courses this winter, such as Aunt Alix and I went through, it would draw their attention and interest, especially if you were to give the example, and have the lectures once a week in your own house.[9]

As typhoid spread through the Greek Army, Queen Olga asked for nurses to go to Lamia, 10 miles from the coast, where wards were overflowing with cases. Constantine, Sophie and Olga visited the military hospital where they saw some heart-rending sights. Queen Olga showed much tenderness and compassion for a man who was obviously dying. As the priest arrived to give him the sacrament the royal visitors prayed at the bedside, following the service with reverence.

By June the royal family were living on board the royal yacht *Sphacteria* and the queen and crown princess invited some of the nurses to dine on board. Harriet Boyd was among those who attended. Sophie immediately asked after the soldier who had received the sacrament (he had, unfortunately, died), before quizzing Harriet about the American hospitals, particularly the John Hopkins hospital in Baltimore. Miss Boyd later recalled Queen Olga's 'real charm and … great gift for showing personal interest', as well as Sophie's obvious concern for the sick.[10]

Olga and Sophie visited the English hospital at Chalcis, spending two hours touring the wards where they were very favourably impressed, and the queen left some money so that a man suffering from rheumatism could have medicinal baths. The royal visitors were also shown the nurses' quarters, where cubicles were made from wires strung across the room, to which blankets or rugs were fixed with safety pins to afford some privacy. The old wooden crate used as a combined wash stand and chest of drawers also caused some amusement. This hospital was renowned for its efficiency, in stark contrast to the military hospital, where some of the men were suffering from typhoid. Olga and Sophie were so disgusted with the dirty conditions there that the queen ordered 200 patients to be sent to Athens, taking some with her on the royal yacht. The Empress Frederick was concerned that her daughter would catch a disease. 'Please do find time to bathe in the sea on your way *to* and *from* hospital to avoid infections,' she urged, 'and drink a glass of milk with a drop of brandy.'[11]

In October, the Empress Frederick asked Queen Victoria if 'the red enamel cross with your cipher in gold and the dark blue bow' (which she herself had been awarded some years ago) could be given to Queen Olga and Crown Princess Sophie. Queen Victoria promised to enquire.[12] The statutes of the Royal Red Cross were then changed so that the queen could bestow it on anybody, regardless of nationality, and it was awarded to both women in December 1897. Sophie also received the Order of St John of Jerusalem and, unexpectedly, a decoration from the kaiser.

Ironically, it took a failed assassination attempt to restore the royal family's popularity. In February 1898 two gunmen fired on King George and his daughter Marie as they drove along the Phaleron Road in their carriage. Both were unhurt and their coolness under fire raised the royal family's reputation. During the First World War, people in a Yorkshire town would be very glad that a Greek gunman failed to hit his target.

★★★

In 1908 Prince Ferdinand, the 47-year-old ruler of Bulgaria, remarried. The effeminate, sybaritic Ferdinand (whose father Prince Augustus of Saxe-Coburg-Gotha was a cousin of both Queen Victoria and Prince Albert) had been chosen by the Bulgarian government as their sovereign prince in 1887. The British ambassador's wife reported that he wore bracelets and powered his face. 'He sleeps in pink surah nightgowns trimmed with Valenciennes lace', she added for good measure.[13] He loved to run precious stones through his fingers and had a preference for handsome blond chauffeurs. His first wife had died in 1899 after giving birth to her fourth child and since his mother's death, Ferdinand needed someone to appear beside him on official occasions. He did not need somebody who would demand affection.

When Ferdinand told Grand Duchess Vladimir of Russia that he was looking for a wife she lost no time in contacting her cousin Princess Eleonore, elder daughter of the late Prince Heinrich IV of Reuss-Köstritz. Although aged forty-eight and not conventionally pretty Eleonore was 'full of the solid German values of efficiency, uprightness and dedication to duty'.[14]

Eleonore, born in 1860, had led a fairly humdrum existence as a minor princess in an obscure German court, but on visits to her cousin in St Petersburg her interest in nursing and hygiene led her to visit the hospitals. Deciding to study nursing properly, she enrolled on a course and received a certificate as a qualified nurse.

Early in 1904, Japan, angered at Russia's penetration into the Far East, launched a surprise attack on the Russian naval base at Port Arthur, Manchuria. Within hours Russia and Japan were at war. Eleonore volunteered her services on the Red Cross hospital train organised and equipped by Grand Duchess Vladimir. The train left St Petersburg with a staff of four doctors, eight sisters of mercy, four medical students and medical and office personnel, and equipped with the latest technology: beds for heavy and light injuries, a pharmacy, operating rooms, consulting rooms and staff accommodation. Travelling between Vladivostok, Harbin and Irkutsk, it brought the wounded from the front to General Kuropatkin's headquarters at Harbin, where the headquarters of the Russian Red Cross in the Far East were established.

Also nursing in Manchuria was Princess Alice of Bourbon, the 28-year-old daughter of Don Carlos Duke of Madrid and descendant of the kings of Spain, recently divorced from her husband Prince Friedrich of Schönburg-Waldenburg. When the Russians suffered defeat after defeat, Alice and Eleonore worked to restore order as heavy losses threw the ambulance services into disarray.

Eleonore worked in a Russian hospital and superintended a field ambulance, 'sharing all the risks and hardships of the campaign',[15] reported *The Times*. Newspapers showed photographs of her 'serving tea to an early casualty on a stretcher'[16] and reported that she proved both courageous and efficient, often working with splints and bandages under fire. In May 1905, a newspaper correspondent noted the arrival of 'Princess Reuss' at Kun-Tu-leng station, where she 'had just arrived to join the Red Cross'.[17] The following day she inspected hospitals with General Kuropatkin. The vigorous, independent princess soon earned the sobriquets 'Queen of Charity' and 'The German Florence Nightingale'. The *New York Times* called her 'Europe's Royal Nurse' who watched over the cots of the wounded during the Russo-Japanese War and the later Balkan War.[18] She was decorated on the field for her services to General Kuropatkin's army.

With the war over, Princess Eleonore perhaps saw the Bulgarian marriage as another opportunity for her hospital and charity work. She and Ferdinand certainly made a strange couple.

Ferdinand and Eleonore were married on 28 February 1908, but Ferdinand showed little enthusiasm for a bride who was neither young nor beautiful. Displaying the necklace he had chosen as Eleonore's wedding present he said unkindly, 'this will suit her austere bosom.'[19] When they visited King Carol of Romania during their honeymoon Ferdinand insisted that the double room be changed for separate bedrooms. Any illusions Eleonore may have had were shattered, and she soon found herself virtually abandoned. Nevertheless, she proved an excellent stepmother to Boris, Cyril, Eudoxia and Nadejda, who were aged between 14 and 9. 'She knew life and had faced it squarely,' recalled Queen Marie of Romania. 'She had an altruistic spirit, was practical, energetic', but, added Marie, 'to say that she was happy would, I think, be an exaggeration'.[20]

A few months after their marriage, Ferdinand proclaimed himself Tsar of Bulgaria. Eleonore was now the tsarina, although the press generally called her the queen. She used her rank and wealth to help those less fortunate, especially in rural areas where the peasants still resorted to sorcery and primitive remedies to cure their ailments.

In 1910, she started the Queen Eleonore Fund to build hospitals for deaf and blind children. Then, to see how things were done elsewhere, she visited the School of Nursing of the Assistance Publique at the Salpêtrière Hospital in Paris. Eleonore inspected everything from the kitchen and dining room to the laboratory and massage department, in which she expressed a special interest. She also questioned the pupils, saw the surgical instruments and looked over some of the students' bedrooms. During tea in the drawing room the queen was asked to sign a photograph taken when she was working as a Red Cross nurse in Manchuria.

With Eleonore's support, the Bolgarski Tcherven Krest (Bulgarian Red Cross, established in 1885) began training courses in nursing for charity women. In Sofia they founded a society called Samarjanka (Samaritan Woman), where under instruction from Red Cross doctors the women did sanitary work, nursing and were trained to assist the doctors. Courses soon spread to other Bulgarian cities.

Eleonore's efforts were soon to bear fruit when war broke out.

★★★

In October 1912, the newly formed Balkan League of Greece, Bulgaria, Serbia and Montenegro declared war on Turkey, with the object of carving up Turkish-owned Macedonia to enlarge their own countries. Within two weeks the allies defeated every Turkish army in Europe and the Ottoman Army collapsed.

As Bulgarian troops poured south into neighbouring Thrace and headed towards Constantinople, Queen Eleonore founded a hospital in Sofia in which she nursed, helped by German nuns. She spent many weeks moving between the hospital and the front, reorganising and superintending the inadequate arrangements for the care of the sick and wounded. Her urgent appeals for aid were answered in London by the Bulgarian Relief Fund, which collected food, blankets, clothes and money. The British Red Cross sent X-ray apparatus and an operator, along with two personnel units. On their arrival in Bulgaria, Queen Eleonore welcomed them warmly, giving each a signed photograph, and 14-year-old Eudoxia and 13-year-old Nadejda presented flowers. The queen then sent her equerry to see the party off at the railway station, where they discovered that she had thoughtfully supplied provisions for their long journey to Kirk Kilissa.[21] As refugees flooded in from Macedonia the queen telegraphed her thanks to Britain, adding that 'the need of further help is urgently felt'.[22]

The queen was also helping families reduced to destitution or left without support while their breadwinners were at the front. 'Am most grateful for generous gifts on behalf of the wounded soldiers,'[23] she telegraphed in response to donations made to the Red Cross by the American public. The work of the Women's Sick and Wounded Convoy Corps was greatly appreciated by Eleonore, who presented them with a miniature ambulance unit as a mark of thanks.

In March 1913 the Bulgarian Army captured the Ottoman stronghold of Adrianople after a five-month-long siege. Eleonore immediately went to nurse the soldiers, working as an ordinary nurse in the overcrowded hospitals, often staying late into the night to tend the wounded and dying as cholera, dysentery and typhus raged through the wards. She won great acclaim both for her nursing skills and as a director of the Bulgarian Red Cross.

Ferdinand ordered her to stop – he hated hospitals or anything to do with illness, detested the smell of antiseptics and anaesthetics, and particularly disliked the smell of Eleonore's clothes when she came back from the hospital. Although he 'recognised the importance and the necessity of having a consort who could deal with "all these abominations"',[24] for many weeks after she returned from Adrianople he refused to see her. When she began supervising the hospital management, inspecting supplies before they were sent out and organising relief for the families of those killed or wounded, his patience snapped. Possibly jealous of his wife's immense popularity, he ordered that no more stores should be despatched to the soldiers in the field and those donated by the public were to be sold at auction. Eleonore is said to have wept when she heard the news. 'I am of no account at all, then,' she exclaimed sadly.[25]

★★★

The Greeks, again commanded by Crown Prince Constantine, marched from victory to victory, anxious to avenge their defeat by Turkey in 1897. To Queen Olga and Crown Princess Sophie, chief patrons of the Greek Red Cross, fell responsibility for raising funds and distributing relief. 'Cannot your people do something for the sick and wounded?' Sophie telegraphed to her aunt, the widowed Queen Alexandra. The queen immediately approached the Red Cross Council. Soon personnel were despatched, a Balkan fund netted donations totalling £41,000 and gifts of clothing and blankets flooded in.[26] America proved a fertile ground after Queen Olga made a direct appeal to a Greek-American newspaper in New York. At Sophie's request New York's *Atlantis* newspaper also launched an appeal, which eventually raised $95,541. From Salonika, where she was nursing, Queen Olga immediately wired her thanks, saying she was 'profoundly touched' and 'grateful to all generous givers'.[27]

Sophie, who was expecting her sixth child, had less participation in actual nursing this time but another Greek princess was very much involved. This was Alice, the wife of George and Olga's fourth son Prince Andrew, a great-granddaughter of Queen Victoria.

Princess Alice of Battenberg was born at Windsor Castle on 25 February 1885. Her mother Princess Victoria was the eldest daughter of Princess Alice of Hesse; her father Prince Louis of Battenberg had become a naturalised British subject in 1868 when he joined the Royal Navy. Little Alice was a great beauty but she was profoundly deaf. Her no-nonsense mother soon ensured that the princess could lip-read in four languages.

In 1903 in Darmstadt, Alice married Prince Andrew of Greece in what was one of the last big royal gatherings before the First World War. By 1912, she was the mother of Margarita, Theodora and Cecile. Her husband served in the Greek Army and when war broke out Alice decided to set up a hospital.

On 20 October 1912, Alice accompanied Andrew and his brothers to Larissa and, with the help of Sister Margarethe and Sister Anna from the Alice Hospital in Darmstadt, began to sort out her hospital. In the military hospital Alice found some wounded soldiers from a recent skirmish at Elassona. Wealthy volunteers were doing 'magnificent work between Larissa and the front carrying despatches, officers, ambulance ladies, wounded and special stores over the Turkish artillery road, using their own motors with remarkable skill on the long, stony gradients with sharp turns among the precipices',[28] but the fourteen-hour journey over a mountain pass littered with huge boulders caused the wounded even more suffering. Alice realised that it would be impossible to bring severely wounded men to Larissa under these conditions. When news arrived of the army's rapid advance, she decided that her hospital would have to be near the front at Elassona.

Alice was informed that there would be no large battle there for at least two days, so there would be time to move everything, including her 'first-class operation room'. She quickly commandeered a car and, accompanied by her surgeon Meerminga and his assistant, as well as Mme Agyropoulo (wife of the local prefect) and Sister Margarethe, she set off. The journey took nearly five hours: ' … we set off at 11 o'clock and reached Elassona at 4.30 p.m. over impossible roads; we nearly fell over precipices and stuck twice in sandy river beds for an hour', she told her mother.[29] Everywhere they were greeted by delighted people overjoyed at being liberated from the Turks.

However, to Alice's horror a fierce battle was already raging at Elassona. She immediately commandeered a school and pillaged as much bedding as she could from Turkish houses. With beds of sorts now ready for 120 men she sent for her nurses, who would have to travel overnight from Larissa, and requisitioned a car from the general staff to send Meerminga off to the battlefield. There was no time to lose.

Alice described the scene:

… although the army had very good surgeons and men nurses with lots of bandages to make the first bandages on the battlefield, they had no means of transport to the nearest town, nor *one single plan* for improvising a hospital, with food and bandages, in such a town; and the Red Cross of Athens and other countries were so slow, they had not a single hospital nearer the war zone than Athens, for the Larissa hospital I myself forced the Military Authorities to fit out an operation room in 24 hours.[30]

There was nobody to organise transport, feed those who were able to walk or tend to the more severely wounded. For this she blamed the French General Eydoux and the head doctor Arnaud. Queen Olga and the princesses had been urging them for weeks to get things ready quickly. The French had assured them that everything had been done, but the royal ladies had been sure they were lying, Now Alice had seen proof.

Gunfire could be heard in the distance until 6.30 p.m., when the battle ended. Two hours later Meerminga arrived with the first casualties. The only nurse available was Sister Margarethe, so Alice and Mme Agyropoulo donned aprons and caps and prepared to help as the wounded began arriving after a journey in heavy rain. First the surgeon examined the wounds – 'ghastly ones from shells, then fractured bones and ordinary Mauser wounds etc' – then they put on fresh bandages. After the pain of this, the men were given a glass of brandy, followed by hot milk to make them sleep, which luckily most did after their exhausting journey on the bad roads.

For the next five hours, Alice helped the doctors by the light of a few 'miserable lamps' and tried to organise food and drink for hundreds of drenched, exhausted men. 'I found a small spirit lamp in a corner of one room and took spirits of wine from a lamp in another and a small Turkish coffee pot with water, and I possessed one tin of condensed milk which had to do for 250 men.' She had to cook with insufficient water in a tiny pot, sandwiched between a surgeon operating on one side and a dying man on a stretcher who wanted to hold her hand for comfort. With her free hand she tried to stir the pot while the blood from the operation trickled onto her: 'We helped the doctors in fearful operations, hurriedly done in the corridor amongst the dying and wounded waiting for their turn, for we could not spare a single room.' Later in this letter Alice described 'the corridor full of blood, and cast-off bandages knee high'.[31]

This work went on for three days and three nights, during which time she managed to snatch just a couple of hours' sleep in a freezing cold peasant's house. There was no chance to even change her clothes and all she had to eat was a crust of dry bread with a small cup of Turkish coffee. Alice had the only operating room near the battlefield and as more and more casualties arrived she commandeered four additional houses in which to put the less badly wounded. They were given a light meal and placed on mattresses on the floor and covered with blankets, using their greatcoats as pillows. Later a man came to help with the cooking, boiling the water in a huge kettle over an open fire. Finally two Greek Red Cross nurses took over, but only after all the wounded had arrived and Alice and her colleagues had done the initial work. This work was not without its dangers. In November *The Times* reported that two Turkish prisoners cut the throat of an attendant in a hospital at Elassona.

Alice was now a first-class nurse. 'I, who had never set my foot in hospitals, because I could not stand the sight of wounds and pain,' she wrote in disbelief.[32]

On 25 October, Alice arrived in the west Macedonian town of Servia, where Crown Prince Constantine asked her to set up a hospital. The Turks had already scattered in confusion and disorder so instead of the expected battle she had the joy of a reunion with Andrew.

The following day she joined King George and his sons as they made a ceremonial entry into the conquered towns of Elassona, Servia and Kozani. That night, and for several more, Alice had the luxury of a proper bedroom and embroidered bed linen trimmed with lace.

Half an hour from Kozani was a new military hospital. All the necessary bedding and hospital equipment had arrived but the Turks had rummaged through the storerooms, leaving everything in an awful mess. Alice found charwomen to wash the walls and floors before soldiers erected the bedsteads. She and Mme Agyropoulo worked for two days putting mattresses, pillows (some of which they had to make themselves) and sheets onto the 200 beds. 'We hung up the lamps and washed the mugs and put one by each bed, also spittoons, and we put shirts and under-drawers in a cupboard for each room etc.'[33]

The Greeks achieved a great victory at Kailar on 26 October. Alice and her nurses donned aprons and caps and snatched half an hour's sleep before the first wounded arrived. During that night over 175 men were bandaged and 160 more were put into a separate wing. The next day Alice had to assist at an amputation, done in one of the wards and screened from the sight of the other patients. She gave the chloroform, prevented the man from biting his tongue and then handed the cotton wool and basins to the surgeon. This was probably her worst experience, although once the terrible feeling of disgust had passed she found it all quite interesting. Afterwards Alice saw the amputated leg lying on the floor completely forgotten and suggested that perhaps someone should take it away, at which point Mme Agyropoulo promptly picked it up, wrapped something round it, put it under her arm and marched off to find a place in which to bury it. Unfortunately she had left the bloodstained end uncovered, and as she marched through the hospital people were heaving with revulsion. Alice shouted after her but Mme Agyropoulo did not hear. After the tension of recent days Alice suddenly saw the funny side and burst out laughing.

By November Alice was in Verria, west of Salonika, where she spent four cramped nights in a railway station awaiting more wounded. Through field glasses Alice could see the nearby fighting as Constantine's men cut off the Turkish retreat. The battle ended with a Turkish rout and Alice went to the hospital to receive the casualties. Her dedication and organisational ability surprised and delighted the entire family; Alice, said Sister Anna, was setting 'the finest example'.[34]

Salonika was liberated on 9 November after 400 years of Turkish rule. Two days later King George made a ceremonial entry into the city and celebrated the victory with a *Te Deum* in the Byzantine Cathedral, with Alice in his entourage. She and Andrew settled into a villa formerly owned by the Sultan and were joined by Queen Olga, who arrived from Athens with a party of doctors and nurses. The queen immediately began visiting the hospitals, giving what comfort she could, frequently using her own money to help families. Despite the fact that the short-sighted queen was having treatment for her eyes, she soon had female prisoners making blankets for the Greek soldiers and was planning a new maternity hospital in the town.

Another arrival was Nona Kerr, lady-in-waiting to Alice's mother, who came with three nurses from London's Charing Cross Hospital. Alice and Nona set to work organising the Salonika hospitals. Typhoid and dysentery were rife, hygiene was sadly lacking and the hospitals were in a dreadful state. Nona noted that Alice looked terribly thin.

Early in December, after a much needed rest, Alice and Nona set off to Preveza to establish a hospital which could, if necessary, follow the army. They then inspected some improvised hospitals at Philippiada, Alice covering her face with a thick veil to hide nettle rash.

Back in Athens, they found Crown Princess Sophie furious because some of her nurses had been sent from Cairo to Salonika by Alice, who had not asked permission.

Alice spent Christmas in Salonika, where she inspected a refugee camp and ensured that the homeless were properly fed. Andrew and their daughters Margarita, Theodora and Cecile were with her but by now both the prince and princess were in need of a tonic.

In January, Alice visited Epirus where she had intended to sort out the hospitals but, in a fit of pique, Constantine suddenly entrusted all the town's military hospitals to his brother George's wife Marie. Constantine was not amused at what he considered to be Alice's interference, feeling that this work should be done by Sophie. 'Why the devil is Alice coming here to mix up everything as she did in Saloniki [sic]?' he thundered in front of the hospital staff.[35]

By the end of February Alice and Nona were in Eminaga. There was more fighting in the first week of March and around 100 wounded men to take care of but by now the war was nearly over. On 6 March, Janina, the capital of Epirus, was taken by the Greeks. The Turks were soundly beaten and had to give up all their European possessions except Constantinople.

On 18 March 1913, 68-year-old King George took a walk through Salonika accompanied by his aide-de-camp. They had just passed a rather squalid café when a raggedly dressed man standing outside pulled out a revolver and shot the king in the back. He died instantly from a bullet in his heart. The assassination shocked all Europe. Constantine returned immediately to Athens to take the oath as king.

After the funeral Alice left to visit her family in England. In London the Greek community showed 'their admiration and deep gratitude for the heroic devotion with which she nursed, during both wars, the sick and wounded Greek soldiers'.[36]

Alice's work had not gone unnoticed at Buckingham Palace either. On 7 November the War Office announced that King George V had awarded the Royal Red Cross to Princess Andrew of Greece, 'in recognition of her services in nursing the sick and wounded among Greek soldiers during the recent war'.[37]

★★★

In June 1913, a second Balkan war broke out when Bulgaria, dissatisfied with its share of the spoils from the first conflict, attacked its former allies Greece and Serbia, launching an assault on the Serbian forces in Macedonia. As the Greeks and Serbs penetrated into Bulgaria, Turkey joined the fight and Romania attacked Bulgaria from the north. In Bulgaria there was widespread famine as refugees fled from the Greeks in the south and the Turks and Serbians in the east and west. Once again Queen Eleonore's appeals for help resulted in donations from America and the Bulgarian Relief Fund in London. Eleonore's good works, executive abilities and lack of pomp made her immensely popular with the people, while the soldiers saw her as an angel of compassion and solace.

The Romanians crossed into Bulgaria on 3 July. In command was King Carol's nephew Ferdinand, whose wife Marie sprang from an exotic heritage. Princess Marie of Edinburgh was born on 29 October 1875 at Eastwell Park in Kent. Her father, the handsome, bluff Prince Alfred, Duke of Edinburgh, was Queen Victoria's second son; her mother, the proud, autocratic Grand Duchess Marie Alexandrovna, was the daughter of Tsar Alexander II of mystical Russia. Princess Marie grew up at Clarence House, London and in Malta where her father commanded the Mediterranean fleet. In 1893 she made an arranged marriage with 27-year-old Crown Prince Ferdinand, heir to his childless uncle King Carol, a German prince chosen in 1866 to reign over Romania.

Marie was homesick and unhappy. She had no independence and what little she saw of Bucharest was a dull imitation of other European capitals. Only in the countryside, with its lush green meadows full of flowers, mountains and trees, did she find true enchantment. Nor did Marie find much comfort in her dull, unattractive husband and, although by 1913 she was the mother of Carol, Elisabeta, Marie (Mignon), Nicholas, Ileana and Mircea, there were rumours that Marie was having affairs.

When the second Balkan war broke out Marie donned a Red Cross nurse's uniform and set off to visit the troops and the Red Cross hospitals along the River Danube.

By 12 July the Romanian Army was just outside Sofia but King Carol forbade the troops to enter the capital of a fellow monarch. There was little armed resistance from the Bulgarians but the Romanians encountered something just as deadly as cannon fire – cholera, which brought panic in its wake.

The Bulgarians had contaminated the water supply by throwing the bodies of cholera victims into the water wells situated in the Romanian Army's path. Marie, appalled by what she saw in the hospitals, was fired with a fervent desire to ease the men's suffering and to be of use. Her friend Elise Bratianu had volunteered to nurse with the Red Cross but was forbidden even to cross the Danube. Elise told Marie, who secretly crossed to the Bulgarian side on a pontoon bridge and visited one of the hospitals. Here she found Romanian men 'almost abandoned and dying for the want of nursing and proper care'.[38] A leader, a rallying point, was needed. The Romanian aid organisations were simply not equipped to deal with this kind of disaster and the doctors were fighting a losing battle. Dr Jean Cantacuzène and his assistant Dr Slatineanu quickly convinced Marie that as crown princess she was ideally placed to help.

Marie immediately asked King Carol's permission to take over the administration of the cholera camp of Zimnicea, situated at one of the principal points where Romanian troops would re-cross the Danube on their way home. Her first step was to launch an appeal, which brought in a huge amount of provisions, and 'extras' unobtainable in military camps. She also asked for volunteers, turning to an old friend, Italian-born Sister Pucci, head of the nuns of St Vincent de Paul, who brought with her a great number of sisters to do the nursing. They pitched a large tent in the middle of the cholera camp equipped with camp beds and rough deal boxes for seats.

Marie spent two weeks in the camp accompanied by her lady-in-waiting Mme Mavrodi and Helene Perticari, the wife of one of the king's aides-de-camp. 'It is true that I know nothing about sickness,' Marie wrote in her memoirs, 'but I did not pretend that I had come as a nurse; but what I could be was a leader, an upholder, one to whom everybody could turn for help.' She organised, encouraged, inspired and soon became the 'pivot around which everything revolved'.[39]

Conditions were appalling. The men lay on straw pallets on the floor in huge wooden barracks with only dim lighting. They had no mattresses and very little in the way of bed linen. Work was hindered by impossible roads, slow means of transportation and fierce heat, broken by almost tropical rain which turned the field and the space between the beds into a sea of mud. When the sun shone the heat inside was torrid, when it rained the floors were wet and water dripped down the walls. Every day Marie, wearing riding boots under her white nurse's uniform, brought cigarettes and cheer to the men, and had hampers of flowers delivered from the gardens at the royal palace of Sinaia. The men thrust the stems through the identity card pinned above them on the walls; those who could not move held them and smelt the blooms. When they died, Marie laid flowers on their graves.

When Marie was exhausted she sat on one of the crude boxes and ate a skinny chicken cooked by Sister Pucci, who worked with bare feet, ankle-deep in mud, her blue skirts looped up and her white nun's wimple looking like the wings of a seagull. Marie called the sisters '*Mes Soeurs Cyclamen*' because their headdresses reminded her of the flower.

The doctors greeted Marie with scepticism, watching as the young woman who had known only palaces gritted her teeth to stand the sights and the smells of a cholera camp. Although she had a loathing of illness, Marie soon proved that she could endure the strain and the horror; she even braved the barracks known appropriately as 'Hell', where the very worst cases were placed. Those not already stricken with cholera had to be isolated at neighbouring camps and then examined before being demobilised. These men were angry, unable to realise why they could not go home. Marie regularly brought anything she could find which would lift their spirits. The commander, Colonel Rujinski, soon became her ally and friend.

At the far end of the field was a wooden laboratory where Dr Cantacuzène's pupils were hard at work preparing serum and making analyses to fight the epidemic. Marie visited but never stayed long, fearing her presence would hinder this vital work. Dr Cantacuzène's sister Constance set up a temporary hospital near Marie's camp and took some of the worst cases, who were nursed in proper beds.

Before Marie left the camp she was joined by Crown Prince Ferdinand for a requiem in the field. The troops stood in a huge square and everyone – priests in their vestments, Sister Pucci and her nuns in their white wimples, doctors and soldiers – came together in prayer. Afterwards Marie went through the ranks and decorated every man with a flower.

The brief experience of the cholera camp opened Marie's eyes to wider issues. 'My life and interests have changed … ,' she told her mother, 'I don't feel myself at all, I am a changed person.'[40] It enhanced Marie's reputation in Romania and stood her in good stead for her next and more prolonged experience of war.

***

The Queen Eleonore Cross was established in 1913 as an award for Red Cross work during the Balkan Wars. The cross, superimposed on a silver ring with the Red Geneva Cross in the centre and the Bulgarian crest at the top, was in the personal gift of the queen.

The problem of finding adequately trained nurses during the wars prompted Queen Eleonore to turn to America. In 1913 she met Mabel Thorp Boardman, director of the American Red Cross and Nursing Service. Early the following year it was announced that Eleonore hoped to travel to America to study the country's handling of economic and social problems. The visit, said *The Gettysberg Times* on 10 March, 'is the result of the deep interest which King Ferdinand and Queen Eleonore have long held in the United States, which has been strengthened by the association of the king and queen with the American doctors who were in charge of the Bulgarian hospitals during the recent war'. Unfortunately the visit was postponed and never took place.

Eleonore was planning to open a Nurses' Training Centre in the State Alexander Hospital in Sofia and wished to have four young Bulgarian women trained in America. At the same time she wanted to engage a superintendent to start the training school while these young women were being trained. She hoped that the government would then include the school's expenses in the regular hospital budget.

The American Red Cross recommended Helen Scott Hay and offered to pay her expenses. Miss Hay had trained in Chicago, later becoming superintendent at the Illinois Training School for Nurses. In 1914 she was given the post of Director of American Red Cross Nursing Personnel and sent to Europe. She worked firstly in Russia, where she was received by the Dowager Empress, and then in the Balkans.

Queen Eleonore invited Miss Hay to help attract young women for the planned training school, and together they visited nearly all the big hospitals in Bulgaria prior to the school being established. Miss Hay published articles about nursing and public health in America, emphasising the need for Bulgarian women to be thoroughly trained in these areas. She described a public health nurse as 'someone who brings together professional skills, theory and sympathy for the poor'. The nurses should befriend mothers and children, becoming familiar with the lives of the poor in order to assist them. Above all the aim was to reduce cases of tuberculosis, epidemics in schools and infant mortality.[41] Two nurses from the Henry Street Settlement in New York came to teach American Red Cross methods to a group of Bulgarian girls. Among the trainees were Eleonore's step-daughters Eudoxia and Nadejda. As Queen Eleonore and Miss Hay worked to improve nursing in Bulgaria events elsewhere were leading Europe into war.

★★★

'Some damn foolish thing in the Balkans', Bismarck had predicted, would start a European conflict. On 28 June 1914 his prophecy was fulfilled when the heir to the Austro-Hungarian throne, Archduke Franz Ferdinand, was assassinated with his wife at Sarajevo in Bosnia, which Austria had annexed in 1908. The deed was committed by a Serbian nationalist group with help from Belgrade. Within a month, Austria declared war on Serbia, the Serbs appealed to Russia for help and, thanks to a network of international treaties, the war engulfed Europe. On one side were the Entente powers of Britain, France and Russia, who were later joined by Italy; opposing them were the Central Powers of Austria-Hungary and Germany, who were joined by Turkey in October. All over Europe royal and aristocratic women turned castles and palaces into hospitals ready to receive the wounded.

Greece was neutral, but Queen Olga was in Russia and she immediately went to nurse at the hospital at the Life Guard Barracks of the Combined Cossack regiment near her childhood home Pavlovsk. 'I spend every day in the hospital, apply the dressings and enjoy all those little talks with my dearest soldiers,' she wrote:

> I returned home from the hospital at 9 p.m. only ... Around 11 p.m. I fell asleep, and around one in the morning went back to the hospital where the soldiers were transported. All of them were in a bad condition, all were on stretchers, frozen to the bone and tired of all the shaking during their trip. I returned home at 4 p.m.; slept less than five hours and feel ok. I am in a fog.

The queen was then in her mid-sixties.[42] Her son recalled that she:

> performed the duties of an ordinary nurse, returning to the palace only for meals. In this labour of love and charity, my mother found her true vocation, and she gave herself up to it with all her heart and soul, either by assisting the doctors or by cheering up the sick and wounded with the sweetness of her presence. Nothing would give her greater pleasure than when, after dressing some poor fellow's wounds, the doctor declared himself satisfied with her work.[43]

Queen Olga continued nursing until Russia was engulfed in revolution in 1917.

★★★

Bulgaria at first remained neutral. Queen Eleonore sent cases of Bulgarian cigarettes to the British, French, Russian and Austrian wounded. It was, she said, neutral charity. She received Josephine Sykes Morgenthau, wife of the American Ambassador to Constantinople, who shared Eleonore's interest in social work and asked the queen to intercede on behalf of Armenian women and children brutally treated by the Turks. As Turkey was keen to gain Bulgaria as an ally the timing was propitious.

In October 1915, Bulgaria declared war on Serbia, entering the conflict on the side of Germany and the Central Powers. As the wounded arrived Eleonore worked unsparingly in Sofia's Klimentinskata Hospital, founded by Ferdinand's mother in 1891. A witness recalled that she possessed 'a special gift for relieving suffering'.[44]

Early in October, Austro-German forces captured Belgrade, while Bulgarian troops attacked from the west. Queen Eleonore then answered an appeal for help from some British nurses caught up in the fighting.

When the Bulgarians captured Skopje on 22 October, a group of fifty-four nurses headed by Leila, Lady Paget (whose husband Sir Ralph was the British Red Cross Commissioner in Serbia), decided to remain with the Serbian wounded. As the first British relief workers to become prisoners of war they were given 'a great amount of liberty, and Lady Paget was allowed independent use of her stores in helping the refugees'.[45] She was confident that her past friendship with Queen Eleonore (whom she met during the Balkan War and who had praised Leila Paget generously) would secure reasonable treatment of her Red Cross unit while she continued to tend the Serbian casualties. Then at the end of November the Germans arrived. Leila wrote privately to Eleonore begging the queen to use her influence to ensure their repatriation.

In February, the British nurses were taken to Sofia, where Leila was the queen's guest in the royal palace. The other nurses were lodged in hotels by the Bulgarian Red Cross and during their four-week stay were allowed to go about town and visit the 400 interned British prisoners. Queen Eleonore received Lady Paget several times. During one of these interviews the queen was asked to intercede for the release of two British soldiers who were unfit to return to the front: one was blind and the other had lost a leg. The queen arranged for them to return home. Lady Paget and the British nurses eventually reached London in April 1916.

America entered the war in 1917 and Helen Scott Hay was called back to Washington. By this time Queen Eleonore was seriously ill. Every summer since her marriage she had spent some time at Euxinograd, the royal palace on the Black Sea coast which she dearly loved, and on 12 September 1917 she died there after a long illness. British and French prisoners of war, in whose welfare Eleonore had taken such interest, were among the many who sent wreaths to the funeral.

Marie of Romania had nothing but admiration for Eleonore. 'She served her people with generous abnegation, [and] was a wonderful sister of charity during the Balkan and later the World War,' she wrote.[46] As the war took its toll many European princesses donned Red Cross uniforms and volunteered as nurses. Among them were some of Queen Marie's relatives in Russia.

Notes

1. Julia Gerlardi, *From Splendour to Revolution* (St Martin's Press, 2005), p.119.
2. Epton, *Victoria*, p.197.
3. Allsebrook, *Born to Rebel*, p.39; Arthur Gould Lee (ed.), *The Empress Frederick Writes to Sophie*, (Faber & Faber, 1955) p.248.
4. *The Times*, 16 April 1897.
5. *The Times*, 24 April 1897.
6. *The Times*, 27 & 28 April 1897 .
7. Gould Lee, *Empress Frederick*, p.249.
8. Gerlardi, *Splendour*, p.167.
9. Gould Lee, *Empress Frederick*, p.257.
10. Allsebrook, *Born to Rebel*, p.74.
11. *The Nursing Record & Hospital World*, 19 June 1897; Gould Lee, *Empress Frederick*, p.252.
12. Agatha Ramm (ed.), *Beloved and Darling Child* (Alan Sutton, 1990), p.208.
13. Theo Aronson, *Crowns in Conflict* (John Murray, 1986), p.83.
14. Gordon Brook-Shepherd, Royal Sunset (Weidenfeld & Nicolson, 1987), p.62.
15. *The Times*, 13 September 1907.
16. Moorehead, *Dunant's Dream*, p.179.
17. *The Times*, 27 May 1905.
18. *The New York Times*, 29 March 1914.
19. Stephen Constant, *Foxy Ferdinand: Tsar of Bulgaria* (Sidgwick & Jackson, 1979), p.212.
20. Marie, Queen of Roumania, *The Story of My Life*, Vol. 2, p.253.
21. *British Journal of Nursing*, 14 December 1912.
22. *The Times*, 9 November 1912.
23. *The New York Times*, 6 December 1912.
24. Constant, *Foxy Ferdinand*, p.212.
25. *The New York Times*, 29 March 1914.
26. Dame Beryl Oliver, The British Red Cross in Action (Faber, 1966), p.218.
27. *The New York Times*, 6 December 1912.
28. *The Times*, 6 November 1912.
29. Letter from Princess Alice, 26 October 1912, quoted in Hugo Vickers, *Alice, Princess Andrew of Greece* (Hamish Hamilton, 2000), p.94. Extracts from the letters of Princess Alice of 26 October 1912 and 2 November 1912 quoted by Vickers are used here by kind permission of HRH The Duke of Edinburgh, who owns the copyright.
30. As above, 26 October 1912. Quoted in Vickers, *Alice*, pp.95–6.
31. As above, 26 October 1912. Quoted in Vickers, *Alice*, pp.96–7.
32. As above, 26 October 1912. Quoted in Vickers, *Alice*, p.97.
33. As above, 2 November 1912. Quoted in Vickers, *Alice*, p.98.
34. Vickers, *Alice*, p.100.
35. Vickers, *Alice*, p 103
36. *The Times*, 10 November 1913.
37. *The Times*, 8 November 1913.
38. Marie, Queen of Roumania, *Story*, Vol. 2, p.305.
39. Marie, Queen of Roumania, *Story*, Vol. 2, p.307.
40. Hannah Pakula, *The Last Romantic* (Weidenfeld & Nicolson, 1985), p.167.
41. Kristina Popova, 'Between Public Health & Social Work', in *Social Work and Society International Online Journal*, Vol. 9, No. 2, (2011).
42. Quoted in Gerlardi, *Splendour*, p.302.
43. Nicholas, Prince of Greece, *My Political Memoirs, 1914–17* (Hutchinson, 1928), p.167.
44. Aronson, *Crowns*, p.181.
45. *The Evening Post*, 20 May 1916.
46. Marie, Queen of Roumania, *Story*, Vol. 2, p.253.

4

'To Lessen Their Suffering Even in a Small Way'

By 1914, Queen Victoria's descendants had spread widely through the courts of Europe. Her grandson King George V was on the British throne; in Germany was another grandson Kaiser William II; among the queen's granddaughters were Queen Marie of Romania, Queen Sophie of Greece and Queen Victoria Eugenie of Spain. Two more of the queen's granddaughters were in Russia – Alix and her elder sister Ella, daughters of Princess Alice of Hesse.

Ella was one of the most beautiful princesses in Europe. In 1884 she married Grand Duke Sergei Alexandrovich, a son of Tsar Alexander II, and took the Russian name Grand Duchess Elisabeth Feodorovna. The marriage remained childless but the couple built schools and hospitals on their country estate Ilinskoe and did everything they could to help those less fortunate. In 1891, Sergei was appointed Governor General of Moscow but he proved unpopular and in 1905 was assassinated by a terrorist's bomb.

After her husband's death Ella divested herself of all her worldly goods in order to fund the building of a convent of which she would be Abbess. She then purchased a 4-acre estate on the Bolshaya Ordynka, a major boulevard on the far bank of the Moscow River opposite the Kremlin. The cornerstone of the convent church was laid on 22 May 1908 in the presence of the imperial family.

The Martha and Mary Convent of Mercy began its activities on 10 February 1909. The sisters were deaconesses, 'not ordained but distinguished by their dress ... employed in works of mercy'.[1] In a last gesture of worldly flair Ella had her pearl-grey robe and white veil designed by the religious painter Michael Nesterov, who also painted the interior frescoes of the convent church.

The ground floor of the two-storey main house contained service rooms and storerooms, with a kitchen and dining room for the sisters; on the floor above was the hospital, with twenty-two beds (including a separate ward for those seriously ill), operating rooms, a bandaging room and bathrooms. Some of the sisters lived on the attic floor. Ella occupied three small rooms in an adjacent building, sleeping on a wooden bed with a hard pillow and no mattress. On the other side of the main house was a pharmacy providing medicines, either free or at very low cost for those able to pay, an outpatients' clinic with its own library, and a dental surgery. Living quarters for more sisters were situated above.

In the courtyard, a fourth house contained classrooms for the eighteen girls of the orphanage, a library and rooms for the priest-confessor Father Mitrofan. The winter garden was converted into the hospital chapel. When the original six sisters had grown to thirty, an additional house with more living quarters, a dormitory for the orphanage, workshops and a laundry was built with donations from wealthy Muscovites. Surrounding the property was a beautiful English-style garden, with lilacs and laburnum bushes, where the patients could recuperate in the fresh air. An adjacent piece of land bought by Ella in 1909 provided both a guesthouse and a house for the poor.

Normally nuns in Russia would neither nurse nor teach and only in extreme circumstances were they permitted to leave the cloister. Ella wanted her nuns to be something between a monastic order and a nursing institution. Their day began at six in the morning and usually lasted until eleven at night. Besides their spiritual duties they took food to the poor and, having attended a short course in first aid, could give immediate medical attention when necessary. They worked in the clinic giving massages and injections, taught in the orphanage school, or worked in the kitchen. Ella ensured that they had adequate food, rest and an annual holiday, although due to the physical demands placed upon them she only accepted candidates aged between 21 and 40. One of her closest companions was Barbara Yakovleva, 'Sister Barbara', 'a small, dark-haired unassuming woman in her early thirties', who is said to have been widowed during the Moscow riots of 1904–05.[2]

The sisters working in the hospital attended more advanced courses on medical treatment, given by the head doctor A.I. Nikitin, and other courses by Professor Kornilov and Doctors Bereskin, Miasoedov and Tchernavski; they completed their training in the convent hospital. The six consultation rooms in the clinic were served by thirty-four physicians every week, all of whom volunteered their services free of charge. During 1913 over 10,000 patients were treated in the outpatients' clinic. The hospital was considered a model institution and soon had such a high reputation that other Moscow hospitals sent their more serious cases there.

Ella was an ideal nurse, with an immediate empathy towards the sick and suffering. She fought to overcome her revulsion of the operating theatre and was soon competently assisting Doctors Berskin and Ivanov during surgery. 'Well-known surgeons at other hospitals wondered at the Grand Duchess's nursing skills and frequently asked for her help in difficult cases.'[3] Ella usually had just three hours' sleep before getting up to make the round of the wards, and the sisters were ordered to summon her immediately if anybody was dying, whatever the time of day or night. She sometimes spent the whole night at the bedside of a dying patient, trying to ease their suffering both medically and spiritually. Some died in her arms.

Often she took on the task of nursing the very worst injuries. A cook with terrible burns from an oil stove was brought in by some nurses, who thought there was little that could be done medically for the woman. Gangrene was setting in, only the palms of her hands and the soles of her feet had escaped injury, and they thought it would be kinder to let her die in the convent. Ella disagreed: 'God willing, she will not die here,' she replied. Despite the awful smell, the grand duchess changed the dressings twice a day, taking two hours each time in order to spare the woman as much pain as possible, airing her robes after every session to rid them of the stench. To the surprise of the doctors the woman slowly recovered and a *Te Deum* was sung when she was finally discharged.[4]

One young girl was admitted for a trepanation of the skull (a procedure whereby holes are drilled in the skull to relieve pressure on the brain) and Ella nursed her devotedly. On the far side of the garden were several residential patients in summer huts. In one was 'a sick little girl' with her sister; while in another was a soldier and a poor little hunched-backed boy. Nearby were what Ella described to her niece as 'sanitairs in tents', while in 'a wee home' a little way away were eight paralysed soldiers.[5] In 1914, as war became inevitable, Ella ensured that her hospital was ready to receive wounded soldiers.

★★★

The outbreak of war saw a huge outpouring of patriotic fervour in Russia. As anti-German hysteria swept through the capital, Tsar Nicholas II changed the German name St Petersburg to the Slav name of Petrograd and the imperial women, accustomed to wearing expensive clothes and sparkling family jewels, put these aside to take their place in the operating theatre, or by the bedside of a dying soldier.

The grand duchesses organised hospitals, sanitary trains and relief work, as well as medical supply depots and field chapels for the front. Yet such was the initial disorganisation, said the French Ambassador, that 'some twenty-five trucks of medical supplies' gathered by Ella 'were mistakenly sent to the wrong front, and field chapels needed in the east were sent in the opposite direction'.[6]

The Russian Red Cross and the hospitals were financed by the imperial family. Nurses were called 'sisters of mercy' and addressed directly as *sestra* (or sometimes by the affectionate diminutive *sestritza*). Aristocratic ladies flocked to train as sisters but many fled when their nursing duties became unexpectedly demanding. 'Some of them joined just because the uniform was becoming,' recalled the British Ambassador's daughter, 'some of them never even got as far as passing the exams.'[7] The president of the Russian Red Cross was the tsar's mother the Dowager Empress Marie Feodorovna. Her main focus was raising money, leaving the practical work to younger members of the family. One of the most active was Marie's daughter-in-law Alix, Ella's sister.

The death of her mother when she was only 6 had turned Alix from a bubbly child to a shy, withdrawn and awkward young woman. Deeply religious, she hesitated about converting to Orthodoxy in order to marry Nicholas II in 1894. The decision caused her much heart-searching and their hasty wedding, brought forward by the sudden death of Nicholas's father Alexander III, seemed to superstitious Russians like a bad omen. 'She has come to us behind a coffin,' they whispered.

On her marriage Alix became Empress Alexandra Feodorovna, but although the couple were supremely happy, she lacked charm and was disliked by society. The empress rarely smiled and her face and hands flushed red when she was agitated. She suffered from sciatica and childbearing proved difficult. The tsar needed a son to succeed him but Alexandra bore four daughters – Olga, Tatiana, Marie and Anastasia. When Tsarevich Alexei was finally born in 1904 he suffered from haemophilia and Alexandra blamed herself for passing on the disease. As the doctors were powerless to help she turned to faith healers and *Staretz* (wandering holy men) like Gregory Rasputin. 'Our Friend', as she called him, was the only person who seemed able to relieve Alexei's sufferings, and his influence over Alexandra grew. The stress and anguish of Alexei's illness undermined her own health, leaving her prey to a string of psychosomatic illnesses. She drew her husband and children further and further into their own little world at the Alexander Palace, Tsarskoe Selo, 15 miles from the capital, where she often spent days resting on a couch in her mauve boudoir.

The outbreak of war changed all this. Overnight, Alexandra was transformed. To the amazement of her relatives she forgot all her ailments as she organised hospitals and sanitary centres reaching from Petrograd and Moscow in the north to Charkoff and Odessa in the south. Even the large State Rooms of the Winter Palace eventually became wards and operating theatres. A series of large *skladi* (storage depots) opened, where ladies made bandages and packed medical supplies, warm blankets and clothes for the soldiers. Small *skladi* operated all along the Austro-German frontier to supply the hospitals on the front line.

The centre of the empress's personal activity was the large group of evacuation hospitals near Tsarskoe Selo. A wing of the huge Catherine Palace was converted into a hospital for officers under the management of Princess Elizabeth Narishkin-Kurakin. Princess Vera Ignatievna Gedroits MD was the hospital's surgeon, with Sister Lyubushcha as the senior nurse.

Princess Gedroits was a remarkable woman. Born in 1870 in Slobodishe, Orel Province, into an old Lithuanian princely family, she studied medicine in St Petersburg and at the University of Lausanne before spending five years as assistant to Professor César Roux in his clinic. After the death of her parents in 1900 she returned to Russia with a degree in medicine and surgery and, while working as a factory doctor, studied to gain a Russian medical degree, which she later obtained in Moscow with a doctoral thesis on the treatment of hernias. Princess Gedroits was one of the few Russian women doctors. Her friend Avdieva described her thus: 'a little overweight, she dressed like a man. She wore a jacket and tie, men's hats, a fur coat with a fur collar, her hair cut short.'[8]

During the Russo-Japanese War, Princess Gedroits went to Manchuria with the Russian Red Cross. During her first six days at the front she performed fifty-six complex operations in her own specially equipped ambulance train, or in tents overlaid with clay to keep out the cold. As she later said, 'equipping tents at 22 degrees below zero was no easy task'.[9] She was an extremely competent surgeon and the first to operate on abdominal injuries soon after the men were wounded (others did not operate at all, or did so only after the men had been moved to hospitals behind the front). The princess's methods were adopted by the Russian Army and caused ideas about the correct treatment of such wounds to change. She soon became famous as a female surgeon and war hero and, on her return from Manchuria in April 1905, was received by the empress.

On 31 July 1909, on the recommendation of Alexandra's personal physician Dr Eugene Botkin (and despite her connections with the revolutionary movement), Princess Gedroits was appointed senior registrar of the Tsarskoe Selo Palace Hospital, and she soon became surgeon and friend to the imperial family. The hospital was built during the reign of Nicholas I and was surrounded by alms-houses, a pharmacy, staff quarters, a washhouse and a chapel. At first the upper floor of the main building accommodated thirty officers and 150 lower ranks, with the number of beds for lower ranks increasing to 200 from October 1914.[10] Elizabeth Zinovieff nursed in the Soldiers' Department, 'a large building with two floors' in a small garden planted with lime trees, birch, maple, jasmine and Alexandra's favourite lilac bushes. 'Next door, in the yard, was a separate

building which was the Officers' Hospital,' she recalled,[11] originally a small
pavilion built shortly before the First World War for quarantine cases. In 1914
the empress decided to take it over as a thirty-bed hospital for wounded officers
and she asked Princess Gedroits to equip it. Although it had its own operating
theatre and staff, the head surgeon and the doctor were shared with the Palace
Hospital. The Palace Hospital Annexe (sometimes called the infirmary) was
inaugurated on 10 August 1914 and supported by palace funds. It was an oasis
of peace and calm after the noise of battle and one of the officers said it took
him a long time to become accustomed to the oppressive silence.

The empress hated to see idle hands so it was natural that her family's long
tradition of charity would lead her to nursing. Princess Gedroits had created
a training course for nurses and in August Alexandra, her elder daughters
19-year-old Olga and 17-year-old Tatiana, along with the empress's friend
Anna Vyrubova, enrolled as student nurses under the princess's tutelage. Olga
was Sister Romanova the first; Tatiana was Sister Romanova the second. The
initial pre-war training period for nurses was a year, but shortly after war
began this was shortened to two months to meet increased demand. It was
later shortened to just six weeks.

'Began my lectures at the Alexander Palace … It was agreed that I will read
from 6 to 7 p.m. daily and will just go in my own carriage', Princess Gedroits
wrote in her diary on 27 August.[12] Every morning at nine o'clock Alexandra
and her daughters arrived at the hospital and, after scrubbing their hands in
antiseptic solution, went to the reception wards where the men arrived after
receiving first aid in the trenches or the field hospitals. Under the direction of
trained nurses they washed, cleaned and bandaged wounds. Alexandra's first
patient was the officer E. V. Stepanova who had a simple wound above the
knee. A few days later she brought him a small book of the Gospels inscribed
with the date of her first bandaging.

'Every day they bring there 6 lower ranks and Olga and I dress their
wounds. When we finish doing it we go to the officers' [ward] where Mother
and Anya dress them in turn ',[13] Tatiana told the tsar. After lunch they received
two hours of theory instruction from Princess Gedroits, although occasionally
she was forced to cancel a lecture because the empress was unwell. Sometimes
the grand duchesses were in the ward during the afternoon. 'We were in our
hospital up to 5.30 p.m. and did the dressings in the large hall from 2 p.m.
to 4 p.m.,' Olga explained. 'Then we spent some time with the officers.'[14]
Occasionally, the younger children visited the infirmary. 'Alexei was present at
all dressings,' Tatiana wrote, 'and once he even held a basin for the pus coming
out of the wound …'[15]

One of the nurses who worked closely with Alexandra and her daughters
was Valentina Chebotareva, who had completed formal training before

nursing in the Russo-Japanese War. Valentina was not from the highest court circles but was one of the few ladies at Tsarskoe Selo who had any nursing experience. She was appointed Senior Sister of the annexe and operating room, thereby becoming one of the select group of women working in the tsarina's hospital, an opportunity which would have been closed to her under normal circumstances. She was initially a great admirer of the empress; her opinion changed later, but her feelings for the young grand duchesses, especially Tatiana, never altered. 'It is good here …' Olga remarked one day. 'Is it not strange, we would not have known you, had there been no war?'[16]

Valentina recalled that on arrival at the hospital the empress extended her hand in greeting but remained distant. Princess Gedroits then gave 'a one half-hour lecture in their room' before they went to the bandaging rooms – the empress and Vyrubova to the officers, Olga and Tatiana to the soldiers.[17] Alexandra was soon in her element. Her work not only helped others but took her mind off separations from the tsar when he was visiting the front. 'Looking after the wounded is my consolation', she told him in September. 'To lessen their suffering even in a small way helps the aching heart.'[18] To Alexandra these men were the *real* Russia.

Sometimes there was a long operation but the empress did not flinch. 'We assisted at two operations – she [Princess Gedroits] did them sitting so that I could give her the instruments sitting too,' she wrote to Nicholas on a day when her health was poor.[19] Often there were several operations in one day. The surgeon-princess described working with the empress as a delight:

> She never loses her presence of mind, remains calm and collected under the most trying circumstances, and when she assists at an operation she is positively wonderful, giving her unswerving attention, handing the right instruments at the right moment, and all the time so calm, so gentle, so unobtrusive.[20]

By the end of October, the empress and her daughters had done a full and thorough course of surgical training and were progressing to anatomy and internal illness. Alexandra proudly wrote that she had worked completely alone, only checking with Princess Gedroits that she was following the correct course of action. During the first three months of the war over 600 wounded men passed through the small hospital, as well as thirty-three men with shell shock. As they became well enough, many of them were evacuated to sanatoria in Finland (at that time still part of the Russian empire). Some later came back as outpatients to have their wounds dressed.

Alexandra believed her presence was a help and consolation to these poor men. She had become fond of a young boy who was gradually getting worse. She told her sister, Princess Victoria of Battenberg:

He is contusioned [sic], and in the last week always unconscious, recognising nobody. When I come he regularly recognises me, and then remains with a clear head all day long, suffers hideously – such cramps in the head and whole body – nerves too shattered, poor soul. He is touching with me, I remind him of his mother's kindness and as soon as I come, takes me at first for her (she is dead). When I call him and talk, he stares, then recognises me, clasps my hands to his breast, says he now feels warm and happy.[21]

When sanitary trains arrived from the front she worked until mid-afternoon without food or rest. 'The state of those wounded men was beyond any description', recalled Vyrubova. 'They were dressed not in clothes but in bloody rags. They were covered in dirt from head to foot; many could not tell themselves whether they were alive; they were screaming from the terrible pain.'[22] These poor men had to be undressed and washed, their faces and eyes bathed, so that experienced nurses could instruct the imperial ladies about the treatment of the wounds.

On 6 November Alexandra, Olga and Tatiana went to the building of the Red Cross Society in Leontyevska Street where, together with nurses from the first military graduates, they were awarded certificates as Sisters of Mercy during wartime, signed by Princess Gedroits. These stated that the nurses had listened to a two-month course, undertaken practical exercises and passed the examination of the approved programme. They were now entitled to wear the grey nurse's uniform with a white headdress and apron. 'It was an emotion, putting them on, and appearing with other sisters – 40 – who had finished their course …' Alexandra told Princess Victoria. 'We are continuing lectures about illnesses, medicaments, anatomy etc., to have a fuller course and we all enjoy it.'[23] Alexandra felt fulfilled. 'I never saw her happier than on the day … she marched at the head of the procession of nurses to receive the red cross and the diploma of the certified war nurse,' wrote Vyrubova.[24]

The empress's work was misunderstood. It was usual for high-ranking ladies to hold some honorary position in the many charitable foundations but Alexandra's insistence on becoming a 'common nurse' was misinterpreted as a 'cheap method of seeking popularity' or just simply 'bad taste'.[25] It was not only the nobility who thought so. Many of the common soldiers were embarrassed at being nursed by the tsarina and this feeling was heightened by the fact that she was of German origin. Countess Kleinmichel summed up the general feeling:

… when a soldier saw his Empress dressed in nurse's uniform, just like any other nurse, he was disappointed. Looking at the Tsarina, whom he had pictured as a princess in a fairytale, he thought: 'And that is a Tsarina? But there is no difference between us …' The intimacy which sprang up between the Empress, her young daughters and the wounded officers destroyed their prestige.[26]

It also destroyed the awe with which, as empress, she inspired in them, placing her on a level with other women. She forgot, said Grand Duchess Maria Pavlovna, 'that Russia had thousands of women perfectly able to do this work, while she alone, as Empress, could arouse emotions and inspire loyalties which no-one else could.'[27]

★★★

Grand Duchess Maria Pavlovna was the tsar's cousin. Her mother Princess Alexandra of Greece had married Grand Duke Paul Alexandrovich and died after giving birth to her second child Dmitri in 1891, when little Maria was barely two years old. When Paul was banished for contracting a morganatic marriage, the tsar placed Maria and Dmitri under the care of Paul's brother Sergei, Governor General of Moscow. After Sergei's assassination, Ella assumed guardianship and in 1908 she arranged Maria's marriage with Prince William of Sweden. Maria was unhappy and in March 1914 she obtained a divorce and returned to Russia.

When Dmitri left for the war with his regiment Maria decided to go to the front as a nurse. She turned to Princess Elena, the Serbian-born wife of her distant cousin Prince Ioann Constantinovich, who had begun studying medicine at the University of St Petersburg in 1911 in order to become a doctor (her studies were ended two years later by pregnancy). Elena was forming her own unit, the Marble Palace Hospital Train, for front-line nursing service and Maria asked the empress for permission to go with her. Alexandra agreed on condition that she was accompanied by Natalia Sergeieva as lady-in-waiting.

Only a qualified Red Cross sister was allowed to join a front-line unit, so Maria had to train as a Sister of Mercy. The main Red Cross hospital was the Community of St Eugenia on Old Russian Street 3, Petrograd,[28] part of the care committee of the Red Cross Sisters, under the patronage of Princess Eugenie of Oldenburg, a distant cousin of the tsar and a well-known philanthropist. Maria did practical training there every morning, while in the evenings she studied theory and attended lectures given by eminent physicians. Maria 'worked for a long time under the superintendence of Professor Walter [a well-known Petrograd surgeon] and Dr Schwartz, in one of the hospital barracks'.[29] Instead of just doing the rounds of the wards and talking to patients, she now had to become familiar with the sight of wounds and learn how to bandage them. After three weeks the grand duchess passed her examination and was presented with a certificate by her former governess Evdokia Dzhunskovskaia, Lady Patroness of the Eugenia Community of Sisters of Mercy and a longstanding member of the Red Cross.

A special mobilisation committee had been formed in the charge of the Red Cross sisters, and the medical institutions proceeded to the front in four batches. Maria left in the third, consisting of a field hospital of the Greek colony and a hospital for 200 people in the name of the Society for Sales of Russian Metallurgical Factories, bound for the East Prussian front. With Elena and Maria were eight nurses, two doctors, twenty orderlies, a superintendent and a representative of the Red Cross, as well as the necessary equipment for field operations – 'an ambulance and other wagons, field kitchens, cauldrons, horses and tents' and Elena's car. Maria and Elena shared a compartment. In her memoirs Maria described her field kit: 'a few grey uniforms, white kerchiefs we wore as head-dress, aprons, white hospital smocks, cotton underwear and cotton stockings – all packed in one suitcase.' That night, for almost the first time in her life, Maria took out her own nightdress and pillow and undressed without the help of a maid.[30]

At Gumbinnen, Maria and Elena drove out to find a location for the hospital. The town was deserted. Unbeknown to them, the Russian Army had been heavily defeated at the battle of Tannenberg and the inhabitants had fled, leaving all their possessions behind. Dmitri and Prince Ioann (Elena's husband) then appeared, saying that General Rennenkampf had moved his headquarters west to Insterburg in Poland, where they themselves were stationed. Elena's hospital train therefore followed.

At Insterburg they found an old school, the largest building available, which they cleaned ready to set up the hospital. Two classrooms on the upper floor became wards, while other rooms were transformed into bandaging rooms and operating theatres. The nurses lived on the lower floor where Maria shared a modest, small, stone-floored room with Natalia Sergeieva. Apart from their camp beds, the only furniture was some packing cases on which to sit.

The first few days were quiet. Maria went shopping with Elena and was delighted to discover that her uniform 'produced a different kind of respect and trust than her position as a member of the Imperial family'. She was also pleased to find that it 'broke down barriers and smoothed out differences in rank'.[31]

Most of the soldiers had no idea who she was. One morning in the town a soldier approached and asked if she could put a fresh dressing on his hand. Maria had a clean bandage in her pocket, so they sat down near the square. As she unwound the dirty bandage one of General Rennenkampf's officers approached with a camera, addressed Maria by her title and asked if he could take a photograph. Maria blushed in confusion but when she had finished bandaging, the soldier, now having learnt her identity, knelt and kissed the hem of her skirt.

Elena was head of the hospital unit, while Maria worked as an ordinary nurse. From the very beginning she loved the work and was known in the wards for her cheerfulness. Most of the patients were young, good-looking cavalry men. One of Maria's duties was to wash patients who were unable to take care of themselves. One sub-lieutenant petulantly refused to wash himself and insisted she do it, trying to hinder her as she did so. Maria refused to talk to him and afterwards, when he sent the orderly to fetch her under a feeble pretext, she refused to go. Later that evening some wounded Guards officers were brought in. Maria dressed their wounds, changed them into hospital clothes and went to have supper. While she was eating, the orderly came to report that the young sub-lieutenant was having hysterics. The other officers had disclosed the identity of his nurse and he was so ashamed of his behaviour that he now lay there sobbing. Only on the day of his discharge did he pluck up courage to apologise.

Maria also witnessed her first death. One afternoon two men were brought in on stretchers, one with a very weak pulse. Maria sent for the doctor, meanwhile calling for camphor and a needle from the bandaging room. Suddenly the man began to choke blood. Maria started to unbutton his collar but by the time the doctor arrived it was too late.

Maria's initial war service lasted only two weeks. By September General Rennenkampf's army had lost the battle of the Masurian Lakes and was retreating hastily. Every day, Zeppelins dropped bombs on Insterburg as the Germans tried to blow up the railway station. The artillery fire grew closer, explosions rocked the air, shells and shrapnel fell nearer and a continuous stream of wounded arrived. Orders came to transfer all the wounded to sanitary trains and pack up the hospital ready to retreat. Maria made several trips to the station, walking on the hard cobbles beside the springless wagons which jolted the wounded along to the railway line. As the station had been almost completely destroyed, the men were laid on stretchers on the pavement while planes continued to fly overhead. She received the St George's medal for her work that day.

Once the wounded had been moved Maria helped to pack up the hospital. Then, as she tried to snatch a few hours' sleep, she was woken by Natalie Sergeieva saying there was a Zeppelin dropping bombs over the city. They hurried into the yard, where Maria found the rest of the hospital staff standing, helpless, as explosions rocked the surrounding area. Later they learnt that a bomb had exploded between the hospital and General Rennenkampf's headquarters next door. It was decided that for safety reasons Maria would not leave with the unit in marching order. The grand duchess and Princess Elena, expecting her second child, were evacuated by car with Rennenkampf's staff.

Back in Petrograd, Maria worked in the nursing home of the St Eugenia Chapter of the Red Cross for Sisters of Mercy, living in a small, simply furnished room close to the matron's apartment. She refused to have a maid, as it was against the rules for a sister and she wished for no exception. Maria spent three weeks working in the bandaging room in the mornings and the public dispensary in the afternoons. She then worked as a nurse in the overcrowded hospital, dressing wounds in the surgical ward, nursing a patient who was dangerously ill or an officer who had just undergone surgery, and writing letters home for the men. For a long time Maria managed to preserve the secret of her identity, the patients simply called her 'nurse'. Whenever time permitted she continued to attend evening lectures to increase her knowledge. However, it had become obvious that having the tsar's cousin working near the front line was more of a liability than a blessing. Soldiers who could otherwise be usefully employed had to be diverted to ensure her safety. The St Eugenia Chapter was organising a large hospital at Pskov to work at the rear of the army and Maria was therefore appointed head nurse. It was a position that both served Maria's desire to be of use while befitting her status. Sixty-year-old Theodosia Zandina, who had nursed during the Turkish war, was appointed as her assistant. Before Maria left, the convalescent officers presented her with a bouquet tied with white satin ribbon. On it was engraved in gold letters: 'To our beloved Sister, from the wounded officers.'[32]

In the middle of October the hospital unit of twenty-five nurses, five doctors, eighty orderlies and a superintendent was ready to leave for Pskov, headquarters of General Ruzskii's Northern Army. The unit went in marching order, Maria followed two days later. Pskov would be her home for the next two-and-a-half years.

★★★

The tsar's sister Grand Duchess Olga Alexandrovna already had some nursing experience. Olga married Prince Peter of Oldenburg (the son of Princess Eugenie, who did so much for the Russian Red Cross) in 1901. It was an arranged marriage; the bride was 19, the bridegroom 33. Peter was a gambler with little interest in women, but at least Olga was able to remain in her beloved Russia instead of making her home abroad with a foreign prince.

Princess Eugenie owned the huge estate of Ramon south of Moscow. When Olga and Peter visited, the grand duchess often helped the two doctors and four nurses in the sizeable hospital which Eugenie and her husband Prince Alexander had opened in 1880. There was usually plenty to do, Olga recalled:

So it wasn't in the slightest bit strange that I was to be found there almost every single day. I liked being there and would read to the patients or chat with them. At especially busy times I would also go along to the operating theatre and do what I could do in the place of a nurse. I learnt a lot from these visits – things that I would have much use of later in life.[33]

Olga was also one of the trustees of the Pokrovskaya Society, founded by the Oldenburg family in 1858, whose hospital and institutions had expanded by 1900 to include 100 Sisters of Mercy, a pharmacy and out-patients' department, consulting rooms, laboratories, a women's gymnasium [school] and a refuge for the homeless.

In 1903, Olga met Nicolai Kulikovsky, an officer in her brother Michael's regiment the Blue Cuirassiers. It was love at first sight but, although Kulikovsky came from a prominent military family, he was a commoner. This did not worry Olga, who had no use for pomp and ceremony, and she immediately asked her husband for a divorce. Peter refused to sully the family name by providing 'evidence' of his supposed adultery (the husband was always the guilty party), saying he might consider the matter again in seven years. As Olga and Kulikovsky were seen frequently together in public, Peter took the unusual step of appointing Kulikovsky as his aide-de-camp and giving him rooms in their St Petersburg palace, which thus became the scene of an extraordinary *ménage à trois*. This was the situation in August 1914.

When Kulikovsky's regiment was called to the front Olga wanted to find a way to be near him and also make herself useful, so she asked the tsar's permission to go to the front as a Sister of Mercy. Early in August, Olga, with her fellow nurse and travelling companion Tatiana Andreevna Gromova, left with the Parish Hospital of St Eugenia, the general Red Cross Hospital patronised by her mother-in-law. There were eighteen nurses, five doctors and enough equipment for 200 beds. Their destination was Rovno, 1,550 miles south of Petrograd.

'We are travelling in a second-class carriage,' Olga wrote to her niece Tatiana, 'there is a corridor down the middle – compartments on one side and arm chairs on the other, which are used as beds in the night. We wash in turns. Everyone is terribly kind to me.' They spent the morning hunting bugs and the doctors came into their compartment to chat. During the long journey they were provided with hot food once a day at one of the stations. 'We are on the way to Kiev,' she added, 'and from there we do not know where they will send us.'[34]

On 6 August they reached Rovno, a small town of narrow, dirty streets and a few shops near the Polish-Austrian border. The understaffed Red Cross field hospital was in a former artillery barracks, with the military hospital on the other side of the road. The place was swarming with stray cats, one of whom was quickly adopted by Olga. She shared a room with Tatiana Gromova, who the grand duchess soon grew to like for her cheerful personality. Gromova, born around the mid-1880s, had trained as a masseuse, a physical training instructor and a hospital nurse. In 1910 she gave treatment to Grand Duchess Anastasia, who had a weak leg. 'I am really fond of Tatiana Andreevna,' Olga told Marie Nicolaeivna in October, 'we live very comfortably together.'[35]

'Sister Olga' was Second Sister, there was no undue deference. She stuffed mattresses with hay and sewed them up, put the blankets out in the sun to air and ensured everything was ready to receive the first wounded. They were not long in arriving. To the sound of creaking cart wheels and horses' hooves on the hard road the first dusty, blood-stained men arrived. As the nurses began cutting the stiff, blood-soaked clothes away more casualties were brought in and it quickly became apparent that their 200 beds were insufficient. The most lightly wounded were placed on mattresses in the corridor. Olga and her colleagues were soon working more than fifteen hours a day, preparing the entire dressing material from morning to night with barely a break. For the first few days they hardly slept, as the wounded were brought in during the night. For some nights afterwards Olga heard those creaking cartwheels in her sleep and jumped out of bed to see if more wounded were arriving.

'The backs of my legs are very tired so I am lying on the bed and writing to you – waiting for supper – it is already about 9 o'clock,' she told Marie Nicolaievna. 'There has just been a wonderfully touching vespers in one of the wards, where the light casualties are … Those who could, stood – others sat, and those who couldn't were lying down.'[36]

Olga took pleasure in seeing the men recover and was sad when any died:

Many of our patients have left, and at first I missed them, because they were mine; but now I have become fond of (and loved) three dears – two without legs and a third seriously wounded in the thigh and injured in the blood vessels, which is really dangerous – God give that he will get well again. One without a leg was in the Combined Guards' battalion in 1905–1907 and was incredibly pleased to see me and to remember with me all the places like Gatchina, Tsarskoe Selo, Christmas, etc …[37]

She wrote letters home for those unable to do so, although they always asked her not to say that they were wounded. 'Unlucky legs and arms are fractured, stomachs, chests and head are injured by shots, and somehow it all has to be taken care of,' she told her niece. 'If it is very bad, and their sufferings are unbearable – we anaesthetise them with chloroform – then it is easier to do everything.'[38] When difficult bandages had to be changed Olga held the patient in her arms while the doctor worked.

The men could not believe that the tsar's sister was a simple hospital nurse. 'Which Sister bandaged your wounds?' the head surgeon asked one man. 'That snub-nosed little one over there,' he replied, pointing towards Olga. The surgeon looked rather uncomfortable but Olga 'laughed gaily at the wounded soldier's ingenuous designation'. Another man sat with tears trickling down his cheeks after Olga's identity was confirmed by the doctor.[39]

In late September the soldiers were delighted when the tsar visited Rovno. Only one man was upset. His weak eyes were bandaged and he would miss his only chance of seeing the sovereign; however, Olga obtained the doctor's permission for the bandages to be taken off just for a moment when Nicholas reached his bedside.

Nicholas returned to the hospital on 29 October, before going to the military hospital opposite. In one of the beds was a young boy under guard, who had been court-martialled and sentenced to death for desertion. Olga learnt that when he had more or less recovered he would be shot, so very quietly she told her brother the sad story. As the tsar approached the bedside the boy slipped out of bed and knelt at his sovereign's feet. Nicholas gently put his hand on the boy's shoulder and uttered words of forgiveness, and then dismissed the guard. Everyone was moved to tears.

Fresh casualties arrived every day and there was a constant shortage of medical supplies, clothing and bed linen. She told Marie:

> We have had a lot of work in recent days as there were about two hundred new casualties here. Among them were many different Cossacks: Terskies, Kubans and Don Cossacks ... There was one terribly dear and very young wounded volunteer Cossack, who I took care of myself as I did not entrust him to anyone else and did not permit anyone to touch him and growled and clenched my teeth when any of the nurses decided to help me to dress him! For him that was very nice and flattering so he laughed a lot – and his comrades did that too – and when we left, we gave each other a firm handshake and he said "I will never forget you!"[40]

One day they fed nearly 1,000 casualties in the dining room. Olga worked at full speed, carrying the enormous teapots, distributing bread, cleaning the tables and feeding the men. 'Which one of you is the sovereign's sister?' she was asked, and she blushed as she pointed to herself with a guilty look.[41]

Early in 1915 she was promoted to First Sister of the Red Cross community in Rovno. 'Later, in recognition of her tireless work ... the hospital was named after her.'[42] In mid-March, as the Austrians rapidly retreated, the Russians captured Lvov in Galicia, the small Austro-Polish part of Western Ukraine. A few days later the seemingly impregnable fortress of Przemyśl was taken. In Russia there was jubilation. Olga immediately travelled to Lvov and rode by Nicholas's side as he entered the captured city. 'The people gave us a tumultuous welcome and flowers were thrown from every window,' she recalled.[43] She never forgot that triumphant ride.

★★★

In January 1915, Anna Vyrubova was seriously injured in a railway accident. Her legs were crushed, her head was pinned down by a steel girder and her skull and spine were badly injured. The tsar and tsarina hurried to the hospital, where Princess Gedroits told them Vyrubova was dying. There was nothing they could do.

Gregory Rasputin heard the news the following day. He drove immediately to the hospital, took the dying woman's hands and called out her name. As she slowly opened her eyes he ordered her to 'wake up and rise'. She made an effort to get up and then spoke to him in a feeble voice. 'She will recover, but she will remain a cripple,' predicted Rasputin, before staggering from the room and collapsing from sheer effort of will.[44]

Vyrubova recovered but from that time used crutches or a wheelchair. To the dismay of many, Rasputin's influence over Alexandra, which had waned at the beginning of the war, was restored. Rasputin's frequent visits to Vyrubova were not welcomed by Princess Gedroits, who once seized him by the shoulders and pulled him into the hallway, slamming the door in his face.

With Nicholas away visiting the front, Alexandra became closer to the young boy (see pp.68–9) and when he died she was heartbroken. Once again her health collapsed and she spent six weeks in bed with complete exhaustion.

The strain was beginning to tell. Sometimes she sat talking to the wounded and embroidering while her daughters worked on the wards. Sometimes she was simply unable to go at all. The war aged Alexandra. 'My hair is also changing colour fast – such miseries one daily sees & lives through – & always the same courage,' she told her brother Ernie, the Grand Duke of Hesse. 'Many an officer have we had back wounded 2, 3 times again for us to nurse – good Lord what wounds from the explosive bullets!' The Austrians were using 'dum-dum bullets' which exploded and fragmented on impact, leaving particles of metal behind which had to be extracted from the enormous lacerated wounds.[45] These lethal bullets, which had been banned in 1875, caused damage that surgeons looked upon with horror.

The empress described a typical day:

> … with Olga to the big palace to see a very seriously wounded officer (through the lungs). At 10 Tatiana fetched us (after her lesson) and they dropped me at Ania's.

At 10.30–1.00 we worked at our hospital, with officers and men, and operations, rather often appendicitis, etc, too. Then I would go and sit with that poor officer again, for an hour or more, then pass through the other wards. After tea, rested, if did not have audiences or officers to bid goodbye, before returning to the ward. After dinner, off to Ania or to the hospital, or to both according to necessity … [46]

One evening she went back at midnight to see the seriously ill officer Smirnov. Ensign Pavlov recalled that in the winter the empress sent in regular supplies of fresh flowers and fruit: 'in the spring, cherries and peaches; in summer, strawberries, melons and watermelons; and in autumn pears and grapes.'[47]

In August, a patient died during an operation. 'What silence came,' Valentina Chebotareva recalled. 'The Sisters, and Olga and Tatiana, were crying. The Empress, as the sorrowful angel, closed his eyes, stood a few seconds and quietly left the room. Poor Vera Ignatievna [Gedroits] instantly went to her room.'[48]

For Easter 1915, Nicholas gave Alexandra the Red Cross Egg made by Fabergé. Inside this austere egg is a triptych with a miniature of the Resurrection, flanked by miniatures of St Olga and St Tatiana painted in enamel on gold. On the exterior are portraits of the Grand Duchesses Olga and Tatiana wearing Red Cross uniforms.

Nicholas also gave a Fabergé egg to his mother. The simple white egg with a red cross in the centre has a central band with Church Slavonic lettering in gold saying 'Greater love hath no man than this that a man lay down his life for his comrades.' The 'surprise' inside is a folding screen showing miniatures of the five Imperial nurses – Grand Duchess Olga Alexandrovna, Grand Duchess Olga Nicolaievna, Empress Alexandra Feodorovna, Grand Duchess Tatiana Nicolaievna, and Grand Duchess Maria Pavlovna the younger.[49] Yet for the Romanovs time was running out, as the country spiralled into chaos.

Notes

Until 1 February 1918 Russia used the Old Style Julian calendar, which was thirteen days behind the west in the twentieth century. Unless otherwise indicated, all Russian dates are Old Style.

1. *The Martha-Mary Convent and Rule of St Elizabeth the New Martyr* (Moscow, 1914. Reprinted by Holy Trinity Monastery, Jordanville, 1991) p.49.
2. Christopher Warwick, *Ella, Princess, Saint & Martyr* (John Wiley, 2006), p.249.
3. Lubov Millar, *Grand Duchess Elizabeth of Russia: New Martyr of the Communist Yoke* (Nikodemos Orthodox Publication Society, California, 1991), p.140.
4. E.M. Almedingen, *An Unbroken Unity* (The Bodley Head, 1964), p 74; Millar, p.140.
5. Quoted in Warwick, *Ella*, p.254.
6. Millar, *Grand Duchess Elizabeth*, p.173, quoting Paleologue.
7. Merie Buchanan, *Petrograd, The City of Trouble 1914–1918* (Collins, 1918), p.128.
8. k.finkelshteyn.narod.ru/Tzarskoye_Selo.
9. John Bennett, the *British Medical Journal*; k.finkelshteyn.narod.ru/Tzarskoye_Selo.
10. This building is now the N.A. Semashko Town Hospital No. 38.

11. Elizabeth Zinovieff, *A Russian Life* (Y.N. Galitzine & J. Ferrand, 1997), pp.115, 117

12. k.finkelshteyn.narod.ru/Tzarskoye_Selo.

13. Letters of Grand Duchess Tatiana, 5 September 1914. www.alexanderpalace.org.

14. Letters of Grand Duchess Olga, 21 October 1914. www.alexanderpalace.org.

15. Letters of Grand Duchess Tatiana, 30 November 1914. www.alexanderpalace.org.

16. Gregory P. Tschebotarioff, *Russia, My Native Land* (McGraw-Hill, USA, 1964), p.59.

17. Tschebotarioff, *Russia*, p.55.

18. Joseph T. Fuhrmann (ed.), *The Complete Wartime Correspondence of Tsar Nicholas II and the Empress Alexandra* (Greenwood Press, Connecticut, 1999), p.15.

19. Fuhrmann, *Complete Wartime Correspondence*, p.24.

20. Anon, *Russian Court Memoirs 1914–1916* (Herbert Jenkins, 1917), p.50.

21. Baroness Sophie Buxhoeveden, *The Life and Tragedy of Alexandra Feodorovna, Empress of Russia* (Longmans Green, 1930), p.193.

22. Yuri Shelayev, Elizabeth Shelayeva & Nicholas Semenov, *Nicholas Romanov: Life and Death* (Liki Rossi, 1998), p.103.

23. Buxhoeveden, *Life and Tragedy*, p.193. One of the grand duchesses' uniforms is preserved in the Pavlovsk Museum.

24. Anna Vyrubova, *Memories of the Russian Court* (Macmillan, 1923), p.110.

25. Alexander N. Bokhanov, Dr. Manfred Knodt, Lyubov Tyutyunnik, Vladimir Oustimenko, Zinaida Peregudova, *The Romanovs: Love, Power & Tragedy* (Leppi Publications, 1993) p.275.

26. Countess Kleinmichel, *Memories of a Shipwrecked World* (Brentano's Ltd., 1923), pp.216–17.

27. Maria of Russia, p.196.

28. The Municipal Hospital No. 46 is now located in the building.

29. Anon, *Russian Court Memoirs*, p.53.

30. Maria of Russia, *Education of a Princess*, pp.167–8.

31. Maria of Russia, *Education of a Princess*, p.175.

32. Anon, *Russian Court Memoirs*, p.54.

33. Paul Kulikovsky, Karen Roth-Nicholls & Sue Woolmans, *25 Chapters of My Life*, (Librario, 2005), pp.57–8.

34. N.K. Zvereva, *Avgusteishie sestry miloserdiia* (Veche, Moscow. 2006), pp.255–6.

35. Zvereva, *Avgusteishie*, pp.261–2.

36. Kulikovsky, Roth-Nicholls & Woolmans, *25 Chapters*, p.77.

37. M. Udaltsov, *Belikaya Knignya Olga Aleksandrovna Romanova-Kulikovskaya* (Forum, Moscow, 2011), p.67.

38. Zvereva, *Avgusteishie*, p.257.

39. Anon. *Russian Court Memoirs*, pp.52–3.

40. Udaltsov, *Belikaya Knignya*, pp.69–70.

41. Zvereva, *Avgusteishie*, pp.262–3.

42. Ian Vorres, *The Last Grand Duchess* (Hutchinson, 1964), p.148.

43. Vorres, *Last Grand Duchess*, p.148.

44. Robert Massie, *Nicholas and Alexandra* (Victor Gallancz, 1968), p.316.

45. Petra H. Kleinpenning, *The Correspondence of the Empress Alexandra of Russia with Ernst Ludwig and Eleonore, Grand Duke and Duchess of Hesse* (Books on Demand, 2010), p.329.

46. Buxhoeveden, *Life and Tragedy*, p.196.

47. www.pravaya.ru/govern/391/2311.

48. k.finkelshteyn.narod.ru/Tzarskoye_Selo.

49. Alexandra's egg was sold by the Soviet Government and later presented to the Cleveland Museum of Art. The dowager empress's egg, for which the tsar had paid 3,559 roubles, was confiscated by the Provisional Government and taken to the Armoury in the Moscow Kremlin. Records show it was sold in 1933 to Lillian Pratt. For more on both eggs see Tatiana Fabergé, Lynette Proler & Valentin Skurlov, *The Fabergé Imperial Easter Eggs*, (Christie's, 1997), pp.222–4.

5

Towards Revolution

In March 1915, Grand Duchess Olga Alexandrovna's hospital was moved 130 miles south-west to Lvov in Austria-Hungary. Olga liked the town very much, particularly admiring the magnificent churches.

New casualties arrived every day. There was heavy fighting in the area and Olga could hear the cannons thundering in the distance as she worked around the clock. At Easter she distributed eggs and tobacco pouches to the soldiers, giving them the traditional three kisses and the Easter greeting '*Khristos Voskres!*' – 'Christ is Risen!' Some men from the Akhtyrsky Hussars were among the wounded. This was Olga's regiment, she had been appointed their Honorary Commander-in-Chief on her wedding day. 'I dress their wounds myself every day,' she told Tatiana. 'I do not leave that to anyone! ... If there is no more bandaging to do in the evening I go over to sit with them in a small room – where the window is wide open, and we sit there together in the dusk and chat about life in general ...'[1]

Soon the earlier rejoicing turned to despair as Lvov and Przemyśl were lost again. Many of the tsar's subjects came under German occupation and refugees fled before the German advance. As the Russians retreated, all their western fortresses, all of Poland and part of Lithuania were lost, together with 3 million men.

On 8 May, Olga's hospital was evacuated. The wounded had to be sent off quickly, along with the army, with only the very worst cases being transferred to another hospital which would remain behind. Sitting in an automobile on a flat train wagon on the way to Tarislov, Olga wrote by candlelight to Nicolai Kulikovsky: 'We ... are after all evacuating to Proskurov – but are ordered not to hurry in a panic as it could be that we will soon be ordered to go back again. How foolish all this is. All trivialities in life are so unbearable ...'[2]

In Proskurov the hospital was once again in a barracks and the nurses were accommodated in empty railway carriages at the station while it was made ready. There was considerably less work to do so Olga visited the Akhtyrsky Hussars just over the nearby Austrian frontier. While visiting the trenches she came under Austrian artillery fire and, for her courage, was awarded the St George's medal by General Mannerheim. In August, as the situation worsened, Olga's hospital was moved once more. This time they went north-west to Kiev.

★★★

As Russian troops retreated from Galicia and Poland people began to whisper about the 'German' empress and her 'German' sister. As Ella drove back to the convent one day the mob threw stones at her car, smashing the windscreen.

In August the tsar took the fateful decision to take over as Commander-in-Chief of the army and immediately left for Stavka (headquarters), 500 miles from the capital. Left behind in Petrograd, the empress now became increasingly involved in the government of the country. Behind her stood Rasputin. When the situation failed to improve, people remembered that she was German and that the kaiser was her cousin and she therefore must be betraying information to the enemy. The outcry against *Nemka* ('the German woman') grew louder.

In the infirmary the atmosphere changed, as the empress was no longer regarded with the same respect. Alexandra's attendance at the hospital was now intermittent, although Olga and Tatiana played ping-pong or chequers with the convalescing officers in between their nursing duties. 'Everything was simple and cosy,' recalled Valentina[3] but some members of the nobility were troubled by their over-familiarity with the patients. Photographs were circulated showing the grand duchesses sitting with the wounded men and Valentina was concerned for the girls' reputations. As Countess Kleinmichel explained, 'in the state of mind which existed after the defeats of 1915, everything presented itself as a weapon to be turned against this unhappy family who wished only to do good'.[4]

Calm, considerate and industrious, the hard work of a nursing sister came naturally to Tatiana. All who saw her at work admired her professionalism and soon even the doctors agreed that she was a born nurse. She rose at seven every morning to have lessons before the car took her to the hospital. After lunch came more lessons, before she returned to the ward. In the evening the girls came to clean the instruments, happily scrubbing them with soap and alcohol before carrying them to their containers, often helped by the more able-bodied men. The officers were surprised that the grand duchesses should risk ruining their hands when there were orderlies to do this work.[5]

Valentina Chebotareva described Tatiana as 'a wonderful sister'. When an emergency incision proved necessary she collected and boiled all the instruments, prepared the sheets, moved the tables and had everything ready in twenty-five minutes. 'The operation went smoothly,' but the patient later died.[6]

'Today Tatiana Nicolaievna arrived first,'Valentina recorded one October day in 1915. 'She ran with me into the kitchen where we prepared the bandages. The Empress laughed ... Poor Olga Nicolaievna is very sick – [she has] developed a strong anaemia, laid for a week in bed, but with permission comes to the hospital for half an hour for arsenic injections.'[7] Arsenic was often used as a tonic for depression or nervous illnesses.

Given the grand duchesses' sheltered upbringing, it was inevitable that they would form attachments to some of the patients. Olga had become seriously fond of a 3rd Lieutenant with the 13th Erivan Grenadier Regiment, Ensign Dmitri Shakh-Bagov, a dark-eyed 22-year-old Caucasian whom she called 'Mitya.' Olga noted in her diary every time she treated him.

Tatiana's favourite was Sub-Lieutenant Vladimir Ivanovich Kiknadze, a Georgian from the 3rd Guards' Rifle Regiment who came into the hospital in the second part of 1915. Tatiana especially liked to play ping-pong with him and she also met his sister. Olga often sat on Shakh-Bagov's bed and one day both grand duchesses *and* Kiknadze sat on Shakh-Bagov's bed looking at photograph albums. Princess Gedroits was angry.

Valentina took her duties as informal chaperone very seriously:

> Soon after the end of the dressings Tatiana Nicolaievna goes to do injections and then sits alone with K. [Kiknadze] ... The sweet face of Tatiana Nicolaievna hides nothing, she is pink, excited. But it is not good, all these attachments. I think it is horrible. The others are actually jealous and I can imagine what they say in the town. Vera Ignatievna [Princess Gedroits] will send K to Evpatoria, thank God. Let us keep them far from sin. Vera Ignatievna said to me she heard that Shakh-Bagov, when he was drunk, showed someone Olga Nicolaievna's letters. That is the last straw! Poor children!'[8]

In June Shakh-Bagov was discharged and soon returned to the war. Ivan Beliaev recalled that Olga sat for more than an hour with her head down sadly into her sewing machine. A month later, when a letter arrived from Shakh-Bagov, Olga was excited. For a long time she searched for the knife he used the day before he left the hospital and was deliriously happy when she found it. She also kept the page of the calendar for the day he left. Then the hospital received a letter saying he was wounded again and had asked to come back. Olga snatched up the letter with a loud cheer. When he returned she immediately brightened.

The empress encouraged these friendships. 'I asked Anya to invite Rita [Khitrovo, Olga's friend, also a nurse] and Shakh-Bagov and Kiknadze and Demenkov for the children at 4.30, to spend a cosy afternoon, as they don't go to the hospital today,'[9] she told Nicholas in November 1915.

According to Valentina, Olga's great wish was to live a normal life in a village without any formality. Alas for a young girl's dream. The last time she saw Mitya was on 27 December 1916. Tatiana's romance fared no better. In October 1916, Kiknadze was sent to the Crimea. It is unlikely that they ever met again.

★★★

Since October 1914, Grand Duchess Maria Pavlovna had been established in the provincial town of Pskov, 200 miles south-west of Petrograd and 150 miles from the front. Her hospital was on the lower floor of the Ecclesiastical School for Girls, where Maria had a 'small but cheerful room' in the apartment of the directress.[10] Once again she helped scrub the floors, clean the furniture and get the hospital ready. Initially it had 250 beds but gradually this increased to 600.

Maria was nominal supervisor of twenty-five women but the grand duchess had been brought up to obey, not to command, so at first the orders were issued by the experienced Theodosia Zandina. With no duties in the wards, Maria helped in the bandaging rooms, where casualties arrived in goods trucks with only provisional bandaging covering their wounds. After a while the doctors gave Maria the most difficult and important dressings to do.

She also assisted the surgeon. Soon, 'no operation was ever performed without me,' she claimed, even in the middle of the night. Later, when the doctors had so many casualties they were unable to cope, she performed small operations herself, extracting a bullet or amputating a finger, and sometimes she administered anaesthetic.[11]

Shortly after Maria commenced work at the hospital the empress paid a 'surprise' visit. Dressed in nurse's uniform Alexandra, Olga, Tatiana and Anna Vyrubova were welcomed by the directress and pupils of the Ecclesiastical School before being taken up to the hospital. The men, who had been informed that the empress was coming, were disappointed to see four nurses enter the ward all dressed exactly alike. Maria watched as Alexandra spoke to each patient. 'No matter how sincerely the Empress sympathized with the men's suffering,' she wrote, 'no matter how she tried to express it, there was something in her, eluding definition, that prevented her from communicating her own genuine feelings and from comforting the person she addressed.'[12]

With little to do, Maria tried to take over the hospital's executive functions. After discovering how lavishly the doctors and supervisors distributed the food supplies she decided the expenses were too high. With the help of a nurse she began supervising the monthly expenses and deliveries to the kitchens. The Petrograd Red Cross disapproved. Evdokia Dzhunkovskaia descended on Pskov where, ignoring all Maria's plans for reform, she lectured her on everything from provisioning and accounting to the regulations for the nurses' uniforms. For the grand duchess it was a humiliating defeat.

In quiet periods Maria was able to take the occasional holiday. Her brother, stepbrother and father (his banishment lifted) visited and she sometimes went to Petrograd. During one of these visits she assisted at an operation performed on Dmitri who, suffering from an unspecified ailment, had spent most of January 1915 resting at his estate of Usovo on the banks of the Moscow River. In February, in order to improve his health, the doctors decided to remove his tonsils. 'I got up around 11.00 and had coffee in bed,' he wrote in his diary. 'Maria came, of course. My throat operation is set for tomorrow at 11.00 … they say that it is nonetheless painful.'[13]

The following day the operation was performed in Dmitri's home:

> Today I got up around 10.00 and had coffee in bed. Maria came. The two doctors – Polyakov and Ostrogorsky – arrived around 11.00. They arranged the sitting room a little, moving the furniture and carpet out of the way and [replacing them] with a bed and oil cloth. Polyakov had brought his medical orderly with him. They all put surgical gowns on, and Maria helped them. First they painted my throat with cocaine …

The grand duke was given no proper anaesthetic before Polyakov performed the operation:

> There was really relatively little blood in my throat, and Maria held my head It was all over pretty quickly, but my head was phenomenally painful. It felt as though they had made my head explode into pieces. I had to lie in bed with a compress on my head, and I stayed there all day. I started to feel a little better towards evening. Maria tended me all day with incredible and touching devotion. She almost never left my bedside. I got up for a minute in the evening. I felt very weak. I ate nothing but a piece of [illegible] and cold water. I hope this will soon all be past.[14]

Maria was rapidly becoming a competent nurse and was immensely proud of her work.

★★★

By August 1915, Grand Duchess Olga's hospital was established in an old grammar school in Kiev. Olga had briefly visited the city the previous year on her way to Rovno and now she was delighted to be back. From Kiev she corresponded with her sister Xenia who had remained in Petrograd. The letters give a vivid account of Olga's daily life in the hospital.[15] The conditions were good and Olga was popular with her colleagues. Apart from Tatiana Gromova, these included the nurses Olga Vassiliev, Vera Pommerg and Emilia Tenso, and the doctors, whom she called by their nicknames of 'Risti', 'Pupka' and 'the Gaffeur'.

'We are very busy,' she told her niece Tatiana, 'and yesterday afternoon around 6 o'clock 50 men were brought to us … We worked intensely for an hour and then carried them on stretchers – or some went on foot – upstairs and put them to bed and gave them supper. They had a good appetite!'[16] In her free time Olga enjoyed looking at the wax exhibits at the Anatomical Museum and later read some useful reports on the subject. Often she painted while Pupka read aloud, but sometimes she was so tired that she just stretched out under an apple tree to ease her aching legs.

With fighting taking place all the time she was worried about the safety of Nicolai Kulikovsky. In March 1916 she went to Petrograd and made it plain that she wanted to divorce Peter and marry Kulikovsky.

As the advance began, the hospital was ordered to make room for new casualties. Fifty soldiers left and over 200 newly wounded men arrived. By the end of the month they had 350 newly wounded soldiers and eleven officers. Inevitably there were deaths. One man asked Olga to open the window so that he could hear the church bells better. Olga did so. She could hear nothing but the soldier died with a smile on his face.

At 5.30 a.m. one day in May, Olga was woken by a policeman's voice in the street calling for people to receive the wounded from the train. She dressed quickly and rushed to help. From 8 a.m. they worked for thirteen-and-a-half hours, barely stopping to swallow lunch. There were so many casualties that some were put in the corridors. Some men were very badly wounded and on Whit Sunday Olga put little green trees in the wards to cheer them up.

Olga's mother the Dowager Empress Marie Feodorovna had moved into the Maryinsky Palace in Kiev, unable to stand the atmosphere in the capital where Empress Alexandra reigned supreme. Empress Marie now became a regular visitor to the hospital.

The wards were full but men continued to arrive and there was a desperate need of linen. Olga only had time for a brief walk with her mother in the palace garden, where she picked some of the prettiest roses to cheer up a soldier who was feeling poorly after an operation. She then worked until seven in the evening. Her face was pale, her eyes were sunken and she felt so tired she was close to tears. Three Akhtyrsky officers were among the casualties: one shot through the throat, shoulder and back; one through the leg; and one through the shoulder. The temperature most days was 93 degrees and on the long, hot summer nights Olga and a colleague took their mattresses outside and slept on the balcony. Olga told Xenia that she had nightmares in which the bandages she put on kept falling off.

The terrible operations continued all month, including a remarkable one to remove a large piece of shell. Some of the recent arrivals were so badly injured that they had been left on the battlefield for dead. One morning the Empress Marie arrived unannounced and they had to shield her from the sight of the terrible wounds.

'Just now we have so much work that for more than a month I did not get out neither for a walk nor for a ride,' she told the tsar on 4 July. 'There are so many wounded, nearly 500 beds.'[17] Soldiers were lying on stretchers in the corridors but the exhausted doctors and nurses had to carry on. Olga's letters describe men with parts torn off, throats torn open, eyes missing, mouths shot through and dreadful injuries in the bowel. One man died from peritonitis. She helped at all the operations (including an amputation) and during one was so drenched with blood that she had to go and change her clothes.

To Olga's joy, at the end of August a telegram arrived from the tsar telling Olga that her marriage had been annulled. The grand duchess had waited so long for this moment that she wanted to marry as soon as possible.

In mid October Olga developed an abscess in her throat. To swallow was agony and she was unable to speak or eat. Old Dr Trofimov came to treat her and twice daily Pupka changed the huge compresses and prescribed something for her to gargle with. The nursing sisters brought flowers, Tatiana Gromova fussed around and in the evenings Pupka read aloud. Even the cat never left her bed. When Nicolai Kulikovsky arrived she was still in bed, waiting for the abscess to burst. It was with relief and joy that Olga finally reported to Xenia that the abscess burst on the night of 25 October.

Olga was still bedridden when the tsar and Tsarevich Alexei visited Kiev three days later. The visit caused quite a stir in the hospital. This was the last time Olga would see her brother and nephew. The following day she got up for the first time since her illness. Still unable to work, she decided to marry on 4 November.

News of the impending nuptials soon spread and in the wards she was greeted by shouts of 'good health to the bride'. When a huge double bed was brought into the hospital, blocking the corridors as two men tried with difficulty to manoeuvre it, there was much laughter. It was a present from the dowager empress, but Olga found it too soft to sleep on so she gave it to the wounded.

Olga and Nicolai Kulikovsky were married at the Kiev Vassily Church on Tryokhsviyatitel Street, one of the oldest churches in Russia. Afterwards, back at the hospital, the nurses and doctors threw hops and oats at the newlyweds, while inside all the able-bodied patients stood on the stairs. Supper was a lively affair, as the fruit wine made by the apothecary soon had the staff tipsy. 'At about 8 Mama, Sandro [Xenia's husband] and the Akhtyrskys left us, and then the company went mad! One of the doctors played the piano and the others all danced (I also) …' Olga wrote to the tsar. Tatiana Andreevna and nurse Voevodina danced the traditional 'Russkaya', a beautiful Russian folk dance, and one of the young doctors got drunk and spent the rest of the evening lying on a bed being sick.[18] At ten o'clock the newlyweds left for their honeymoon. A few days later the grand duchess proudly signed her letter to Xenia, 'Olga. Mme Kulikovsky'.

★★★

By the autumn of 1916 the front was only 125 miles from Pskov. There were heavy losses after further offensives, every day brought more operations and between September and December the number of beds was increased again. Maria's feet swelled up from standing all day and her hands became red and sore from frequent washing, but she gave no thought to her tiredness as she worked to alleviate the terrible suffering.

One day Dmitri passed through Pskov unexpectedly. Maria was in the operating theatre when she was informed of his arrival. She quickly washed her hands and rushed out, giving no thought to her appearance and not bothering to look in the mirror. 'What have you been doing?' he asked, looking at his sister's bloodstained overalls. 'Murdering someone?'[19]

One of the many problems was how to transport the wounded from the station to the hospital, a distance of some 2 miles, without ambulances. The lightly wounded could be sent on foot accompanied by nurses, others were placed on stretchers and carried along the road. Although older schoolchildren helped to carry the stretchers, two journeys were sometimes necessary and one bitterly cold day Maria's feet became frostbitten.

During the winter of 1916, Maria organised a small party of nurses to work at the front. Travelling south-west to Dvinsk, she found a suitable building and worked for a day with the nurses. A sanitary train bearing her name was the contact between Dvinsk and the Pskov hospital some 166 miles away.

At Dvinsk, Maria witnessed at first hand how war weariness had increased among the soldiers in the trenches. The mood in the Pskov hospital had changed as well. Soldiers were reluctant to return to the front, there was a serious lack of food and medical supplies, and even the nurses were rebellious.

Nevertheless, these were the happiest years of Maria's life. 'Each day brought me wider contacts, fresh impressions, new opportunity to escape from the old restrictions ...'[20] she wrote. She also became an acute observer of political questions, sharing her relatives' increasing unease and fear about the growing influence of Rasputin over the empress. In Petrograd the ministers now reported directly to Alexandra and the cabinet had ceased to function. A solution would have to be found.

★★★

'I miss my hospital so much – but what's to be done?' Alexandra lamented in January 1916[21] when bad health forced her once more to rest. In the absence of the empress her elder daughters continued to give out medicines, make the beds and do the dressings.

In February, Ensign Simeon Pavlov was admitted to the infirmary with one leg completely shattered and the other severely wounded in the knee. There was talk of amputating his leg but Alexandra insisted that they 'rely on the will of God and leave him a leg'. So, he said, 'I stayed with both feet.' His Certificate of Injury stated that his operation was carried out by Princess Gedroits with the assistance of the empress, and that the dressings were done by Alexandra and Tatiana. Later the empress visited him. Pavlov said he would never have recognised her if the ward sister Olga Grekova had not announced her arrival. 'Before me stood a tall slender lady 50 years old [she was 43] in the plain grey dress of a sister and a white nurse's headdress ...' he recalled. 'The Empress greeted me and asked where I was wounded [ie, which front] ...' He described her face as classically correct, 'beautiful, very beautiful,' but a beauty that was 'cold and without passion. And even now, grown old with time and with fine wrinkles around the eyes and the corners of her lips, her face was very interesting, but too strict and too thoughtful.' He also noted her clear complexion and the red spots forming on her cheeks. He was especially struck by her eyes, 'large, light grey with a hint of steel ...'[22]

The grand duchesses often came back in the evenings to play a game with the patients called 'rouble'. 'This game was essentially very simple,' Pavlov recalled, 'and all that was necessary was under the outstretched palms of your hands on the desk to hide the silver rouble so well that the other party could not guess who had the rouble and in which hand.' Play was divided into two teams, with Olga and Tatiana (and occasionally Marie Nicolaievna) as leader. 'It is difficult to convey the atmosphere of ease and very genuine and sincere joy that reigned at the table during the game,' he wrote. 'It was continuous noise and laughter, jokes and witty remarks.' The ease with which the two young women joined in, with 'absolutely no formality and tension', struck him forcefully and inspired limitless respect and devotion.[23]

The wounded organised concerts and occasionally Olga was persuaded to provide accompaniment on the piano. When the men returned to the front the grand duchesses encouraged them to write.

Although happy in the infirmary the grand duchesses disliked visiting the Catherine Palace where everything was strict and formal. 'We have to watch every step, because there we are focused on,' Olga said.[24] They could never go as simple nurses.

To celebrate her hospital's second anniversary in August 1916, Alexandra asked that the infirmary's name be changed to Her Majesty's Own Hospital No. 3, to end the current confusion between the Palace Hospital and the hospital of the Catherine Palace. She was delighted when the Holy Synod presented her with a testimonial in recognition of her work, as well as an icon and a *Gramota*, a letter of recommendation which was 'something like the Papal gift of the Rose'.[25] Alexandra was the first empress since Catherine the Great to receive the Synod by herself.

As the year drew to a close the infirmary was quiet. 'There is not much work now ...' Olga told her aunt, Grand Duchess Xenia, on 30 November:

In our absence, three new patients arrived, one wounded in the head and shell-shocked and what with the concussion and everything else, he is quite deaf and unable to speak ... Another is serious with an abscess on the kidneys which has already been lanced, but he is still weak ...[26]

Tatiana gave chloroform for the first time and the empress visited Novgorod. This would be the last of Alexandra's hospital tours. Baroness Buxhoeveden recalled that 'there was no warmth in the welcome, though the Empress did not realise it'.[27]

On 17 December came the news that Rasputin had disappeared. A few days later his corpse was found under the ice of one of the tributaries of the River Neva. He had been murdered by a group of conspirators headed by Prince Felix Youssoupov, husband of the tsar's niece Princess Irina, and Grand Duke Dmitri Pavlovich, the tsar's cousin.

It was February 1917 before Alexandra returned to the hospital. 'Maybe it was necessary to kill him,' Valentina Chebotareva heard Olga exclaim one day, ' – but not so terribly – we are a family, one is ashamed to admit they [the murderers] are relatives.'[28]

The tsar returned to the front on 22 February. The following day Olga and Alexei went down with measles, followed by Tatiana, Anna Vyrubova and Anastasia. Busy nursing the invalids in the Alexander Palace, still wearing her Red Cross uniform, Alexandra hardly noticed the bread riots and disturbances in Petrograd.

★★★

As the revolutionaries neared the Alexander Palace, the empress threw a fur coat over her nurse's uniform and, accompanied by her 17-year-old daughter Marie, went outside to talk to the troops defending the building. Walking along the ranks the empress told them that she trusted them completely and that the life of the tsarevich was in their hands.

Meanwhile, stranded in Pskov and unable to reach Petrograd, TsarNicholas II was finally convinced by the Duma, the Soviet and the generals that it was too late for concessions. Unwilling to plunge his country into civil war, on 2 March he abdicated for himself and Alexei. It was the end of the Romanov dynasty.

When the news was broken to the empress by Grand Duke Paul she was in nurse's uniform tending her sick children. Ensign Pavlov recalled that Alexandra phoned the hospital to ask after the wounded. Called to the telephone, Princess Gedroits 'sobbed like a helpless child'.[29]

Alexandra was still wearing her Red Cross uniform when General Kornilov came to the Alexander Palace to place her under arrest. 'From now on, we are to be considered prisoners: shut up – may see nobody from outside,' she wrote in her diary.[30] Confined in the Alexander Palace and recovered from measles, Tatiana pined without work. 'It is so strange to sit in the morning at home, to be in good health and not to go to the change of bandages!' she wrote to Valentina in April.[31] As the girls had worked as Sisters of Mercy, the commandant felt unable to deprive them of the joy of exchanging Easter greetings with their former patients and colleagues. Tatiana wondered why nobody wrote directly to the empress – but the commandant had asked all the nurses not to do so.

After the imperial family had been exiled to Siberia, Valentina Chebotareva wrote in her diary:

> I greatly regret that I was unable to kiss Tatiana and take leave of her personally –
> but kindness from [Alexandra Feodorovna] I find difficult to bear. I feel terribly
> sorry for her and yet it is all so painful that I cannot find the warm feelings of
> old, after all she is the awful cause of all the misfortunes of our land, she ruined
> her entire family, the unfortunate [one] – sick of soul, sick with mysticism and
> arrogant pride.[32]

★★★

In Pskov, General Ruzskii brought Maria news of the tsar's abdication. The atmosphere in the hospital changed; she had already noticed that people avoided her and complaints from the men were more frequent. The general advised her that in view of the revolutionary excitement in the town she would be well advised to attend the *Te Deum* in the cathedral. Nobody stood aside for her and for the first time in her life Maria found herself fighting her way through a crowd.

The notorious Order No 1 abolished discipline in the army, making soldiers no longer subordinate to their officers. Only two doors, one of them glass, separated her rooms from the main hospital where there were 300 lightly wounded soldiers, plus eighty orderlies. Maria could no longer be certain of their loyalty. One morning, as she was bandaging a patient, he jumped off the table and hit her on the chest. After the soldiers took the Oath of Allegiance to the provisional government the head doctor asked Maria to leave.

General Ruzskii had managed to secure a compartment for his staff on a train bound for Petrograd. Maria was to travel with them. All the nurses came to the station to see her off, kissing her hand as they had done in former times. Maria and Theodosia Zandina left Pskov in a sealed compartment in an overcrowded train. Two weeks later a group of hospital orderlies, who had formed their own Soviet, arrived in Petrograd to ask Maria to return to the hospital and assume authority. The grand duchess was flattered but despite the fact that she missed her hospital work Maria refused.

★★★

Abbot Seraphim saw Ella shortly after the tsar's abdication. She was thin, exhausted and unable to speak without crying. The grand duchess could see the abyss into which the country she had so faithfully served was falling, her only wish now was to continue to serve and to die in Russia. There was no news from the Alexander Palace and 'the telegrams she sent were returned'.[33]

She continued to nurse some critically ill women in the convent hospital and forbade the doors of the outpatients' department to be locked despite looting and disturbances in the city. One morning a group of drunken, dishevelled men recently 'liberated' from prison burst in. 'One of them saw her and shouted that she was no longer Her Imperial Highness and who was she now?' Ella calmly replied that she was his servant. In that case, he said, she could dress the abscess on his groin. Without protest she got hot water, ointment, lint and bandages, fetched him a chair and knelt down before him.

Very carefully she cleaned and dressed the wound, telling him he should not neglect it but should come back next day so that gangrene did not set in. The man was stupefied. 'And who the hell are you then?' he asked again. 'I have already told you – I am your servant,' Ella replied calmly. The men left, muttering as they did so that she was nevertheless 'a German'.[34]

In May some former convicts drove up waving red flags, saying they had come to search the convent and arrest Ella for harbouring German prisoners and weapons. The grand duchess remained calm and led them towards the church. Requesting them to leave their rifles at the door she invited them to follow her inside, where Father Mitrofan conducted a short service. Ella's demeanour so impressed them that they conducted only a rudimentary search and told her to stay and nurse the sick.

Later that day members of the provisional government came to advise Ella to move into the Kremlin for security. Ella refused, also declining an offer to help her leave Russia from the German kaiser, transmitted via the Swedish minister. 'I could never leave my sisters,'[35] Ella said. She continued to tend her patients.

★★★

In Kiev the mood turned ugly. The police were abolished, prisoners released by the mob roamed the streets, obscene graffiti about the emperor and empress appeared on the walls and the imperial double-headed eagle was torn from buildings. Olga, who was pregnant, hardly dared go near the hospital. She complained to Xenia that 'uncertainty is always the most trying thing for one's nerves. Mine are in a bad state.'[36]

Although the dowager empress's presidency of the Red Cross had been removed immediately after the revolution, she persisted in visiting the hospitals. Then one day, the gate of Kiev's main hospital remained firmly closed. The head surgeon, supported by his entire staff, rudely informed her that she was not required. Shaken, the 69-year-old lady finally agreed to leave at once for the safety of the Crimea. With her went Olga.

On a bitterly cold evening after work Olga silently boarded a special train on a deserted siding:

> I wore nothing but my nurse's uniform. To avoid all suspicion I had not put on a coat when I left the hospital. My husband covered me with his greatcoat. I had a very small dressing-case in my hands. I remember the moment when, looking upon that small case and my crumpled skirt, I realised that I owned nothing else in the world.[37]

★★★

At Ella's hospital fewer and fewer patients were admitted and there was a severe shortage of food and medicine. 'Official allocations of bromide and quinine were most spasmodic', there was no iodine and it would not be long before the sisters would have to rip up sheets to make bandages.[38] People still flocked to the outpatients' clinic, some to find courage, others to bring small gifts of food to the convent.

On 25 October the Bolsheviks took power. The red flag flew on the Kremlin and churches were desecrated. Ella's sisters nursed the wounded from the running battles on the streets and she forbade them from leaving the convent. The *Cheka*, the Communist Secret Police, were established in Moscow. One word out of place was enough to have a charge levied and any of the strangers coming daily to the clinic could be a *Cheka* spy. Ella felt responsible for her sisters and for the sick entrusted to her care.

One day the *Cheka* arrived with a search warrant. Ella explained that there were sick and aged people in the buildings and asked that the search be carried out with as little disturbance as possible. This was done and the men quietly departed. 'It looks like we are not yet quite worthy to receive a martyr's crown,' Ella remarked.[39]

Sometime later an official from the Food Commissariat came to assess the convent's needs, saying that special rations would be allowed for the patients. 'That promise was kept, and supplies arrived with a staggering punctuality.'[40] Lengthy questionnaires arrived, 'demanding ages and the social status of all the nuns and the patients'. These were completed and returned, no more was heard. 'The Health Commissariat made spasmodic allocations of quinine, aspirin, surgical spirits, lint and bandages.' and twice a week a lorry arrived with food and provisions. People continued to smuggle in butter and eggs, but tea had become a distant memory.[41]

Soon the Bolsheviks tightened their grip. Patrols along the road were doubled and all visitors were questioned before they could enter the convent. Some of the patients were transferred to another hospital and Ella learned that the orphans would be removed to a state institution.

Then, during Easter 1918, Ella was arrested.[42] She was informed by the *Cheka* that for her own safety she would be immediately removed from Moscow. With only half an hour to put the convent's affairs in order there was no time to visit the hospital, but Ella asked Father Mitrofan to continue working in the community while he was allowed to do so.

Only two of the weeping sisters were allowed to accompany her – Katherine Yanisheva and Barbara Yakovlova. The remainder were forcibly separated from

Ella as she was taken to the waiting vehicle. Just before entering, she turned and made the sign of the cross.

★★★

Ella was arrested for simply being a member of the Romanov family. Maria Pavlovna and Olga Alexandrovna finally escaped from Russia but the empress and Ella were not so lucky.

In July 1918, the tsar, tsarina, their five children and four attendants died in a hail of Bolshevik bullets at Ekaterinburg. The next day Ella was thrown alive down a Siberian mineshaft with several male members of the Romanov family, including Prince Ioann (the husband of Maria Pavlovna's fellow nurse Princess Elena). Grenades were thrown in after them. Before she died Ella tore off part of her veil to bandage Ioann's wounds. Grand Duchess Elisabeth Feodorovna was later canonised by the Russian Orthodox Church and her statue now stands above the west door of Westminster Abbey.

Notes

1. Kulikovsky, Roth-Nicholls & Woolmans, *25 Chapters*, pp.122–3.
2. Private collection.
3. Gregory P. Tschebotarioff, *Russia, My Native Land* (McGraw-Hill, 1964), p.57.
4. Countess Kleinmichel, Memories of a Shipwrecked World (Brentano's Ltd, 1923), pp 217–18.
5. Tschebotarioff, *Russia*, p.59.
6. www.//kfinkelshteyn.narod.
7. Ibid.
8. Ibid.
9. Joseph T. Fuhrmann (ed.), *The Complete Wartime Correspondence of Tsar Nicholas II and the Empress Alexandra* (Greenwood Press, Connecticut, 1999), p.306.
10. Maria of Russia, *Education of a Princess*, p.187.
11. Maria of Russia, *Education of a Princess*, p.191.
12. Maria of Russia, *Education of a Princess*, p.194–5.
13. Diary of Grand Duke Dmitri Pavlovich, 7 February 1915. Private collection. Copy at Harvard. Kindly translated for me by Dr William Lee.
14. Diary of Grand Duke Dmitri Pavlovich, 8 February 1915. Private collection. Copy at Harvard. Kindly translated for me by Dr William Lee.
15. Olga's letters to her sister Xenia, transcribed and translated where necessary by Coryne Hall and Karen Roth-Nicholls, are in private hands. A copy of the transcript is in the author's possession. Information about Olga's time in Kiev is taken from these unpublished letters from which it is currently not possible to quote.
16. Kulikovsky, Roth-Nicholls & Woolmans, *25 Chapters*, p.128.
17. Patricia Phenix, *Olga Romanov: Russia's Last Grand Duchess* (Viking, 1999), p.94.
18. *Kejserinde Dagmar* exhibition catalogue, p.186.
19. Maria of Russia, *Education of a Princess*, p.213.

20. Dr Marion Mienert, *Maria Pavlovna: A Romanov Grand Duchess in Russia and in Exile* (Lennart-Bernadotte-Stiftung, Germany, 2004), p.102; Maria of Russia, p.229.
21. Fuhrmann, *Complete Wartime Correspondence*, p.350.
22. www.pravaya.ru/govern/391/2311.
23. Ibid.
24. Ibid.
25. Buxhoeveden, *Life and Tragedy*, p.233.
26. Prince Michael of Greece, *Nicholas and Alexandra: The Family Albums* (Taurus Press, 1992), p.224.
27. Buxhoeveden, *Life and Tragedy*, p.223.
28. Tschebotarioff, *Russia*, p.61.
29. www.pravaya.ru/govern/391/2311; www.//kfinkelshteyn.narod.
30. Greg King & Penny Wilson, *The Fate of the Romanovs* (John Wiley, 2001), p.57.
31. Tschebotarioff, *Russia*, p.191.
32. Tschebotarioff, *Russia*, p.193.
33. Warwick, Christopher, *Ella, Princess, Saint & Martyr* (John Wiley, 2006), p.290.
34. E.M. Almedingen, *An Unbroken Unit* (The Bodley Head, 1964), p.107.
35. Almedingen, *An Unbroken Unit*, pp.110–12.
36. Phenix, *Olga Romanov*, p.113.
37. Vorres, *The Last Grand Duchess,* p.154.
38. Almedingen, *An Unbroken Unit*, p.114.
39. Almedingen, *An Unbroken Unit*, pp.115–16.
40. Almedingen, *An Unbroken Unit*, p.116.
41. Almedingen, *An Unbroken Unit*, pp.117–18.
42. The generally accepted date is 27 April. See Warwick, *Ella,* p.297 footnote. The Communists closed the convent in 1926.

6

'I Hear We Have a Princess Here'

As British aristocratic ladies rushed to set up hospitals and nursing homes, there was a desperate need for both but a shortage of nurses. Queen Alexandra's Imperial Military Nursing Service had only 463 trained nurses and, although voluntary organisations such as the Territorial Nursing Services were augmenting it rapidly, help was urgently needed.

Among those who volunteered were two relatives of King George V. His niece Alexandra (Princess Arthur of Connaught) worked in England; Princess Louise of Battenberg went to France.

Lady Alexandra Duff was born on 17 May 1891 at East Sheen Lodge, Richmond, the daughter of Princess Louise (eldest daughter of the future Edward VII) and the Duke of Fife. From childhood Alexandra was interested in nursing, but young people of her rank were discouraged from knowing about illness, so she nursed her dolls instead. 'It was indeed a joy when we were visited by our family doctor,' she wrote in her book *A Nurse's Story*, 'as I was then able to get some professional advice for my precious dolls.'[1]

Louise became Princess Royal in 1905 and Edward VII raised the rank of her daughters Alexandra and Maud to princess. When the Duke of Fife died in 1912 without a male heir a 'special remainder' allowed Alexandra to become the 2nd Duchess of Fife. The following year she married Prince Arthur, son of Queen Victoria's son the Duke of Connaught. The couple set up home in London and on 9 August 1914 Princess Arthur of Connaught (the title by which she was usually known) gave birth to a son, Alastair.

Five days earlier war had broken out and Princess Arthur was determined to find work in a hospital. The princess never thought there was even a remote possibility of enrolling in a nursing course but she went along to Ascot Racecourse where Aileen, Countess Roberts (daughter of the field marshal), had adapted the grandstand as a hospital for fifty wounded men, with a depot for hospital supplies in the Silver Ring Stand and a workroom in the bar. Princess Arthur worked as a kitchen maid in the old cloakrooms of the Silver Ring Stand, now a scullery, 'doing the washing up, and all kinds of odd jobs, as well as preparing vegetables, making bread, laying the tables for meals, and waiting on the patients'.[2] The hospital was clean, airy and well adapted but the scullery was gloomy. It was suggested that she would find it more interesting to become a nurse. As soon as the princess returned to London she eagerly took up the suggestion.

Prince Arthur immediately approved the plan and took her to St Mary's Hospital, Paddington, to see the matron, Miss Ruth Darbyshire. The princess realised that the work would bring her into contact with the more squalid side of life, but after looking round she decided to enrol.

In 1915, while Prince Arthur was serving with the Scots Greys and undertaking important missions for the king, his 24-year-old wife began general training at St Mary's Hospital under the pseudonym of Nurse Marjorie. Nobody knew her identity and she tried desperately to fit in and not look as conspicuous as she felt. Miss Darbyshire was strict about uniform – hair had to be hidden neatly beneath the cap, sleeves had to be down and cuffs on. One morning Princess Arthur was reprimanded because her dress was too short.

St Mary's had no preliminary training school, so the princess learnt as she went along. The work was rough, the hours long but she was in her element. She had been brought up to obey in the strict Victorian tradition, so was prepared for the discipline of hospital work. She helped on the soldiers' wards where the men were suffering from mustard gas poisoning. Her first dressing involved cleaning out an eye socket and replacing the glass eye. Her second involved a bayonet wound. Like many nurses she came down with hospital throat (a septic throat and a high temperature) but escaped the other bane of the time, the poisoned finger. Towards the end of her training she even slept at the hospital, occupying a small room in the nurses' home with an iron bedstead and a hard mattress, an old cane chair with a hole in the seat, a broken blind and torn linoleum. It was a long way from life inside the royal homes, but at the end of her shift the exhausted princess was too tired to notice.

Working in the operating theatre involved long hours standing on hard floors in a hot room without letting either concentration or attention to detail lapse. As the day of her first operation approached, some unpleasant childhood memories of having teeth extracted resurfaced, and the princess was afraid that the smell of the anaesthetic would make her feel faint. However, when the day arrived she was so interested in watching and listening to the surgeon that she forgot her fears completely.

At Christmas the nurses decorated the wards and the students produced short plays or sketches to entertain the wounded men. The nurses' only relaxation throughout the year was Christmas dinner.

Later Princess Arthur worked in the gynaecological wards. Midwifery training was given in a maternity hospital in the East End, which at that time was considered a rough area of London. The princess went there by taxi, although she was warned that the unusual sight of such a vehicle in that district might excite the local people. However, she was confident of reaching her destination unharmed, as a nurse's uniform induced respect in even the roughest quarters. A row of poor houses overlooked the narrow road leading to the hospital entrance and the vehicle was soon surrounded by a crowd of eager people pushing forward to see who was arriving. Spotting her uniform, the people immediately parted to let her through.

Working in casualty, Princess Arthur was busy all the time, and she took a little while to grow accustomed to this because it was so different from working on the wards. The sister-in-charge was known to the nurses as Granny. She was an old Irish lady whose real name nobody knew, and nobody could remember a time when she had not been there. Although she criticised all the nurses in turn, she was also kind-hearted and wise, ensuring by the simple method of repetition that her ideas would be remembered and, above all, carried out.

In casualty there was an element of surprise – one never knew what injuries would be brought in next. There was certainly room for the unexpected. One day, as Princess Arthur and the sister were having their tea, it suddenly became apparent that one of the waiting women was about to have a baby. There was no maternity ward, so, half pushing and half lifting, the princess manoeuvred the woman into a room and onto a couch. Behind her came sister, protesting that the woman couldn't possibly remain there but must be taken to Queen Charlotte's maternity hospital. Shortly afterwards the woman gave birth to premature twins who, sadly, did not survive.

Another time a woman came in wearing 'a mangy black coat'. Her face was swollen, her eye was black and it transpired that she had got into a fight in a pub while drinking with friends. Yet she tried to preserve her dignity – when Princess Arthur asked what had happened, she replied that it was jealousy: 'The cat bashed me because I was wearing me fur coat!'[3]

Suppertime provided a welcome break, even in the nurses' dining room with its yellowish plaster peeling from the walls. The princess found the meals 'monotonous and badly cooked. The evening meal consisted of day nurse's supper, stew and rice pudding, and night nurse's breakfast of weak tea and a kipper with bread and margarine.' Although Princess Arthur was able to have one meal a day at home, she was often hungry.[4]

The shortage of students because of the war gave her the opportunity to gain further experience. She was soon extracting teeth (something she admitted disliking), helping the casualty surgeon and setting fractures. She specialised in the removal of needles, or pieces of needles, embedded in the skin and once amputated a thumb under a general anaesthetic.

In the evenings, volunteers from the St John Ambulance Brigade came in to learn how to deal with various accidents. They were well prepared for air raids: seats in the hall were moved to make room for stretcher cases, while extra rooms were prepared where dressings could be done. Night after night the air-raid warning sounded but nothing happened. Then, one evening in August 1917 two bombs were dropped near the hospital, one of which demolished a house. Nineteen cases were brought in that night.

The patients had no idea that 'Nurse Marjorie' was King George V's niece and occasionally someone tried to give her a tip. One man followed her around the room trying to give a half-crown piece while she kept the tables and chairs between them to prevent him pressing it on her. Eventually he was persuaded to put it in the hospital box.

Towards the end of her training Princess Arthur was offered the post of staff nurse in a military hospital. She refused, wishing to complete her course. She also refused an offer to nurse in France, as it would interfere with her final examinations. She passed her nursing exams and received a Certificate of General Training, but the end of the war in 1918 did not signify the end of her career. She had found her true calling during the conflict and would devote the rest of her life to nursing.

Princess Arthur once said that if the war had not ended by the time she left St Mary's as a qualified nurse, then she would nurse in France. Another great-granddaughter of Queen Victoria had done exactly that.

★★★

Princess Louise of Battenberg was the only British royal lady who nursed in a hospital in France during the First World War. She was born on 13 July 1889, the second child of Princess Victoria of Hesse (the eldest daughter of Princess Alice) and Prince Louis of Battenberg, a relative of the Hesse family who had forged a career in the Royal Navy. By 1912, Louis had risen to the position of First Sea Lord but shortly after the outbreak of war was forced to resign his post because of his German origins. Princess Louise had an elder sister, Alice (later Princess Alice of Greece, mother of the Duke of Edinburgh), who became a devoted nurse during the Balkan War, and two younger brothers: George (later Marquess of Milford Haven) and Louis ('Dickie', later Earl Mountbatten of Burma).

Tall and slim, Louise had none of her sister's classic beauty but she was nevertheless attractive. Shy in public, in private she was vivacious and always ready to laugh. Louise also possessed what her aunt Empress Alexandra of Russia described as a self-sacrificing nature. 'She was the kind of person who would give her last crust to help someone in need,' said Lady Zia Wernher.[5]

After Prince Louis's resignation in October 1914, the family moved to Kent House on the Isle of Wight. With Alice married, George serving on a battlecruiser and young Dickie away at naval college, Louise decided she wanted to help the war effort.

Louise and her friend Alicia Knatchbull-Hugessen worked for the Soldiers' and Sailors' Families Association, later transferring to Smoke for Soldiers and Sailors, an organisation started by Lady Denman at her home in Buckingham Gate, London, to send tobacco and cigarettes to the troops. Louise had fallen in love with 'a very nice young man' and they planned to become engaged; however, before they could do so he was sadly killed in the first few months of the conflict. Louise was heartbroken and her parents, who 'had liked him very much', were also upset.[6]

It was probably to forget her heartbreak that Louise decided to work in a military hospital. She therefore approached Lady Oliver (later Dame Beryl Oliver), head of the Naval and Military Voluntary Aid Detachment (VAD) department, which administered the combined nursing staff of St John Ambulance and the Red Cross.

The VAD was formed in 1909 to provide supplementary aid to the Territorial Medical Service in time of war. They provided the personnel to carry out transport duties, staffed the rest stations, provided a workforce for the temporary and general hospitals and did clerical work and cooking. Comprising both men and women, they formed part of the military organisation. All were required 'to be in possession of First Aid and Nursing Certificates of the St John Ambulance Association', and all were trained 'to make use of local resources for the improvisation of stretchers, for methods of transport and for converting local buildings into shelters and rest stations for the sick and wounded.'[7] By the beginning of the war, 50,000 women had joined. They were usually middle-class, 'daughters of the local gentry, landowners, army officers and clergy' or women with an aristocratic background.[8] Most had never had any real paid employment. In the spring of 1915, the War Office decided to employ VADs in the hospitals so that more fully-trained nurses could be released for duty abroad. From the summer of 1915 the War Office allowed VADs to serve in hospitals abroad as well. They were paid £20 per year, served for one year or for the duration of the war, lived in the nurses' quarters and were under the supervision of the matron.[9]

Louise felt that her fluent French and German would be most useful in a French military hospital near the front. Volunteers for France had to be at least 25 years old (Louise had reached that age in July 1914) and the women were recruited and sent out by the British Committee of the French Red Cross.[10] In February she visited Rouen where her mother's unofficial lady-in-waiting Nona, now Mrs Richard Crichton, was nursing in one of the hospitals. Having thoroughly enjoyed her visit, Louise decided that this was what she wanted to do. Although she was somewhat frail in health, having suffered from slight curvature of the spine as a child, in March 1915 Louise planned to join the team of nurses organised by Lady Viti Paget, wife of Admiral Sir Alfred Paget, who was going to France to nurse in one of the Anglo-American hospitals for French soldiers. 'We have been rushing about all today and been very successful in our shopping,' Princess Victoria of Battenberg wrote to Nona on 24 March. 'We called on Lady [Viti] Paget … Passport, journey, all is settled and Louise is off tomorrow with that certain 10 o'clock train. All Lady Paget tells me about the circumstances at Nevers is satisfactory and Louise seems really looking forward to going there now.'[11]

The next morning, armed with an *Ordre de Mission* from the French Red Cross, which allowed her free railway travel in France when exchanged for a Transport Order, Louise set off cheerfully. Although not bound by the regulations imposed by the British Red Cross and the War Office, VADs serving in France usually took with them a camp kit, so such things as 'gumboots, garters, mackintosh, sou'wester, black cashmere stockings, folding bed, chair, table, washstand and bucket' may well have formed part of her equipment.[12]

Louise's destination was L'Hôpital Anglais at Nevers, a town on the River Loire in Burgundy, about 160 miles south-east of Paris. Although it was situated on the outskirts of Nevers, surrounded by fields, there was nothing picturesque about the hospital No. 40 Autonome. It was housed in some quite plain modern buildings which were created as offices and depots for the PLM Railway Company in the middle of a railway repair yard for the Paris–Lyon railway. As the railway lines ran almost up to the building, third-class railway carriages had been adapted to take four stretchers in each compartment so that the wounded could be brought directly to the hospital. It was founded by Anglo-French hospitals and afterwards maintained by Mr Robert Woods Bliss of the US Embassy in Paris and his wife Mildred (née Mildred Barnes, his stepsister). Mildred organised the American Distributing Service to transfer medical supplies to French hospitals and funded several vehicles for the Ambulance Corps. She was awarded numerous decorations for her war relief work during the First World War.

The hospital opened in December 1914 with 110 beds, which later increased to 170. Being modern it had pleasant sunny wards, bathrooms, a heating system and an X-ray room next to the operating theatre. It was headed by the distinguished English surgeon Dr Leslie Haden Guest (later Lord Haden Guest), and the staff were mainly British but many of the hospital orderlies were French, as were the girls who came in to mend clothes and look after the linen.

There was no accommodation in the hospital for the nurses, so Louise and Lady Paget had a nice room in a house with a large garden about five minutes' walk from the hospital. The others were lodged in chalets nearby. Among Louise's colleagues were Ida Wheatley and May Eardley-Wilmot, whose father Admiral Sir Sydney Eardley-Wilmot was an old friend of Prince Louis. The hospital staff called each other by their surnames. All the VADs came from upper-class homes and spoke French, some of them extremely well.

The first thing Louise required was two inoculations, which she recovered from very easily. Then, dressed in her uniform of a plain dress and a large white apron, her head covered with a white cap and a long veil, she was ready to start work.

Soon three cattle trucks full of wounded from the Argonne arrived, most of them serious cases. The orderlies brought out the more serious casualties on stretchers and laid them down side by side. They were given a drink and a warm blanket while the doctors moved among them asking about their wounds and examining the labels tied to their tunics. 'A red label means a severe wound; a blue label a less severe wound, though often serious; and the slightly wounded have a white label.' The latter were rare.[13] One of the biggest killers was gangrene, caused by bacteria in the soil dug out for the trenches. Typhoid was also widespread and many men died from infections in places where isolation units were not the top priority. The wounded arrived caked with Flanders mud from the trenches. Some did not even reach hospital; they drowned as the trenches collapsed. Those who survived long enough to reach a hospital had bone injuries from gunshot wounds and shrapnel. There was little that could be done for abdominal wounds apart from giving them morphine, most of them died. Penicillin had not yet been discovered but blood transfusions were in their infancy and so were rarely given. As the war dragged on the Germans began using poisoned gas. Depending on the amount used it could cause blindness, or in severe cases dissolve the lungs so that the men drowned.

As the wounded arrived Princess Louise was keen to lend a hand. 'I wish you ... could have seen her,' Lady Paget wrote to Prince Louis, 'kneeling beside a man washing him and looking after him. She was flushed with excitement at the joy of being able to help! So many women would have shuddered at the sight of his feet and been put off by the horrible smell ...'[14] Then the men were put to bed, their uniform and belongings were packaged up and labelled and they were finally able to have some much needed rest.

Louise scrubbed floors, made beds and bathed the patients. She thrived on discipline and the daily routine, although, her mother reported in May, she was looking 'rather thin in photos but very well and her feet which felt tired standing about at first, are getting accustomed to the work. She and Lady Paget (not the feet) have several hours of duty each day.'[15] Louise and her colleagues worked as probationers under trained nurses, beginning with simple dressings, but soon she was removing pieces of shrapnel from wounded men and assisting at amputations. She also picked up some rather unrefined French slang words used in the trenches.

To the surprise of her parents, Louise took her turn on night duty, going from bed to bed straightening pillows, holding a cup of water to the lips of a parched man and perhaps giving an injection where needed. Four o'clock in the morning was the worst time, 'the hour when life beats most feebly in the bodies of men', when those near death usually succumbed.[16]

Regular letters came from home (those from her father beginning 'my dearest Shrimp' or 'my beloved Shrimp')[17] and both parents visited during 1915. For her birthday that July, which the wounded men helped her to celebrate, Louise's parents gave her a picture of a pretty view of Nevers, painted by a struggling local artist who was grateful for the commission.

Princess Victoria visited Nevers in September. 'Louise is so well and cheery,' she reported, 'thoroughly at home in her hospital, liking the work, on a good footing with her co-workers and a quite motherly one with her wounded – a sensible, capable, independent young woman – more tolerant and patient than I expected.' Victoria was proud of her daughter, although at the same time saddened by the realisation that Louise was no longer in need of her guidance. The hospital was very short staffed and Victoria became 'a sort of maid of all works' helping wherever she could. She thought the hospital primitive but much better off than the French ones in the town. They were expecting another fifty-nine wounded, so their time together was limited, but at least Victoria's maid was mending Louise's things.[18]

Although Louise had stamina, she was not strong. The nurses often worked thirty-six hours at a time after major battles. They had to keep mirrors away from men with half their face shot away and there was little time to hold the hands of dying men. As well as nursing, they helped severely injured men write to their families. Louise did the same duties as everyone else, including what her father called that 'odious night duty'.[19] In fact, she blended in so well that when a new doctor arrived he had no idea of her identity. 'I hear we have a princess here,' he said to Louise one day. 'What's she like?' 'Very ordinary,' Princess Louise replied, 'like me, sir.'[20]

'Prince Louis of Battenberg's daughter joined Lady Paget to work in the hospital, and has done splendid work, working at the hardest and dirtiest work like any other nurse, and glorying in it, all in a splendid way,' wrote an Australian lady:

> She is addressed as Nurse Louise, though most of them know she is Princess Louise. Lady Paget says she is quite wonderful, and is so sympathetic and kind and patient with the men, and, when any die, with the poor heart-broken wives and mothers, whom she comforts in such a beautiful way. The nurses take turns to represent the hospital at the funerals, and they walk with the chief mourners to the grave and go through sadly distressing experiences with the poor relatives after having nursed the poor men till the end.[21]

Shortly after Louise's arrival a new male nurse began work at the hospital. He was a young artist called Alexander Stuart-Hill. His father, William Hill (Stuart-Hill seems to have been a later addition of the son) was a fishmonger living in Perth, where Alexander was born in 1883.[22] He had won a scholarship to the Edinburgh School of Art, then worked in Europe. When war broke out he was painting in Italy and returned to help the war effort in France, the country he loved best. Princess Victoria described him as 'the quaintest of men – a Parisian painter of the ultra-modern school, Scotch by birth, affected in manner, with a head like the pictures of Shakespeare, witty & shy withal, a thoroughly good fellow, who will do readily the most prosaic & dirty work in spite of beautiful long, manicured nails on his white hands.'[23] Louise's family nicknamed him 'Shakespeare' because his small beard resembled that of the bard. They were unaware that he and Louise were becoming friendly.

In her free time Louise picked berries in the garden with the other nurses, they held dances or musical evenings and in fine weather some of the staff went on excursions to bathe in the River Loire. At Christmas (for which, to her parents' sorrow, in 1915 Louise did not return home) they arranged a play and other entertainment for the men. May Eardley-Wilmot wrote a play in which Ida Wheatley took part, but Louise didn't because she hated performing and was a bad actress, although she did appear in a tableau, representing the Angel of Peace in a white dress with a laurel wreath in her hair.

While home on leave in January 1916 she went to the pantomime at Drury Lane and travelled to Rosyth with her parents to see George, who was a lieutenant in the battlecruiser *New Zealand*. Louise was enjoying her holiday, Empress Alexandra told the tsar, and would probably be returning to Nevers at the end of February.

Louise's father often accompanied her back to the hospital when her leave ended. He was not above pulling strings to make his daughter's journey easier. 'I shall insist on our travelling via Boulogne,' he told her in December, even though the route was blocked, 'we are of sufficient importance and if necessary

I will put on a uniform and you must wear a big Red X somewhere.'[24] He was always delighted to see how pleased the wounded men were when she returned.

By the end of March things were quiet at the hospital. Louise was becoming closer to Alexander Stuart-Hill and in June she asked her parents to invite him to Kent House during her next leave.

Several of Prince Louis's letters to his daughter were about the complicated aspects of travelling during wartime and particularly about finding her a suitable chaperone. Although they were happy to invite Shakespeare to Kent House, Louise could not travel alone with him. Norman Cholmeley, one of the hospital orderlies, had acted as chaperone for the couple before, but he had returned home, so it was arranged that Viti Paget would accompany Louise and Shakespeare to Paris, where Prince Louis would meet them. He would also take her back to Nevers afterwards and visit the hospital.

Many of the best-equipped French hospitals had been captured by the Germans, so their stores, drugs and equipment were in enemy hands. With the manufacturing districts also in German possession it was difficult to obtain sufficient replacements, so Louise often asked her mother to send things out. A new electric hand lantern and two reserve batteries were required and thermometers were urgently needed. When her father received an unexpected cheque for £300 from an American benefactor he paid £50 of this into Louise's account at Coutts for her to use for the hospital.

In the summer of 1916, Victoria paid a twelve-hour visit to Nevers. There was a major offensive and all patients who could be moved had to be sent on to make room for new casualties. Victoria offered to help and 'spent the night escorting wounded men to and from the latrines'.[25]

Louise was often amused by the sometimes unfortunate results of linguistic differences between French and English. A visiting English bishop once spread confusion in the ranks when he decided to bless the troops about to go into battle. '*Que Dieu vous blesse tous*' he said, unaware that *blesser* in French means to wound and that he was therefore asking God to wound, rather than bless, the soldiers. The story went the rounds of the men and it was left to Louise to soothe and explain.[26]

After spending another period of leave staying at Royat, south of Nevers, Louise returned to the hospital in time for a visit from her mother in November. This time Victoria stayed in Louise's cottage, and Norman Cholmeley and Shakespeare came to tea. 'The hospital is nearly full up, about 150 wounded, and a lot came in a couple of days before I arrived,' she told Nona Crighton:

The matron is the celebrated Miss Tubbs over whose dismissal from a hospital there was a fuss last year [until October 1915 Emily Tubbs had been at Endsleigh

Palace Hospital for Officers], most of her nurses striking and leaving out of sympathy for her. She is a good natured person Louise says, a bit casual, but not inefficient and is liked.[27]

Louise returned to England to act as bridesmaid at the wedding of her brother George on 15 November. The bride, Countess Nada Torby, was a daughter of the tsar's cousin Grand Duke Michael Michaelovich of Russia, who had been exiled in 1890 for contracting a morganatic marriage. The duke's wife Sophie, a descendant of the poet Pushkin, had been given the title of Countess Torby, and the couple lived at Ken Wood in Hampstead. Prince Louis told his daughter that Nada's brother Michael ('Boy') Torby, a talented artist who was interested in women's fashion, had 'designed some dresses which are now being made. Blue, of a colour which Mama says will suit you very much,,with a kind of kokoshnik hat …'[28] There was a large turnout of royalty for the wedding at the Russian Church, followed by a service at the Chapel Royal.

After Christmas Louise set out again for Nevers, travelling with another probationer, 'a plain girl in the thirties, who looks quite old and stayed [sic, she means staid] enough for them to travel together without other escort,' explained Victoria.[29] The ship was delayed for several days by fog but at least Louise had a cabin to herself.

Back at Nevers they were expecting many wounded from the fighting in the Champagne region. There was no petrol and the hospital was struggling to get along. The only means of illumination was candles and the wards looked dismal in the flickering light.

Then came rumours of revolution in Russia and the abdication of Louise's uncle Tsar Nicholas. 'No news from Russia from our dear ones. It's terrible and really all Aunt Alexandra's [the empress's] fault,' Prince Louis told Louise.[30]

In the wake of the Russian revolution, King George V was nervous. A mass meeting had been held at the Albert Hall to celebrate the fall of the tsarist autocracy and there were calls to abolish the British monarchy. Above all, the king was being 'attacked as half-German' and for 'surrounding himself with relatives with German names'. He now asked all his relatives with German titles, including the Tecks and Battenbergs, to give these up and assume English surnames. King George had decided to change the name of the House of Saxe-Coburg-Gotha to the more British sounding House of Windsor, while the various branches of the Teck family became Cambridge, Athlone and Carisbrooke.

On 6 June 1917, Prince Louis wrote to tell his daughter that they would have to give up their German titles:

It has been suggested that we should turn our name into English, viz: Battenhill or Mountbatten. We incline to the latter as a better sound … Of course we are at his mercy. We are only allowed to use our German title as the Sovereign has always recognised it, but he can refuse this recognition any moment. If so we are plain Mister, which would be impossible …

Louis made it clear that he was not at all happy about this turn of events. 'You know the rules of the peerage,' he continued, 'the eldest son bears the 2nd title … but the sons and daughters are Lord – and Lady – surname. I fear this will trouble you.'[31]

Prince Louis and Princess Victoria now became the Marquess and Marchioness of Milford Haven. Victoria, born a Princess of Hesse, could have kept her title but she decided to drop it in favour of her husband's new name. Her Serene Highness Princess Louise of Battenberg became Lady Louise Mountbatten. Although Victoria was sorry her daughter could not be with them when the news was made public, 'I think, however,' she told Nona, 'that she has enough of my nature to take the matter philosophically.'[32]

Victoria was correct. It did not trouble Lady Louise at all; she was too busy tending the wounded. Shortly afterwards she fell ill with mumps and was nursed by Ida Wheatley.

On 27 July Alexander Stuart-Hill came to Kent House for a four-day stay, and around this time he and Louise became engaged. Shakespeare had little money of his own and only the recent death of his father had allowed the couple to consider the possibility of marriage. Alice had arrived from Greece and clarified the situation in a letter to her aunt, Grand Duchess Eleonore of Hesse. 'He is quite well known in artistic circles,' she explained, 'and they predict a famous future for him. But he looks so odd and is such an eccentric that only now, after two years has Louise had the courage to tell her parents, just before I arrived.' Louis and Victoria asked the couple to wait until the end of the war before making an announcement, which would also give them time to scrape together some money. The news was kept strictly between the family and Nona Crichton. They feared that Louise would not be happy and that Shakespeare's artistic temperament might cause problems. There was also the question of his looks. 'I went to London with her [Louise] and met him and went around with the two of them,' Alice continued, 'but everyone turns in the street and laughs at him when they see him … He is very easy to talk to and interesting and she is madly in love with him, but he is so incredibly affected.'[33] Louise described him as 'the one and only person I could ever marry and really be happy with'.[34] Her parents remained unconvinced.

★★★

L'Hôpital Anglais closed in the autumn of 1917, and by the end of October Louise was working at the Princess Club Hospital for Wounded Soldiers in Jamaica Road, Bermondsey, in south-east London. The Princess Club had been started by Princess Marie Louise, the younger daughter of Princess Christian, for working-class girls employed in the factories along the riverfront at Rotherhithe. It was established in 'two fairly large houses adjoining each other, with a so-called garden or open space in the rear' where Marie Louise soon collected enough money to build a club room, bathrooms and a chapel. There was also an antenatal clinic.[35]

At the beginning of the First World War, Marie Louise ejected the girls and turned the building into a military convalescent hospital for officers with 100 beds. It came under the jurisdiction of the War Office so, as the princess put it, there was 'no well-meaning interference from the Red Cross or other bodies'. Princess Marie Louise never donned a uniform, always wearing 'my smartest dress and hat' when she visited the wounded.[36]

The Lady Superintendent was Miss Sophia Stewart Irvine Robertson, a woman in her thirties who had trained at St Bartholomew's Hospital, London, nursed in Bulgaria during the Balkan War and then in Serbia and Montenegro. Between 1916 and 1917 she was matron of the Anglo-Russian Hospital in Petrograd, housed on the Nevsky Prospekt in the palace of Grand Duke Dmitri, where she would have met Louise's aunt, Empress Alexandra, and her daughters.

At the end of October the Marchioness of Milford Haven came to London to have tea at the Princess Club Hospital and visit Louise's ward, where she found her daughter 'quite pleased with her new quarters and work'.[37] By the spring of 1918 the hospital was quiet but a French attack was expected. 'Of course, our losses must be terrible too and I expect you will have plenty of work soon'[38] her father wrote sympathetically. In November 1918 the armistice was signed and the war finally ended. For the moment Louise remained at the Princess Club Hospital but, perhaps for personal reasons, she was anxious to return to France.

Notes

1. Alexandra, Duchess of Fife, *A Nurse's Story* (John & Edward Bumpus Ltd, 1955), p.13.
2. Alexandra, *A Nurse's Story*, p.14.
3. Alexandra, *A Nurse's Story*, p.38.
4. Alexandra, *A Nurse's Story*, p.28.
5. Theo Aronson, *Grandmama of Europe* (Cassell, 1973), p.268.
6. Vickers, *Alice*, p.127.
7. Dame Beryl Oliver, *The British Red Cross in Action* (Faber, 1966), pp.207, 234.
8. Ruth Cowen (ed.), *War Diaries: A Nurse at the Front* (Simon & Schuster, 2012), pp.299–300.

9. This probably applied only to workers of the British Red Cross. See Oliver, *British Red Cross*, p.236.

10. These hospitals are very poorly documented and I am grateful to Sue Light and her excellent website www.scarletfinders.co.uk for help.

11 Broadlands Archives, S385. Princess Louis to Mrs Richard Crighton, 24 March 1915. Viti owed her unusual Christian name to her father's considerable time spent in the vicinity of Viti Levu, an island in the Pacific.

12. Information from Sue Light; Moorehead, *Dunant's Dream*, p.215.

13. Laurence Binyon, *For Dauntless France* (Hodder & Stoughton, 1918), pp.7–8.

14. Broadlands archives. S385. Extract from Lady Paget's letter, quoted in a letter from Princess Louise to Mrs Richard Crighton, 22 April 1915.

15. Broadlands archives, S385. Princess Louise to Mrs Richard Crighton, 12 May 1915

16. Mary Borden, *The Forbidden Zone* (Hesperus Press Ltd, 1929), p.60.

17. Mountbatten Papers, Southampton University. MS 62 MB1/T90. Various dates.

18. Broadlands Archives, S385. Princess Louise to Mrs Richard Crighton, 25, 27 & 30 September 1915.

19. Mountbatten Papers, Southampton University. MS 62 MB1/T90. Prince Louis of Battenberg to Princess Louise, 27 May 1916.

20. Kid Severin & Eva Dickson, *Drottningen, en minnesalbum* (Åhlén & Åkerlands Förlags AB, Stockholm, 1965), p.57.

21. *The Evening Post*, New Zealand, 14 November 1916.

22. The dates are taken from the Scottish census. Alexander Hill appears aged 8 in 1891 and aged 18 in 1901 but is not listed in 1881.

23. Broadlands Archives, S385. Princess Louise to Mrs Richard Crighton, 25 September 1915.

24. Mountbatten Papers, Southampton University. MS 62 MB1/T90. Prince Louis of Battenberg to Princess Louise, 21 December 1915.

25. Fjellman, *Louise Mountbatten*, p.92.

26. Severin & Dickson, *Drottningen*, p.57.

27. Broadlands archives, S3863. Princess Louise to Mrs Richard Crighton, 3 November 1916.

28. Mountbatten Papers, Southampton University. MS 62 MB1/T90. Prince Louis of Battenberg to Princess Louise, 3 Oct 1916.

29. Broadlands archives. S387. Princess Louise to Mrs Richard Crighton, 11 February 1917.

30. Mountbatten Papers, Southampton University. MS 62 MB1/T90. Prince Louis of Battenberg to Princess Louise, 6 May 1917.

31. Mountbatten Papers, Southampton University. MS 62 MB1/T90. Prince Louis of Battenberg to Princess Louise, 6 June 1917.

32. Broadlands Archives, S387. The Marchioness of Milford Haven to Mrs Richard Crighton, 7 June 1917.

33. Quoted in Vickers, *Alice*, p.128 and used here by kind permission of HRH The Duke of Edinburgh who owns the copyright.

34. Vickers, *Alice*, p.128.

35. Princess Marie Louise, *My Memories of Six Reigns* (Evans Brothers, 1956), pp.126–30.

36. Marie Louise, *My Memories*, p.182.

37. Broadlands Archives, S387. The Marchioness of Milford Haven to Mrs Richard Crighton, 23 October 1917.

38. Mountbatten Papers, Southampton University. MS 62 MB1/T90. The Marquess of Milford Haven to Lady Louise Mountbatten, 26 March 1918.

7

A Small Unconquered Corner

For two European queens, nursing held a special poignancy, as they did it not in their country's capital, but in the tiny corner of their respective kingdoms left unoccupied by the enemy. In difficult circumstances sometimes bordering on the impossible, Queen Elisabeth of Belgium and Queen Marie of Romania acted as an inspiration to their beleaguered people.

Elisabeth was a member of the unconventional Wittelsbach family. Born on 25 July 1876 she grew up at Schloss Possenhofen near Munich, the daughter of Duke Charles Theodore *in* Bavaria, son of the head of the Ducal branch of the royal house (the reigning branch were the Dukes *of* Bavaria) and his wife Marie-José of Portugal. Elisabeth – who was named after her aunt, the beautiful Empress Elisabeth of Austria ('Sisi'), wife of Emperor Franz Joseph – was dainty, with fair hair, blue eyes and a dazzling smile. She had boundless energy and quick wits, was a talented musician and, like her aunt, an excellent horsewoman. She was particularly close to her father, who had seen the ravages done to the troops by infectious diseases in the Franco-Prussian War. Charles Theodore studied medicine in Munich, Vienna and Zurich, and eye diseases with a Russian specialist on the riviera. He qualified as an oculist and opened free clinics in Merano, Munich and the castle at Tegernsee, where he performed operations. Elisabeth was one of her father's chief assistants (as was her sister Sophie, who specialised in bacteriology) and gained a rudimentary knowledge of nursing, although she received no proper training.

In 1900, Elisabeth married Prince Albert of Belgium, a grandson of Queen Victoria's beloved uncle Leopold, who became the first King of the Belgians in 1831. One day Albert would become sovereign, as the current king, the immoral, ruthless Leopold II, had only daughters and his heir was his brother Philippe, Count of Flanders, Albert's father.

Elisabeth and Albert moved into in an unostentatious house in the exclusive Quartier Léopold, to where the bohemian princess invited many people from the worlds of the arts, science and literature. She had little time for court ceremonial, preferring to visit the slums in the Marolles district, asking the people about their living conditions and bringing aid to the poor and needy. The fact that in Bavaria Elisabeth had 'taken up nursing' was considered in bourgeois circles to be 'most advanced'. Society sneered that she 'was better at rolling bandages' than curtseying to Queen Marie-Henriette.[1] Extrovert, assured and unconventional, she proved to be Albert's ideal partner in the trials to come.

In 1905, Albert's father died. With the death of Leopold II in 1909 Elisabeth's 34-year-old husband became Albert I, King of the Belgians. The new sovereigns moved to Laeken, 4 miles from the centre of Brussels. In public the bespectacled King Albert seemed awkward, embarrassed and tongue-tied. Yet he was also compassionate, with a devotion to duty and capacity for leadership which showed to better advantage in private. Queen Elisabeth founded trusts, societies and associations to help the sick and needy. She 'spent so much time visiting hospitals, said the king dryly, that he would never be able to claim her full attention until he had broken a limb or contracted a fatal disease'.[2]

By July 1914, Albert was increasingly worried about his powerful aggressive neighbour Germany. Belgium's neutrality was guaranteed by the Great Powers in 1831 but the German war plan involved a lightning offensive against France, which would be reached by crossing through Belgium. With France swiftly defeated, the German Army would then turn east to join the Austro-Hungarian Army and crush mighty Russia. All Albert's fears were borne out when the Belgian government rejected the kaiser's ultimatum to allow his army to pass through unhindered. On 4 August, German troops crossed the frontier and King Albert appealed to Britain and France for help. He then left Brussels to become Commander-in-Chief of the army. Meanwhile, Belgium faced the brunt of the German onslaught alone.

★★★

Like most royal families the couple had relatives on the other side of the conflict. Albert's sister Princess Josephine had married her cousin Prince Karl-Anton of Hohenzollern-Sigmaringen and in 1908 they bought Namedy Castle on the Rhine. Karl-Anton served in the army but when war broke out Josephine found herself on the opposite side to her brother, to whom she had always been close. While her husband was fighting with the German Army in Belgium, Josephine turned the castle's Hall of Mirrors into a military hospital, put on a nurse's uniform and tended the wounded soldiers.

Also in Germany was Albert's cousin, Princess Dorothea (Dora) of Schleswig-Holstein-Sonderburg-Glücksburg. She had attended courses on medical care in 1908 and now turned the family castle of Primkenau into a hospital, with a Red Cross flag flying from the roof. Early in August she attended a four-week nursing course at the Bethany Hospital in Berlin, passed her nursing exams and worked in a hospital at Stendal in Saxony. Dora's sister-in-law Empress Augusta Victoria of Germany placed several hospitals under her management. Later Dora served with distinction in a Berlin hospital and then on the front line, where she was considered capable, effective and dependable. By the end of 1917, she was the theatre assistant of Dr Esser, the famous Dutch surgeon.

Elisabeth's cousin, Archduchess Marie Valerie of Austria-Tuscany (daughter of Emperor Franz Joseph), was patron of the Red Cross and well-known for her charity work. She set up a hospital in a barracks at Schloss Wallsee where she devotedly nursed the wounded.

Despite these awkward family connections Queen Elisabeth identified completely with her husband and Belgium. 'It is finished between me and them [Germany], henceforth an iron curtain has descended between us,' she said.[3]

★★★

As the Germans advanced, Lieutenant General Leopold Mélis, Inspector General of Health Services of the Belgian Army, suggested that Queen Elisabeth ask Dr Antoine Depage to 'organise and command the Medical Services of the Belgian Red Cross'.[4] The 52-year-old doctor accepted on condition that he could convert the Royal Palace into a Red Cross hospital.

Antoine Depage and his wife Marie Picard had been part of the royal circle since 1907. He created the first school of nursing in Belgium, organised and directed medical help during the Balkan Wars and in December 1909 was one of the doctors who operated on King Leopold for cancer of the colon. (The king died three days later, although this does not seem to have affected Depage's career.)

At Depage's request the ballroom, throne room and other state apartments were furnished with more than 1,000 hospital beds, their white coverlets neatly turned down ready for the first casualties. At the foot of each was a little Belgian flag, placed there, the queen told the American Ambassador, by her children. Two weeks later, as the Germans crossed the River Meuse, the Palace Hospital had to be abandoned. King Albert ordered the army to retreat to Antwerp, the wounded were evacuated and the royal family followed. On 20 August the Germans occupied Brussels.

Elisabeth moved into Antwerp's Royal Palace, from where she visited the wounded, helped the doctors and organised practical relief for the thousands of terrified refugees. By 23 August three-quarters of Belgium was occupied by the enemy, who looted, destroyed, burned and killed indiscriminately. The remaining quarter was sandwiched between the combatants and the sea. The queen sent her children Leopold, Charles and Marie-José to school in England, away from the constant Zeppelin raids.

In October, Antwerp had to be abandoned but the king refused to leave Belgian soil. He headed for the remaining few square miles of Belgian territory between the River Yser and the Ypres Canal and on 14 October the king and queen reached the royal chalet at Ostend. From this last enclave Albert issued orders that there was to be no further retreat. To her dismay Elisabeth heard rumours that there were two divisions of Bavarian cavalry near Ghent and Ypres under the command of her brother Ludwig William. 'Everything seems too cruel,'[5] she wrote in her diary, lamenting also the late arrival of the British.

On 15 October they moved again. 'On the way I only see horses, soldiers and refugees, on their way to France,' the queen recorded. 'People from the coastal area with bags, suitcases, children, dogs, a real exodus', all fleeing from the Germans. A few days later at the battle of Yser the Belgian Army halted the German advance along the channel coast, saving the French ports. As King Albert said in his dry, self-deprecating way, 'we were cornered into heroism'.[6]

Albert and Elisabeth's destination was the coastal town of De Panne, a former fishing village just north of the French border 8 miles from the front line, where their children had formerly played on the sand dunes during family holidays. It was where Leopold I had first set foot on Belgian soil in 1831. Now a substantial summer resort, it was deserted in winter. One observer described it as 'lonely … with ugly brick and wooden buildings strewn along the beach … nearly everything shabby or half destroyed', with refugees crowding in among the soldiers' barracks. Another said that it consisted of 'ploughed fields, roads leading into sand dunes, roofless houses'. Down the road was a farm and 'a village crouching in the mud'.[7] Even the weather had turned against them, with nothing but grey skies and driving rain.

The king and queen set up home in the modest red-brick Villa Maskens on the coast, almost the last house on Belgian soil. Its owners, a family of Belgian diplomats, had already been evacuated to France. The dunes came almost up to the steps and a policeman guarded the front door.

Conditions inside were Spartan. 'In the bedrooms were twin beds, an old-fashioned lavabo and a large crucifix.'[8] There was no heating or running water, the only firewood was driftwood collected from the beach and for a long time the lighting was provided by carbide lamps. There was no time to change furniture or fittings. The wine cellar served as an air-raid shelter and there was a playroom in the basement for the children when they came from England in the holidays. Their staff and offices occupied two villas next door and the local schoolroom served as the king's office, the headquarters of the Belgian Army.

Queen Mary's brother Prince Alexander of Teck was serving with the British Mission. His wife Princess Alice of Albany (another granddaughter of Queen Victoria) often visited him and knew the Belgian queen well. Elisabeth told Alice that she would not change anything – she did not want to think of it as home. They felt, Elisabeth said, like cuckoos in someone else's nest. She was often seen walking along the beach, deep in thought. Even here they were not safe. 'We are ready all the time to leave again, even at night,' Elisabeth wrote.[9] A few days later, bombs dropped in the vicinity of Villa Maskens.

After the battle of Yser the king ordered the sluice gates opened to flood the Yser valley. This separated the beleaguered Belgians from the Germans by a vast sheet of water and gave them a breathing space. The Belgian Army now formed the extreme left wing of the Allied line, which stretched from Switzerland to the North Sea. Twenty square miles of Belgian soil were all that remained to Albert of his kingdom. 'As long as there is one square foot of Belgium free of the Germans,' declared Elisabeth, 'I will be on it.'[10] Queen Elisabeth's finest hour was about to come.

★★★

For two years Romania remained neutral. Ferdinand I succeeded his uncle King Carol in October 1914 but he hesitated to join the conflict. The dynasty was German, his brothers were fighting for Germany, and Romania was in no position to wage war against the Central Powers. His British-born wife, however, saw things differently.

The flamboyant Queen Marie was anxious for Ferdinand to join the fight. She realised that success could enable the country to gain lands from Austria-Hungary and Bulgaria which many believed were rightly Romania's. Finally, with a heavy heart, in August 1916 he declared war on the Central Powers and left for army headquarters with his eldest son Crown Prince Carol.

Marie was ecstatic. Fired by her experiences in the cholera camp during the Balkan War she was desperate to do 'something useful, something energetic' towards the war effort.[11] Her courage, compassion, vitality, sense of duty and devotion to Romania would all be brought into play during the following two years.

As the Germans bombed Bucharest, the queen and her children moved to Buftea, the nearby estate of her friend Prince Stirbey from where she drove into town to visit the hospitals. She also set up a hospital in the old Palatul Victoriei, which had been her first home when she arrived in Romania. The high-ceilinged rooms were panelled with black marble and dark wood; their only ornaments were some religious paintings by El Greco. The whole palace had a depressing appearance. On Marie's instructions the walls of the large banqueting halls were whitewashed and the hospital was equipped at her expense. Madame Henri Carteg, wife of the marshal of the court, was put in charge and, as mutilated victims were brought in, many ladies volunteered as nurses. Among them was Marie.

Gone were her theatrical veils, cloaks and trailing draperies; gone were the Byzantine-style gowns and elaborate jewelled crosses; gone, too, were the specially designed riding habits which Marie wore to such great effect. Instead Marie donned the white uniform of a nursing sister with its distinctive Red Cross on the left arm. She handed out pictures of herself in this uniform and soldiers died clutching her photograph. Her second son, Prince Nicholas, often accompanied her on hospital visits, while 22-year-old Elisabeta and 16-year-old Marie ('Mignon') chatted to the soldiers and served their food. Even 8-year-old Ileana put a little white cloth on her head and handed out meals.

However, things went badly for Romania. Within a month the country was invaded by the Germans from the north and the Bulgarians from the south. As the Romanians retreated in confusion, over 25,000 soldiers were captured in one campaign alone, while hospitals, stores, provisions, ammunition and weapons were abandoned. When the promised munitions from the Entente failed to arrive, Russia remained their only hope. As the Germans advanced towards Bucharest, Queen Marie wrote to her cousin Tsar Nicholas II begging for help.

At this point Marie's 3-year-old son Mircea contracted typhoid. Every minute she could spare from the hospitals was spent nursing her son but on 2 November Mircea died. It is said that the kaiser, Marie's cousin, refused to bomb Cotroceni Palace while the funeral was taking place in the chapel.

To help assuage her grief, Marie visited the wounded in Moldavia. Mircea's death enabled her to empathise with the Romanian women sacrificing their sons in battle and to help the dying soldiers in the hospitals. The queen's final stop was the town of Adjud, which had a large Red Cross organisation. 'I saw nothing but suffering, suffering, suffering, which did not lighten my heavy heart,' she recalled.[12] As the German advance gathered pace it became clear that Bucharest would have to be abandoned. Marie found her hospital in a panic. Some of the invalids had been evacuated and those who remained were terrified of falling into enemy hands. As the Romanians retreated towards Moldavia the depots and provisions were left behind, with only the most vital things saved where possible.

On 25 November the royal family, their attendants, servants and a pile of luggage left the capital by train. On 6 December Bucharest fell to the Germans. With Russian help the Romanians held the line around Jassy, the provincial capital of Moldavia, 10 miles west of the Russian border. Only a fraction of the country now remained in Romanian hands. Jassy would be Marie's home for the remainder of the war.

★★★

At De Panne, Queen Elisabeth of Belgium realised the urgency of setting up a surgical unit. The only surgical hospital near the army was run by the nuns at Furnes and they had no proper medical training. After the heavy casualties of the battle of Yser the queen asked Dr Depage, who was working at the Red Cross hospital in Calais, to take charge of all the Red Cross field hospitals.

To the east of De Panne at the opposite end of the beach to Villa Maskens was the Hôtel de l'Océan, a large four-storey building used by holidaymakers during the summer. The queen learnt, probably through Ernest d'Arripe, mayor of De Panne, that the hotel was empty and she obtained the owner's agreement to convert it into a hospital. General Mélis was opposed to having a hospital so near the front, citing the risk of losing valuable personnel and equipment if the Germans broke through. However, Depage, director of all medical services, supported the scheme. The queen often had to mediate between Mélis and Depage when tensions arose and without her support the plan would undoubtedly have failed.

King Albert's military attaché Major Gordon was asked to help Depage equip the place. One of the most urgent needs was heating, as the building had none and winter was fast approaching. Gordon and Depage left for England where they learnt that Harrods, the famous department store in Knightsbridge, had in stock a central heating system destined for a Scottish castle and now no longer needed because of the war. It was soon on its way to De Panne.

The bulk of the country's medical supplies was in enemy hands, so the queen rang Harrods on the cross-Channel telephone (a special line was kept open so that she could speak to her children) and ordered what was needed. The equipment was delivered within forty-eight hours. A warehouse was set up next door to Villa Maskens to store the goods which Elisabeth obtained from abroad to distribute to anyone in need. Much of the food came from two nearby farms.

With the aid of money from the Red Cross, the Hôpital de l'Océan opened with 200 beds (and by flattening some of the dunes and adding further pavilions this capacity later reached 1,200 beds, even 2,000 in emergency) on

21 December. The five modern operating rooms erected in the hotel grounds had excellent lighting so that operations could be performed day and night. There were different pavilions for various types of trauma, contagious diseases and infections. The army provided all the personnel except the nurses.[13] As the doctors were commissioned into the army Dr Depage became a colonel, although he never thought of himself as anything other than head surgeon. The Belgian Red Cross also became part of the military establishment, though funds which had been contributed remained under the care of the executive committee. There were few graduate nurses in Belgium at that time and Queen Elisabeth played an important role in the acceptance of lay sisters, many of whom had completed their initial training in London. A group of refugees and Red Cross doctors and nurses banded together to carry on the work of the hospital, which was largely funded by contributions collected by Marie Depage who raised over $100,000 in America.

In May 1915, Marie Depage was drowned in the *Lusitania* on her way back from a fundraising trip for the Belgian Red Cross. Her body was recovered from the Irish coast and buried among the dunes at De Panne, just along the coast from the hospital. It was the queen who comforted Depage and arranged for his son Dr Henri Depage to be brought to De Panne. The following year when Depage was suffering from severe lumbar pain the queen sent him a pelisse (a fur-lined cloak), for which he wrote to thank her.[14] Surviving letters from Depage in the Royal Archives in Brussels attest to their friendship.

★★★

There are many myths about what Queen Elisabeth actually did in the hospital. Her biographer says that she arrived there at nine o'clock every morning and spent the majority of her time nursing or caring for refugee children. (She worked closely with the Swiss Dr Widmer and his American wife Mary Curtat, who founded the Œuvre d'Hospitalisation des Réfugiés Belges, whereby sick children living near the front line were housed safely in private homes in Switzerland.) He also says that she was a 'trained nurse' who held 'a high medical degree', skilful at bandaging and other nursing operations but 'that she was a doctor as well is also amply attested'.[15] This is incorrect. Although Queen Elisabeth followed some courses in basic nursing practice given by Dr Depage, she never held a medical degree and was therefore not a doctor.[16]

The knowledge gained at her father's clinic was insufficient for the operating theatre or looking after maimed soldiers and she had no time to commence any proper nursing training. Nevertheless, she supervised the smallest details, especially concerning hygiene, and could change a bandage or apply a dressing where necessary. The overworked nurses appreciated her visits. At the time when so many doctors treated them as merely maids of all work the appearance of the intelligent, interested queen was a boost to their morale.

Elisabeth did not wear a nurse's uniform, not wishing to be seen usurping the functions of a trained nurse. Instead she wore practical clothes, always white, with a headdress somewhere between a turban and a nurse's cap, described as the 'uniform of a soldier-queen'.[17] Propaganda did, however, play a part. Pictures in the contemporary French magazine *Le Pays de France* show the queen in the operating theatre of a hospital at the front. These were posed. Sometimes a great number of wounded arrived together and operations had to be done quickly. The queen proved a useful assistant, although Depage was known for his tantrums and it is said that during one operation Elisabeth passed him the wrong instrument and he threw it to the ground in anger. 'The fact that she assisted Depage during certain operations contributed to the construction of the myth of the Queen Nurse which developed during the war.'[18]

The queen became a symbol. Her sympathy and care for the men was immense, so that soldiers asked for her when they were dying and many died in her arms. The last face many men saw was that of the tiny queen. The story is told of a young English soldier about to have an operation. Excitedly he pointed to a group of white-clad nurses, saying: 'It's that nurse over there that I want ... Only her. That nurse over there.' The nurse was the Queen of Belgium. In 1915 she wrote to the Minister of War about pay for the injured men, which remained low:

> The men have already offered a lot to the country. Most of them can't receive support because of their family. It is already bad enough that they are injured; into the bargain they can't afford anything extra themselves. I know that you are very concerned about the well-being of the soldiers. Therefore I would be very grateful if you would consider the possibility of raising the pay, paid to the injured in hospitals, during the war.[19]

The republican poet Verhaeran saw in Elisabeth the embodiment of Belgian civilisation, contrasting it with the 'black barbarism of the enemy'.[20] To the public, with whom her popularity was immense, she was 'the heroine of Yser', 'the Mother of the Army', the 'Soul of Belgium'.

★★★

In Jassy, Queen Marie was forced to spend two weeks on the train while her aide-de-camp Colonel Ballif found a suitable house and the basics with which to equip it. The 'sleepy little town'[21] of 50,000 people was now invaded by an influx of Russians and more than 300,000 refugees. The foreign Red Cross units were at their wits' end, and to make matters worse that winter was the coldest on record. Many froze to death in the streets because, as a Red Cross observer noted, 'there was no room for them to die indoors'.[22] Typhus, smallpox and other diseases were widespread and food was scarce. Even the royal family lived mainly on beans.

Marie found Jassy's hastily organised hospitals in chaos. Conditions were appalling and there was no effective head of sanitation. Those with infectious diseases were placed together with the wounded, men were crammed two or three to a bed and the wards were unheated. Men died from pneumonia or infections because there was no hot water to wash the linen and went hungry because there was no fuel to heat the ovens and bake bread. Although there was wood outside the town it could not be brought into Jassy because of transportation difficulties.

The Romanian hospital trains were also unsatisfactory. When the Russian train organised and equipped by Queen Marie's aunt the Dowager Empress Marie Feodorovna arrived, the queen was invited on board. 'We were ... received by a Cossack officer who had the air of a conqueror in his picturesque uniform, a red "*bashlic*" floating like a pair of wings from his shoulder and his belt stuck full of daggers,' she recalled. 'The magnificence of this Imperial train made us feel small, shabby, poor. Here there was everything in unbelievable plenty.[23] On the equally impressive train of the queen's cousin Empress Alexandra Feodorovna, where 'each long white carriage bore the name of its august patroness, and the red cross shone in scarlet brilliance on wall and roof',[24] she was presented with linen for 200 men. The Russian trains had everything soldiers might need at the front. Games and musical instruments were even provided for the convalescents. Marie gratefully accepted the gift of some useful drugs including quinine and aspirin, which were becoming difficult to obtain in Jassy. The Romanians had nothing comparable and the lack of supervision was making itself felt.

Everyone looked to Marie for inspiration and leadership. She did not fail. As 'Head of the Red Cross, Leader of the Refugee Workers, President of the War Invalids Society, and voluntary inspector of all hospitals and camps'[25] she worked day and night. Her old friend Dr Jean Cantacuzène was appointed head of sanitary organisations, but it was too late to stop the spread of typhus. Sanitary equipment was detained in Russia and it took officers from the French Military Mission to bring it out.

Sister Pucci introduced the queen to Dr Cluny, a French doctor specialising in infectious diseases. Soon the Hospital for Infectious Diseases was set up in Villa Greenrul, the home of Marie's English friend Sybil Chrissoveloni outside the town of Ghidigeni. Sybil ran the hospital from her own funds. Marie wanted to establish her own hospital but was finally persuaded to give up the idea and concentrate on helping all the others.

In December, Marie's sister Victoria Melita ('Ducky'), wife of Grand Duke Cyril of Russia, brought much needed medical supplies and provisions. Ducky had a large hospital in Warsaw, an ambulance train that could carry 800 wounded (on which one of the best Petrograd surgeons worked) and a provisions train which fed both troops and refugees in places where food was scarce. She helped organise the Russian motorised ambulance unit, which was soon one of the country's most efficiently run services. During part of the time she was based near Warsaw and throughout the appalling slaughter in Poland, when ambulances were constantly ferrying wounded from the front to the rear, she often worked under enemy fire. 'The amount of wounded is stupendous,' she wrote, 'and the work greater than any efforts can suffice to cope with. One week over 39,000 passed through Warsaw's hospitals and trains.' It was little wonder that she was looking 'worn and harassed, her eyes heavy with overpowering weariness'.[26]

Marie and Ducky drove to the railway station to look for railway carriages that could be turned into Russian hospital trains. Then they distributed St George's Crosses in the Russian hospital in the Notre Dame de Sion Convent. In order to obtain more room for the patients Marie and her sister visited the old Mother Superior, who was exasperated with people trying to commandeer her house. To Marie's embarrassment and Ducky's annoyance she was not very kind about the Russians.

By now there was talk of evacuating to Kherson in Russia, just beyond Odessa. Marie's presence seemed necessary everywhere, helping, encouraging and making the impossible possible. Often she visited eight hospitals in one day. Even on Christmas Day she worked to finish Christmas packets for the soldiers.

By the new year of 1917, Romania was relying for support on the co-operation of Russia, who remained 'her only undefeated ally in the East'.[27] Then came news that the empress's evil genius Rasputin had been murdered by relatives of the tsar and that a revolt by the imperial family against Alexandra was likely. Marie decided that this would be an unpropitious time to go and plead with Tsar Nicholas to help Romania.

***

In Belgium Dr Depage worked with Dr Neuman and Dr Debaisieux to treat the many soldiers suffering from the effects of the mustard gas used by the Germans. The regulations had been altered so that hospitals could be erected nearer to the front line and Queen Elisabeth set up a chain of first-aid posts and hospitals close to the fighting. There was now a three-stage system of first-aid posts, intermediary centres and base hospitals. This efficiency saved many lives.

Yet not even the horrors and deprivations of war could daunt Elisabeth, or stifle her Bohemian artistic spirit. She had a moveable wooden pavilion erected in the grounds of Villa Maskens and furnished it with divans piled high with cushions so that she could meet artists, poets and writers. 'She loved to entertain artistic people from the regiments,' explained Princess Alice.[28] Elisabeth also asked famous musicians and singers to provide entertainment at the hospital and in 1917 she even organised an art exhibition.

Expert horticulturists had grown a rose garden among the Flanders mud and at Easter she brought flowers to the hospital to remind the men of happier times. At Christmas she gave the wounded soldiers presents to lift their spirits, distributing as many as possible herself. The impact on morale was immense.

Sometimes she went to the front where Dr Neuman was working in the cellars of a brasserie in Nieuwpoort. Heedless of danger and in spite of wind, dust and the potholes littering the roads after the daily bombardments, the queen travelled in an ambulance covered with a tarpaulin roof. She usually went after a night attack to ensure that there were not too many seriously wounded, to see whether she could help and if they needed anything. In the afternoon she visited the hospitals at the front taking linen sewing kits bearing the signature of the king and queen, chocolate, cigars, cigarettes, tobacco and, especially, flowers, which she distributed accompanied by a surgeon or his assistant, taking care not to disturb the nurses on duty. The wounds of some of these men were appalling. 'There are heads and knees and mangled testicles,' recalled one front-line nurse. 'There are chests with holes as big as your fist, and pulpy thighs, shapeless; and stumps where legs were once fastened … There are eyes … blind eyes, eyes of delirium; and mouths that cannot articulate; and parts of faces – the nose gone, or the jaw.'[29]

One day, as the queen was being shown round by the head surgeon, a young soldier was brought in with a perforated lung. The surgeon immediately prepared for a difficult emergency operation, but with wounded men constantly arriving there was a shortage of nurses. Without hesitation Elisabeth put on an overall and mask and followed him into the theatre. 'She knew exactly what to do … I did not have to tell her anything,' he commented afterwards.[30] Her daughter Marie-José recalled that Elisabeth often kept the king waiting when she was visiting the hospitals. 'She forgot dinner-time and often only came home when we were already having our desserts', but Albert never complained.[31]

The danger of shells was ever present. Between August 1915 and May 1918 the Hôpital de l'Océan was hit eleven times. When fire broke out in the

Albert-Elisabeth pavilion in 1915, Harrod's offered to bear the cost of the repairs. The queen remained impervious to danger. Princess Alice, who often accompanied her on visits to the hospital or the troops, said she 'never knew Queen Elisabeth to flinch when the shells landed nearby'.[32] When a hospital was hit, Elisabeth was indefatigable in helping the nurses to evacuate the patients, refusing all entreaties to get away to safety herself. Complimented on her courage, she replied that it was the same as any other nurse. 'I do not know what it means to feel afraid,' she said.[33]

From November 1916 until July 1917 the matron at De Panne was the highly respected Violetta Thurston of the British Red Cross, who had worked in Brussels in 1914 and then on Grand Duchess Victoria Melita's hospital train in Poland. Queen Elisabeth spared neither time nor money to ensure that the Hôpital de l'Océan and her medical centre at Cabour were up-to-date and well equipped. Doctor (later Professor) Pierre Nolf, head of the medical services of the Belgian Army and physician to the royal family, became a driving force behind the implementation of the queen's wishes. He had done post-graduate laboratory and practical clinical work in physiology and biochemistry, as well as research into blood coagulation and shock-pathology. Nolf and Depage combined the practical and the theoretical. The ideas Elisabeth absorbed from her association with Depage were pursued with Nolf in later years and enabled the treatment of the wounded to be revolutionised. More than 20,000 wounded were treated in the Hôpital de l'Océan and thanks to this modern hospital the death rate fell from 20 per cent to 5 per cent.[34]

★★★

Despite the freezing cold Romanian winter Queen Marie still travelled round in an open Rolls-Royce. She had no other means of transport. When the car needed fuel her driver had to find an aviation station which had petrol. Not until November 1917 did Marie obtain a closed-top Cadillac from the military section, presented in recognition of her good works so that she could carry out her visits in more comfort.

Early in 1917, Ducky arrived bringing large quantities of food and necessities – 'shirts and trousers, gloves and sheets, dressing-gowns and bandages, medicines, needles and cotton ...' the list was endless, Marie recalled.[35] The hospitals still lacked essentials. At a large military depot Marie was delighted when the commanding officer gave her 100 warm dressing gowns. Urgent requests were sent to the Red Cross in London for 'tents, boilers, sheets, disinfectant, clothing, medical stores of every kind and condensed milk'. A thousand cases of condensed milk were packed in the storehouse in Devonshire House, Mayfair (the Duke of Devonshire had offered the ground floor of his London home as a Red Cross storeroom), and sent to Jassy via Archangel and Odessa, the final leg in a convoy which miraculously was neither looted nor plundered.[36]

At an eye hospital in a former convent on the edge of town Marie and Ducky found Dr Staicovitch in despair at the terrible conditions. In windowless, barn-like buildings 700 men were crammed together in bunk beds with no space between them. There was neither light nor air, the earth floors were a sea of mud and some of the men had typhus. There was also no place to isolate infectious diseases and no sanitary arrangements of any kind. However, thanks to Marie's intervention, when she returned in the summer the place was scarcely recognisable and Dr Staicovitch proudly showed off the improvements.

Despite generous donations from Allied Red Cross organisations the need in Romania was great. The Russians who swarmed into Jassy had to be fed but the money they gave to the peasants in exchange for food soon proved useless, as there was nothing left to buy. In the bitter cold of February 1917, Ileana went out daily with a basket full of bread and biscuits and a thermos of tea and rum, which she gave to any needy people she met on the street.

The queen's 16-year-old daughter Mignon was nursing in a large hospital staffed by French doctors. Mignon had none of her mother's theatricality or sparkle; calm, steady and easygoing, she was an ideal nurse. She worked at the hospital in the mornings and helped Ileana in the afternoons. Queen Marie put her own bread aside for the children to take to the hungry. There were now more sick than wounded and in the overcrowded hospitals the death rate was much higher. Men were sent away without being completely cured and there were no convalescent facilities.

As she had done during the Balkan War, Marie wore high riding boots under her white nurse's dress because of the muddy roads in the more remote villages. One day her car became stuck in deep mud and ten oxen were needed to pull it out. Some of these villages were so isolated that her car could not get through at all, so she had to go by horse and cart. Everywhere Marie went her uniform became a symbol. In a miserable village she found a regiment, 'wretched, dirty, forsaken, buried in mud and melting snow'. Their doctors and officers were either dead or had contracted typhus and the men were 'wandering between crumbling huts, pale, ragged spectres, ghosts of soldiers with ragged faces, with sunken eyes, their clothes in tatters'.[37] She gave them tea, biscuits, sugar, soap and tobacco. For the officers there was tea, chocolate, cigarettes and warm stockings. To the very sick she gave rum, brandy and medicines. In other hospitals she gave holy pictures, prayers, or little crosses to wear around their neck; she cut bread and spread it with jam for dying men; or sat down and read to wounded officers. She found a soldier whose face had been shot to pieces, his eyelids closed and stuck. Marie sat down and gently bathed his eyelids. At night, still wearing her riding boots, she stood in a tub of boiling water shedding her clothes to kill the lice.

Dr Mamulea became head of the queen's supply depots where food, clothing and medicines were stored. It was a good choice and by the spring of 1917 this quietly efficient man was giving good results. Then in March came news of the Russian revolution. With most of Romania still in enemy hands and her allies heavily engaged fighting on the Western Front, King Ferdinand and Queen Marie awaited events with foreboding.

Sick with worry about her Russian relatives, Marie redoubled her efforts in the hospitals. Starting at eight or nine in the morning she often worked until eight in the evening, or even midnight. 'In one day alone, she visited fourteen different regiments in eight different villages, and in a single afternoon distributed one thousand cigarettes.'[38] Queen Marie seldom showed any sign of fatigue, although at night she was exhausted. The Entente continued to give generously (England sent £5,000) and regular transports of provisions arrived from Russia for some time after the revolution.

One of her concerns was the triage, the clearing place at the railway station where the sick were kept on arrival until room could be found in the overcrowded hospitals. This was little more than a dark wooden barracks where men lay huddled together on the floor covered in lice. As the men stretched out their hands, Marie often had to step over corpses to reach them. With the aid of Sister Pucci and Jean Cantacuzène she finally cleaned it up, although typhus continued to spread.

As Easter approached she took food to some of the rural villages stricken with typhoid. In one the wounded were laid out in the sunshine on a grassy bank by a church. There were hundreds of them, literally 'a parade of skeletons', stretching out their bony fingers for her gifts, or to hold her hand briefly for comfort. A legend sprang up that men had been healed just by touching her. As Marie was leaving, 'one of these emaciated phantoms staggered to his feet, and thanked me for coming down from my palace towards their misery on this Easter Sunday'.[39] Little did these men know that Marie now had no palace.

Jean Chrissoveloni (Sybil's husband) was head of the Regina Maria Organisation. The Regina Maria typhus hospital at Voinesti was housed in a huge barn. Marie was proud that her name had been given to this hospital and that her portrait, decorated with flowers, was conspicuous on its walls. She took few precautions and by touching the men too much put herself at great risk of catching the disease, but Marie justified this by saying that she could not be uncertain or show distaste in front of men suffering so cruelly. The doctors tried to persuade her to wear rubber gloves. Marie refused, declaring 'the soldiers all kiss my hand and I really cannot ask them to kiss india-rubber'.[40]

The Regina Maria ambulances were well-run organisations that saved thousands of lives. However, many of the motor ambulances had been lost during the retreat and consequently the army wanted to combine the Regina Maria ambulances with the military units. Marie fought to keep these vehicles, which were vital to fetch the wounded from the front.

Marie took a special interest in the hospitals for tuberculosis and whenever extra provisions could be obtained came personally to distribute them. The Mircea Canteens, a small private organisation feeding the poorest people in the villages, was another of her initiatives.

Opportunities for rest were few but one came in June when it was comparatively quiet. Mignon was happily working with Sybil in Ghidigeni, where she was soon joined by Ileana, so Marie rode, explored the countryside and visited the regiments quartered in distant villages.

★★★

By 1917, Queen Elisabeth's hospital at De Panne was a large complex. Over forty pavilions and barracks were added to the original building, which now boasted its own power plant, laboratories and pharmacy. Forty ambulances were available to bring wounded from the front, the latest medical discoveries were available to the patients, while in the laboratories the doctors were adding to these medical advances. These institutions were soon widely acclaimed and the queen was anxious that the medical personnel should remain with the army and not have to evacuate to France. Other facilities included a butcher, a joinery, a workshop for the manufacture of surgical instruments and both Protestant and Catholic chapels. In the recreation room the original string quartet had grown to the Orchestre Symphonique de l'Armée de Campagne comprising eighty-five musicians.

In the summer of 1917, De Panne became part of the British sector. The area was becoming dangerous, so on 20 July the royal family moved to the even more remote, desolate marshes of De Moeren, 3 miles away. Home was now the nineteenth-century Kasteel Sinte Flora in the district of Veurne, but even here there was danger. Bombs fell in the garden and often a shell burst in the yard.

As the fighting continued, the royal family remained in De Moeren until 1 August. Elisabeth continued to visit the hospital and the trenches every day, driving along roads littered with shell holes. 'How is it possible she is allowed to come here?' a war journalist shouted when he saw the queen near the front line. The queen gave a reassuring smile.[41]

On 28 September the Belgians captured Houlthurst Forest, a long sought-after objective. Casualties were great and every hand was needed.

Queen Elisabeth helped in the advanced surgical stations, working under repeated shelling. At one point King Albert, who was with the army, found her in one of the American Red Cross tents. Neither asked the other to leave the danger zone. Had they done so, they knew the request would have been refused.

Elisabeth visited places very close to the front line to see where she could establish a field hospital. On the way back to De Panne, she recalled, there were 'many trucks on the road, much mud, cars in the canals, everywhere still numerous Germans and Belgians appear.' French cannon blocked the road and one had to be pulled from the canal. Eventually, after a detour, she reached De Panne at midnight.[42] After three days of fighting, the battle of the Crest of Flanders was won and the Belgian Army began to advance. At long last the end was near.

The king and queen made their official entry into Bruges on 25 October. The royal family moved into the vast, red-brick, mock-Gothic Château de Lophen 4 miles south of the town where they remained for the next month. King Albert was now commanding a combined force of Belgian, British, French and American troops fighting their way towards Brussels. Not until after the signing of the armistice on 11 November could Albert and Elisabeth make plans for a formal return to their capital.

On 22 November 1918, Queen Elisabeth, wearing a 'faded grey riding habit', proudly rode on a charger behind King Albert through the gaily decorated streets of Brussels.[43] Behind them rode their children, along with King George and Queen Mary's second son Albert (later King George VI) and Queen Mary's brother Alexander, now Earl of Athlone. It was a triumphant homecoming. People waved flags and banners, cheered themselves hoarse or wept from sheer joy. For Queen Elisabeth the moment was overwhelming.

★★★

By July 1917, the Russians were retreating without fighting and there were fears that Romania could be invaded within days. Queen Marie sent a railway carriage to bring her daughters back to Jassy, Sister Pucci and her nuns prepared to leave for Odessa, Jean Chrissoveloni made plans to evacuate the hospital and Marie continued to pack. For her the worst possible scenario would be to leave for Odessa. Many of her friends were already there but Marie obtained Ferdinand's promise that she would remain with him on Romanian soil until the last possible moment.

Doctors from the American Red Cross arrived with many welcome supplies and provisions which Marie insisted be distributed equally among the needy. Meanwhile she continued to visit the hospitals.

In August, Marie and Mignon travelled by train to Ghidigeni. Mignon had been extremely upset to leave her hospital when many wounded were arriving and every pair of hands was needed, but now she was so excited and keen to get back to work that she got up early in order to be on duty at the normal hour. When Marie arrived later Mignon was already working in the bandaging room:

> Mignon is one of the humble workers. She will do anything and has no wish to shine. She will just as readily wash the windows, sweep the floor, or serve up the meals, as hold a man's leg when it is to be cut off. Mignon has no pretensions.[44]

In fact Mignon was so enthusiastic that she was still working after dinner, so Marie returned to the train long before her daughter. The following day Marie found her working like a Trojan at anything she could turn her hand to. Mignon loved the work so much that the queen decided to leave her there, with Prince Carol guaranteeing her safety.

One of the largest Regina Maria Centres was at Cotofanesti, where there were 1,000 beds in the hospital but too few nurses. On a hill above this hospital a little wooden house was built for the queen so that she could stay there in order to visit surrounding hospitals. This was Jean Chrissoveloni's idea, as he realised the sacrifice Marie had made in giving up the idea of her own hospital.

In October 1917, Marie paid a secret visit to the trenches. She distributed cigarettes to the troops and sat down to smoke and chat with them while they cooked their supper in the dugout. Then came news that the Russian Provisional Government had fallen and Lenin's Bolsheviks had seized power. The increasingly unreliable help from Russia evaporated, along with any chance of a Romanian victory as Lenin, who needed peace at any price, signed an armistice with Germany. With the Germans occupying most of Romania, resistance seemed useless. Marie fought back her tears.

A telegram arrived from King George V saying that Marie and her children were welcome in England at any time. Captain Laycock from British Intelligence was at her disposal if she wanted to send her younger children to safety. Marie suddenly realised that the British knew Romania's position was hopeless.

At the end of January 1918, the Bolsheviks declared war on Romania and seized all their treasure, including Marie's jewels which had been sent to Moscow for safekeeping. A few days later, Ukraine declared independence and signed peace. By February, Romania was encircled by the enemy. There was now no choice but to make peace or face annihilation, but still Marie refused to give up, despite the unbearably harsh German peace conditions.

A preliminary peace was signed on 8 March. Two months later the Treaty of Bucharest was concluded and Romania's war was over.

The foreign missions now left. Nine-year-old Ileana had been acting as interpreter for Colonel Andersen, head of the American Red Cross, as he distributed supplies and organised relief work in the area. He gave the princess a small sum of money with which to help others in need. This simple act was the start of her interest in nursing.

A pro-German government was formed but Marie and her family remained at Jassy. She changed from nurse's uniform into Romanian national dress and withdrew into the country, turning her considerable energy to helping the peasants and returned prisoners of war.

Then, as the tide of war turned in favour of the Entente, the pro-German government fell and the Romanian Army mobilised. In November 1918, the kaiser abdicated and the Austro-Hungarian Empire fell. On 11 November the First World War came to an end. Under the peace terms Romania gained some coveted lands from the former Austro-Hungarian Empire.

On 1 December 1918, the streets of Bucharest were decked with flags and lined with cheering crowds as King Ferdinand and Queen Marie re-entered the city in triumph with their children. Never, thought Queen Marie, had she seen such a parade as this. As she took her place beside the king in the Metropolitan Cathedral, Marie gave thanks for being home at last.

For Queen Elisabeth of Belgium and Queen Marie of Romania normal life could begin again – but those years in the small unconquered corner of their kingdoms would make their names a legend.

Notes

1. Sidney Cunliffe-Owen, *Elisabeth, Queen of the Belgians* (Herbert Jenkins, 1954), pp.44, 54.
2. Theo Aronson, *The Coburgs of Belgium* (Cassell, 1969), p.169.
3. Aronson, *Crowns in Conflict*, p.112.
4. Professor Robert Van Hee, 'Antoine Depage's Relationship with Queen Elisabeth of Belgium', in *Acta Chirugica Belgica*, no. 112 (2013), pp.170–81.
5. Ralf de Jonge, *Koningin Elisabeth: Zwierige vorstin in woelige tijden* (Standaard Uitgeverij, Antwerp, 2007), p.112.
6. de Jonge, *Koningin Elisabeth*, p.112; Aronson, *Coburgs*, p.178.
7. John Jr Van Schaick, *The Little Corner Never Conquered* (Macmillan, 1923), p.63; Borden, *Forbidden Zone*, p.7.
8. Cunliffe-Owen, *Elisabeth*, p.84.
9. de Jonge, *Koningin Elisabeth*, p.112.
10. Van Schaick, *Little Corner* (Macmillan, 1923), p.43.
11. Marie of Roumania, *Story*, Vol. 3, p.59.
12. Marie of Roumania, *Story*, Volume 3, p.79.
13. Medicins de la Grande Guerre, www.1914-18.be/inf
14. 27 December 1916. The letter is quoted in Van Hee, 'Antoine'.

1. Princess Alice of Hesse with her sister Victoria ('Vicky'), Crown Princess of Prussia. The sisters' interest in anatomy horrified their mother, Queen Victoria. (Private collection)

2. Helena, Princess Christian of Schleswig-Holstein. Queen Victoria's third daughter was a staunch supporter of the State Registration of nurses. (Private collection)

3. Queen Olga of Greece, 1875.
Olga nursed both in Greece and in
her native Russia. (Eurohistory.com)

4. Queen Alexandra.
The Danish-born wife of
Edward VII reorganised the
British Army Nursing Services.
(Private collection)

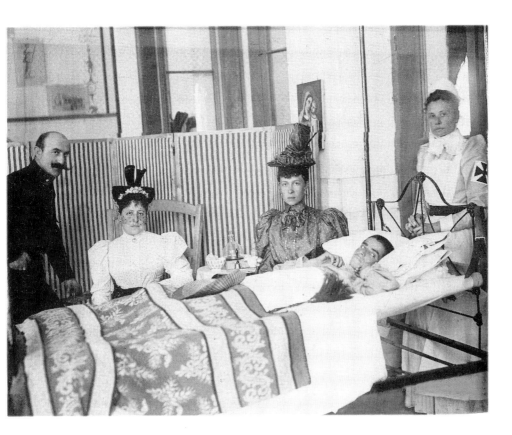

5. Crown Princess Sophie of Greece and Angeliki Kondostavlou at the Crown Princess's hospital during the Greco-Turkish War, 1897. (Eurohistory.com)

6. Queen Eleonore of Bulgaria, 1915. She worked both in the hospitals and at the front. (Mark Andersen)

7. Princess Alice of Greece with her husband Prince Andrew. The princess was a devoted nurse during the Balkan War. (Eurohistory.com)

8. Empress Alexandra Feodorovna of Russia and her sister the widowed Grand Duchess Elisabeth ('Ella'), 1908. The following year Ella founded a convent and hospital in Moscow where she nursed the poor. (Eurohistory.com)

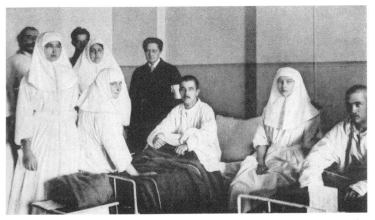

9. From left to right, Grand Duchess Olga Nicolaievna, Anna Vyrubova, Empress Alexandra Feodorovna (seated), Princess Gedroits (*behind, in man's clothes*) and Grand Duchess Tatiana Nicolaievna at the Tsarskoe Selo Infirmary. (Leeds Russian Archive MS 717.3.2.3.)

10. Grand Duchesses Olga and Tatiana playing chess with patients in the Tsarskoe Selo Infirmary. (Eurohistory.com)

11. Grand Duchess Maria Pavlovna ready for service at the Russian front. (Courtesy of Liki Rossii Publishing Co., St Petersburg)

12. Grand Duchess Olga Alexandrovna (*seated, middle*) with the Dowager Empress Marie Feodorovna and nurses from the hospital in Kiev, 1916. (Courtesy of Liki Rossii Publishing Co., St Petersburg)

13. Princess Arthur of Connaught, the royal family's only State Registered nurse. (Ian Shapiro)

14. Lady Louise Mountbatten with her fiancé Crown Prince Gustav Adolf of Sweden, 1923. Louise preferred practical hospital work to being a patron. (Mark Andersen)

15. The unconventional Queen Elisabeth of Belgium with General Joseph Joffre, Chief of the French General Staff, at De Panne, 1916. (Archives du Palais Royal, Brussels)

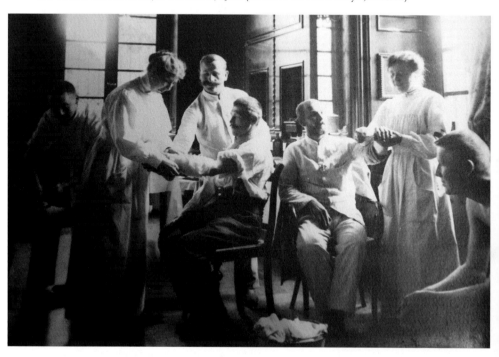

16. King Albert of Belgium's sister Princess Josephine of Hohenzollern-Sigmaringen (*left*) in the hospital of her castle at Namedy. (Collection of the Princes of Hohenzollern, Namedy)

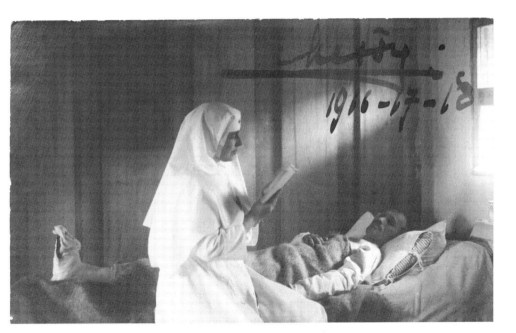

17. Queen Marie of Romania, who was such an inspiration to her beleaguered country during the First World War. (Private collection)

18. Grand Duchess George of Russia unveiling the memorial to soldiers who died in her Harrogate hospitals, 1920. (Ian Shapiro)

19. Grand Duchess George with Princess Margrethe of Denmark *(left)* and nurses from her hospital. (Private collection)

20. Princess Mary with Queen Mary. The queen was astonished at her daughter's transformation. (Private collection)

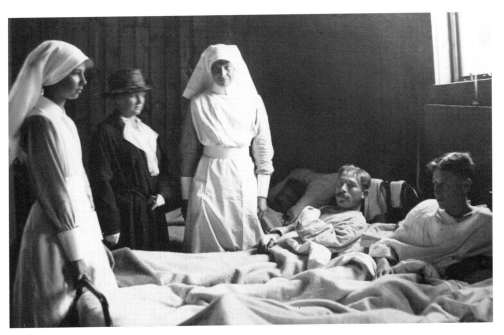

21. The young Princess Marie-José of Belgium *(left)* at the De Panne hospital during the First World War. As Crown Princess of Italy she later nursed in Ethiopia. (Archives du Palais Royal, Brussels)

22. Princess Tsahai of Ethiopia with colleagues from Great Ormond Street. (Museum & Archives Service, Great Ormond Street Hospital for Children NHS Foundation Trust)

23. Infanta Beatrice of Orleans. A granddaughter of Queen Victoria, Beatrice trained as a nurse in her youth. (Archivo Orleans-Borbón. Fundación Infantes Duques de Montpensier)

24. Queen Victoria Eugenie ('Ena') of Spain, who worked hard to reorganise her country's nursing services. (Mark Andersen)

25. Infanta Beatrice of Orleans at the Casa de Maternidad, Sanlúcar, Spain, in the 1960s with ladies of the North American army base at nearby Rota. (Archivo Orleans-Borbón. Fundación Infantes Duques de Montpensier)

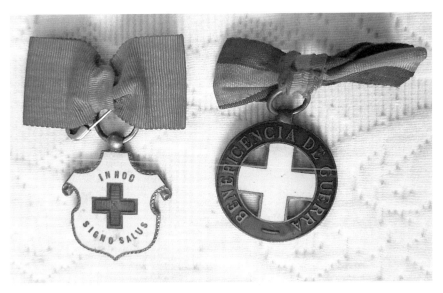

26. *Left:* The Red Cross medal awarded to Infanta Beatrice of Orleans. *Right:* the Cruz de Beneficencia de Guerra awarded for her work during the Spanish Civil War. (Archivo Orleans-Borbón. Fundación Infantes Duques de Montpensier)

27. Prince George and Princess Marina, Duke and Duchess of Kent, with their children Alexandra, Edward and baby Michael, 1942. The Duke was killed in action six weeks after his son's birth. (Eurohistory.com)

28. Princess Katherine of Greece, who helped blinded servicemen in South Africa during the Second World War. (Eurohistory.com)

29. Princess Eugenie of Greece (*right*) with her parents Prince George and Princess Marie and brother Peter. Eugenie took a great interest in the welfare of blinded servicemen. (Eurohistory. com)

30. Princess Ileana of Romania in 1946. She ran her own hospital in Romania until forced out by the Communists. (By kind permission of Archduke Dominic of Austria-Tuscany)

31. Matron Gwen Kirby greeting Princess Alexandra of Kent at Mothercraft House, Great Ormond Street, 1960. (Museum & Archives Service, Great Ormond Street Hospital for Children NHS Foundation Trust)

32. Princess Sofia of Greece working at the Mitera School, Athens, in the late 1950s. (Ricardo Mateos Sainz de Medrano)

33. Princess Margarita of Baden at St Thomas's Hospital in the 1950s. (By kind permission of the Grand Ducal House of Baden)

34. Princess Marie-Astrid of Luxembourg and the stamp issued to mark her presidency of the Youth Section of the Luxembourg Red Cross. (Copyright: Grand-Ducal Court/Tony Krier/All rights reserved)

15. Cunliffe-Owen, *Elisabeth*, pp.90, 85.
16. Information from Professor Dr Gustaaf Janssens, Director, The Royal Archives, Brussels.
17. Information from Olivier Defrance; Gerty Colin, *Les Châtelains de Laeken* (2 volumes. Éditions Luc Pire, Brussels, 2001), Vol. 1, p 172; Borden, *Forbidden Zone*, p.28.
18. Oliver Defrance & Christopher Vachaudez, *L'Album Royal: De Léopold 1er à Baudouin* (Racine, Belgium, 2011), p.102.
19. de Jonge, *Koningin Elisabeth*, pp.120–1.
20. Aronson, *Coburgs*, p.193.
21. Marie of Roumania, *Story*, Vol. 3, p.91.
22. Quoted in Pakula, *The Last Romantic*, p.214.
23. Marie of Roumania, *Story*, Vol. 3, p.92.
24. Florence Farmborough, *With the Armies of the Tsar* (Stein & Day, 1975), p.107.
25. Terence Elsberry, *Marie of Romania* (Cassell, 1973), p.134.
26. Letter to Grand Duchess Helen Vladimirovna, 21 December 1914. Quoted in Arturo Beéche (ed.), *The Other Grand Dukes*, p.13; Van der Kiste, *Victoria Melita*, p.110.
27. Pakula, *The Last Romantic* (Weidenfeld & Nicolson, 1985) p.219.
28. Theo Aronson, *Princess Alice, Countess of Athlone* (Cassell, 1981), p.113.
29. Borden, *Forbidden Zone*, pp.43–4.
30. Cunliffe-Owen, *Elisabeth*, p.91.
31. de Jonge, *Koningin Elisabeth*, p.122.
32. Aronson, *Princess Alice*, p.113.
33. Aronson, *Crowns*, p.155; Aronson, *Coburgs*, p.192.
34. de Jonge, *Koningin Elisabeth*, pp.114–15.
35. Marie of Roumania, *Story*, Vol. 3, p.130.
36. Oliver, *Dunant's Dream*, pp.249–50; Moorehead, *British Red Cross*, p.209.
37. Marie of Roumania, *Story*, Vol. 3, p.148.
38. Elsberry, *Marie of Romania*, p.139.
39. Marie of Roumania, *Story*, Vol. 3, p.169.
40. Marie of Roumania, *Story*, Vol. 3, p.188.
41. de Jonge, p.118. The Kasteel Sinte Flora was used in two episodes of the television drama *Parade's End*.
42. de Jonge, *Koningin Elisabeth*, p.134.
43. Aronson, *Crowns*, p.193.
44. Marie of Roumania, *Story*, Vol. 3, p.218.

8

'Dear Old Harrogate'

'Minny [is] very busy with her hospitals at Harrogate', Empress Alexandra told the tsar in April 1916.[1] 'Minny' was the family's name for Nicholas's cousin Princess Marie of Greece. Born on 3 March 1876, she was the younger daughter of King George and Queen Olga, who had done so much good work for the Greek hospitals.

During the war of 1897, Marie had been very involved with the Red Cross hospitals in Greece. As the foreign Red Cross units arrived to help, various private houses were offered for use as hospitals. One of these was allocated to the Danish Red Cross, which Marie looked after. Their matron Miss Reinhard later stayed on as matron of Queen Olga's private hospital. Marie's hospital had several Turkish soldiers among the patients and she seemed almost surprised to find that they were 'docile, patient and most grateful for all we could do for them'.[2]

By February 1898, the royal family's popularity was at a low ebb after the disastrous war and as Marie drove out with her father in a carriage, an attempt was made on their lives. This failed assassination did nothing to diminish Marie's love for her homeland. Marie would have preferred to spend her life in Greece but in 1900 she bowed to pressure and married Grand Duke George Michaelovich, a distant cousin of the tsar, taking the Russian name of Grand Duchess Marie Georgievna. For him it was a love match, for her a marriage of convenience. Two daughters were born to the couple, Princess Nina in 1901 and Princess Xenia two years later, but Marie's heart remained in her beloved Greece, to which she returned as often as possible. During the Balkan Wars she organised a fund and was able to send a quantity of useful items to the Greek Red Cross.

Before the First World War the grand duchess had paid several visits to England, where she was always known as 'Grand Duchess George of Russia'.

In 1914, she planned another holiday, ostensibly for three weeks, to improve the health of her younger daughter Princess Xenia. The place she chose was Harrogate, renowned for its mineral springs since the medicinal powers of the Tewit Well were discovered in 1571. However, it seems more likely that it was a trial separation from her husband – which, as things turned out, became permanent.

Grand Duchess George, her daughters and her lady-in-waiting Baroness Agnes de Stoeckl arrived in London on 17 July 1914. En route they heard news of the murders at Sarajevo but did not think the European situation would develop into war. By the end of July the grand duchess was in Harrogate. Both the Russian Ambassador and Grand Duke George warned her that the situation was dangerous and she should bring the children home as soon as possible, but she still thought there would be plenty of time. On 4 August, Great Britain declared war on Germany and the grand duchess and her daughters were trapped. 'Feel completely crushed and so anxious. A real hell of a position. May God have pity on His World', she wrote in her diary the following day.[3] With no choice but to remain in England, Grand Duchess George decided to stay in Harrogate and devote herself to the wounded.

She rented a house in York Place and began to look for an appropriate building in which to open a small hospital. She soon found a suitable nursing home at No. 1 Tewit Well Avenue, a large house overlooking the Stray (the public common where the site of the original Tewit Well is still marked by a dome), but without funds to convert it she had to rely on the generosity of local people. She and Agnes de Stoeckl put up posters in the shops and theatres of the town explaining what they were doing. Grand Duchess George, the posters said, would receive donations personally between two o'clock and six o'clock on the appointed day. The townspeople were invited to 'meet the Grand Duchess and *give*'.[4] This first effort at fundraising was not successful – nobody came.

Finally some kind benefactors came to the rescue and provided funds for a twelve-bed hospital. Under the chairmanship of the Mayor of Harrogate a committee was formed comprising Mr Bain, ex-Lord Mayor of Leeds; Mr Herbert Franklin, the surgeon; Dr Mouillot; Mr Stephenson, director of the bank; Mr Haserick; Mrs Boyd Carpenter, daughter-in-law of the Bishop of Ripon; Baroness de Stoeckl and Mrs C. W. Whitworth.

The Red Cross Society in Harrogate was organised by Dr Durward Brown, assisted by Nurse Adam who gave instruction in ambulance work. Lectures and courses on first aid were started in the town and Nurse Adam came to the grand duchess's house to give her and Agnes de Stoeckl practical nursing lessons. Later a doctor came from Leeds to put the ladies through the nursing examinations. They both passed and were presented with certificates as British Red Cross nurses.

The grand duchess went to London to advise the War Office that the small hospital was ready and at their disposal. She then called on her aunt Queen Alexandra at Marlborough House where, besides the queen's unmarried daughter Princess Victoria, Marie found her 18-year-old cousin Princess Margrethe of Denmark, who had been unexpectedly stranded by the war.

Margrethe was the only daughter of Queen Alexandra's youngest brother, Prince Valdemar. On 21 July 1914, she had travelled to France to stay with her maternal grandmother the Duchess de Chartres at Chantilly, near Paris.[5] When war broke out it was impossible for Margrethe to return to Denmark without crossing Germany, so the duchess sent her to England. Accompanying the princess was her lady-in-waiting Augusta Utke Ramsing, born into a Copenhagen military family in 1875.[6] Grand Duchess George was delighted to see her cousin, of whom she had always been fond, so when Princess Victoria suggested that Margrethe go to Harrogate the idea was taken up with pleasure.

On 4 September 1914, Princess Margrethe and Augusta Ramsing left London for Harrogate[7] where Nurse Adam gave them nursing instruction alongside Baroness de Stoeckl's daughter Zoia. 'A cousin of mine established a hospital in Harrogate, and I was trained as a nurse,' Margrethe recalled in an interview many years later. 'It [the training] went quickly but that was also necessary, because all the good nurses were of course sent to the front line.'[8] The *Harrogate Herald* reported that the Danish princess 'devoted a considerable time to nursing'.[9]

The Tewit Well Hospital was under the sanction of the War Office, with Lieutenant Colonel Baron as Officer in Charge. (He was later succeeded by Lieutenant Colonel Shann.) The Harrogate Women's Sewing League, founded by Dr Laura Veale, provided vast quantities of hospital supplies; they had a matron and an 'excellent professional nurse', plus Princess Margrethe, Augusta Ramsing and Zoia de Stoeckl as probationers.[10]

On 24 September the hospital received its first batch of wounded soldiers. The grand duchess had asked for twelve, so when fourteen arrived there was a terrific commotion to find more beds and fit them into the small hospital. The first patients were mainly convalescents sent over from the military hospital in Leeds. Zoia was soon at work washing the hospital's front steps. Nina and Xenia, too young to train as nurses, visited the wounded and brought flowers to cheer them up, and every Sunday Nina also helped Mrs Boyd Carpenter look after the bills.

The success of Tewit Well encouraged the grand duchess to look for a larger building to expand the hospital. She settled on Heatherdene in Wetherby Road, 'a charming place in a garden with big and airy wards',[11] which served as a convalescent home for the Sunderland Royal Infirmary.

On 8 August 1914, Dr Durward Brown (one of the honorary medical officers at the home) had written to Alderman Richardson and the committee of Sunderland Royal Infirmary asking that Heatherdene be placed at the disposal of the Red Cross for the admission of any wounded brought to the district. The reply was disappointing. The home was needed for the infirmary's patients in order to make way for the wounded at Sunderland Royal Infirmary. Grand Duchess George now asked the committee if they would give her this home for war work, and they agreed to do so for a few months. By December 1914, with King George V's help, she had secured it for the duration of the war.

Heatherdene Convalescent Home held fifty-two beds and was under the care of the matron, Christina Macrae. A large room on the ground floor was equipped by the grand duchess as an operating theatre.

At the end of December, fifty wounded soldiers arrived on hospital trains from the front. During meals Grand Duchess George and Baroness de Stoeckl often came to the dining room to talk to the men, who were uncertain as to how they should address a Russian grand duchess. Finally, one of them suggested they should call her 'Sir', as that was how they addressed their commanding officers.[12] It was not all laughter though. Occasionally there were deaths. The *Claro Times* reported on 27 March 1915:

> Among the wounded, who arrived on the train ambulance on Monday, was Jonathan Owen of the 1st Grenadier Guards, who was suffering from severe shrapnel wounds in the leg. Gangrene set in after his arrival in Harrogate, and he died at the Grand Duchess George's Hospital, Tewit Well Road, on Thursday. Yesterday the body was conveyed from Harrogate to the deceased's home in South Wales. The procession from the hospital to the station was headed by the band of the Yorkshire Hussars playing the Dead March from *Saul*. The Grand Duchess with Baron and Baroness Stoeckl were among the following, the Baron wearing the uniform of a Russian officer. The Mayor of Harrogate, wearing his chain of office, was also present. Wreaths were sent by the Grand Duke and Duchess George, the Princesses Nina and Xenia, Baron and Baroness Stoeckl, the wounded soldiers at Tewit Well and Heatherdene Hospitals, and the nursing staff at Tewit Well Hospital.

The fifty-two beds were soon filled, so the grand duchess decided to give up the original twelve-bed Tewit Well hospital and take a bigger house. Luckily, she found one almost next to Heatherdene called Wood Garth, which she renamed St Nicholas after the tsar's patron saint. St Nicholas had a further twenty-five beds and an operating theatre equipped for major surgery. Christina Macrae recommended her friend Miss J. Croll, another Scottish lady and 'a very charming and capable organiser,' as matron.[13] Aided by Sister A. Hawkesford and Staff Nurse J. Whinn, the hospital was run very much in accordance with Grand Duchess George's wishes.

The house at York Place also proved too small, so the grand duchess rented Park Place, a larger house with a park around it. Princess Victoria became a frequent visitor and every evening the ladies brought out their evening gowns to dress for dinner. Princess Margrethe usually left the hospital early so that she would have time to change but the over-enthusiastic Zoia always stayed until the last moment. One evening Zoia rushed in to dinner still in uniform, giving off a strong smell of carbolic. 'Once and for all,' said her angry mother, 'you are to come back in time to wash, and change that evil smelling dress, and look decent. Margarethe does, so why can't you behave like a lady?' Zoia, backed by Princess Victoria, insisted that duty came before everything; the grand duchess and the baroness insisted Zoia must change first. The argument ended with Princess Victoria pouring a glass of water over Grand Duchess George, saying, 'that will cool her down.' A few days later Baroness de Stoeckl justified her outburst when lice were discovered in her hair. 'A few hours later,' she recalled, 'the house was full of doctors, surgeons, specialists and hairdressers, all working on my scalp.' At an official concert that evening Princess Victoria and Grand Duchess George sat behind the baroness, anxiously watching in case something crawled down her neck.[14] According to local lore, while working in the often cramped wards the grand duchess also contracted lice from the soldiers, which she is said to have treated lightly.[15]

Donations to the hospitals were pouring in, especially from Russia. Grand Duke George sent a considerable amount and money also arrived from the Russian Red Cross, which was under the patronage of the grand duchess's aunt the dowager empress. The grand duchess put a small, white enamelled board above each bed with the names of Tsar Nicholas II, Empress Alexandra, Grand Duke George, Princess Nina and Princess Xenia, who had all endowed beds. King George V, Queen Mary, Queen Alexandra, Princess Victoria and the Prince of Wales endowed a bed for one year and their names were also put up. Several people in Harrogate, like Mr Haserick who endowed five beds in each hospital, also had their names displayed.

Grand Duchess George acquired another house in Duchy Road, Harrogate in 1915. It opened on 18 September as St George's Hospital, named after King George V. This provided another twenty-eight beds for a convalescent hospital, while her other hospitals took cases when they first arrived from the front. During that year Grand Duchess George was awarded the Royal Red Cross by the king.

St George's later moved, under the same name, to a larger house on Dragon Parade with Miss Arnold as matron. Now over 100 beds were available.

'We were the only private hospital which received convoys straight from the front. In the end we had 114 beds, 33 nurses, two theatres, and money flowing in,' recalled Baroness de Stoeckl proudly.[16]

The new St George's Convalescent Home for Wounded Soldiers was officially opened in 1916. 'Saturday being the Grand Duchess's birthday, she entertained 100 wounded soldiers to a tea and concert at the Kursaal in celebration of the occasion,' reported *The Times* on 6 March. Grand Duke George had endowed two beds, and others were once again endowed by members of the British royal family and the Russian imperial family.

By 1916, Nina was 15 and Xenia 13. The grand duchess decided to lease a house at 50 Grosvenor Square, London, so that she could see to their further education. She continued to make frequent trips to her hospitals in Harrogate accompanied by her Danish cousin. Princess Margrethe was happy in England. *The Times* reported on 4 February 1915 that she was 'among the visitors at present staying at Harrogate.' Her daughter Queen Anne of Romania recalled:

> One morning, she was washing the steps at the entrance to the hospital. Someone, a gentleman, came up and said: 'I'm sorry to bother you, but I would like to speak to Princess Margaret [sic] of Denmark.' 'Please wait a moment', Mummy replied. She went upstairs, took off the apron she was wearing, put on her dress, washed her hands, and went back to the door. 'So, have you found her?' asked the gentleman. 'I am her!' she replied.[17]

Margrethe remained in England until 1916. 'Father constantly wrote and begged me to come home,' she said, 'but I refused until H.N. Andersen [founder of the East Asiatic Shipping Company and a friend of Prince Valdemar] one day stood in my living room with instructions to bring me home.'[18]

Over 1,200 casualties passed through Grand Duchess George's hospitals, of which 127 were local men. She was always anxious to find room for Harrogate boys so that they could be near their friends at home. Many local ladies were on the nursing staff and the 'bright blue hospital suits' of the convalescents were soon a familiar sight in the town. The grand duchess worked hard, 'cheering the men, meeting the trains, and serving out coffee and cigarettes – sometimes at two o'clock in the morning. She was endlessly keen and eager about the work and the men were … proud to call her their friend.'[19]

The ambulance arrangements were organised by Mr and Mrs Titley. The unit was sponsored by the Harrogate Automobile Club and many well-known local men acted as stretcher bearers. 'When the convoys arrived at the station … the ambulances were drawn up, stretcher bearers ready' and Grand Duchess George,

Baron and Baroness de Stoeckl, and the Baroness's brother Otho (governor of the hospitals) were waiting. Agnes de Stoeckl recalled:

> the tense feeling as the train slowly came into the station and those terrible pale faces looking out of the windows, others lying on their stretchers straining their necks to see the station, knowing they were coming home to a place which would relieve their sufferings; some too ill even to care where they were.[20]

The well-equipped hospitals, which dealt with both medical and surgical cases, received many royal visitors including Queen Alexandra, who came for two days in July 1916, and ex-King Manoel of Portugal in September 1918. In 1917, Christina Macrae and three other nurses from Grand Duchess George's hospitals were given awards for nursing services. In recognition of this, during a visit to Harrogate Queen Alexandra presented Miss Macrae with a Red Cross brooch made by Carl Fabergé, court jeweller to the tsar.[21]

One day Princess Victoria was present when the wounded arrived. 'She and I went from ward to ward,' recalled Grand Duchess George, 'and passing the dining room where the "sitting cases" were eating, we heard the wife of our surgeon, Mrs Franklin, telling the men who we were, whereupon one of them exclaimed: "My word, we are among the nuts!"'[22] The grand duchess 'made the care of wounded British Tommies her war work, and … made many friends and admirers during her stay,' reported the *Harrogate Herald*.[23] Grand Duchess George was very popular with the men. 'She used to spend most of her time sitting and smoking with them, and cheering them with her wit.'[24] In her honour Alleyn Leslie composed the 'Reminiscences of Harrogate Valse'. The four-page music sheet was dedicated to Grand Duchess George whose photograph, along with Princess Margrethe of Denmark, appeared on the front cover. Proceeds from the sale of the sheet music were donated to the wounded. In 1917, W.H. Breare reported in the *Harrogate Herald* that the 'Petrograd March', dedicated to the Grand Duchess George, was very popular at the front.[25]

Air raids were a constant hazard. One evening the alarm sounded in the middle of a fancy dress dinner at Park Place for the grand duchess's birthday. The company all rushed around frantically trying to divest themselves of their outlandish costumes, imagining that the Germans would arrive any minute.

Hospitals need money and many fundraising events were held in aid of Heatherdene Hospital, St George's Convalescent Home and St Nicholas's Hospital. Ladies dressed up in Russian costumes and sold flags and much publicity was given to these events in the local paper. W.H. Breare wrote in his regular column in the *Harrogate Herald*:

I am particularly anxious that there should be a fine response to this appeal, because these institutions, which include the famous Convalescent Home of St George, have done most marvellous work all on their own. You will remember perhaps that there are Heatherdene and St Nicholas Hospitals as well as St George's. These comprise the well-known trio. You have only to ask a wounded lad who is an inmate of either if he is comfortable, and his face lights with an expression not to be forgotten – joy and gratitude eloquently blended. The Grand Duchess has not alone occupied herself with her hospitals; she has entered into every town movement calculated to help war funds, and by her presence influenced large attendances, enthusiasm and success. Harrogate owes much to this graceful, warm-hearted, generous lady. And it would be nice to express our feelings by a bumper collection.[26]

Sports days were organised at Park Place for those able-bodied enough to take part. Events included blindfold squad drill, sack races and a bun and ginger beer race. The grand duchess and her daughters presented the prizes, and on one occasion the grand duchess was joined by Princess Victoria who did the honours. The *Harrogate Herald* reported:

On Thursday and Friday evenings two excellent concerts, arranged by Private Percy Cash, were given at Heatherdene ... by the wounded soldiers, assisted by one or two friends. The Grand Duchess and party were present at the second concert, and at her request the autograph of each of the artistes [sic] was appended to a programme specially arranged by Private F.H. Barstow. The concerts were a great success, and a feature of the programme was the performance of a highly entertaining and finely written farce ...[27]

At Christmas the Wounded Soldier's Entertainment Committee provided Christmas dinner and the grand duchess and her daughters distributed presents from the tree. Often she gave a Christmas tea in the Spa Rooms for the wounded. In return, on her birthday and at Christmas the appreciative men offered her 'charming presents, which touched me deeply: small silver jewel cases, silver frames containing their photographs, silver cigarette boxes, etc.'.[28]

With the outbreak of the Russian revolution the grand duchess's appanage payment (the allowance from Crown properties which provided the imperial family's incomes) was no longer paid and she had to give up the Grosvenor Square house in favour of a smaller property in Regent's Park. She also had to give up her car, travelling instead by bus. After the Bolshevik revolution that autumn all the imperial family's properties were nationalised.

With no more funds to carry on, Grand Duchess George resigned from her work with the hospitals, asking the committee to keep them going or give them to the town, as they had done such good work. The unanimous decision was made to keep them going until the end of the war, with expenses being met by the committee. They also begged Grand Duchess George to remain at the head. She was delighted to do so. Her last Christmas with the men was in 1918, when a big feast was given for all the wounded.

Meanwhile the news from Russia became worse and worse. On 3 April 1918, Grand Duke George was arrested and by July he was imprisoned in the SS Peter & Paul Fortress in Petrograd with three other grand dukes. The four grand dukes were shot on 28 January 1919. 'The Grand Duchess did not hear of her husband's death until it was reported in the papers on 4 February.'[29]

The hospitals closed on 27 March 1919. When the grand duchess took leave of the committee she was presented with an antique silver tray to commemorate all her hard work during her five years in Harrogate. On the back was an inscription: 'Presented to H.I.H. the Grand Duchess George of Russia, by the Committee of her three hospitals at Harrogate as a souvenir of good work in a good cause 1914–1919.'[30]

On 11 April 1919, Grand Duchess George wrote from London to the Committee of Sunderland Infirmary. 'Thanks to your unselfish generosity and to Miss MacRae's wonderful capacities, "Heatherdene" will always remain a happy memory to all those wounded men who were nursed in this hospital,' she said.[31] The *Harrogate Herald* paid tribute to the grand duchess:

> In reviewing all that has been done to ameliorate the suffering of our sick and wounded, we must pay grateful thanks to the Grand Duchess George for undertaking a great and noble work. Merely to enumerate the qualifications of H.I.H. would be an exaggeration to all but those who have closely followed her labours for doing good ... To appreciate the work correctly we must consider pre-war conditions, the demands of war, and the manifold difficulties brought by the war. In pre-war days the provision for institutional treatment of the sick and injured was quite inadequate for the ordinary needs of the civil population. Scarcely a civil hospital but had a long waiting list. The vital importance of preserving health and remedying physical defects had only just begun to be dimly recognised except by the few who had laboured strenuously. Her Imperial Highness realised that the time and necessity had come.[32]

Grand Duchess George never forgot her time at Harrogate. In 1920 she erected a memorial to men who had died in her hospitals. It still stands on the Stray. Below the cross is an inscription:

> In loving memory of the nine men who died of wounds in the hospitals of H.I.H. The Grand Duchess George of Russia in Harrogate during the Great

War 1914–1918: Jonathan Owen, Percy Meadwell, Ramsden Farrar, William Bailey, John E Robinson, Oliver Sewell, William H Thomas, William Fenton Arthur J Crook; and of those who after leaving the hospitals fell on the field of battle. *'I am the resurrection and the life, he that believeth in me though he were dead yet shall he live.'*

She corresponded for years with some of the ex-patients and kept many of their letters and photographs in a leather album, including this poem dedicated to her by a Canadian:

Grand Duchess George of Russia, you have played a noble part,
And I am sure that all your doing it's from your very heart,
The cause it is a worthy one, for our wounded boys we know,
Who are fighting fumes and gases against our German foe,
You've selected a fine mansion in a quiet little spot,
And the treatment that we receive will never be forgot,
And when we're back in Canada which is far across the sea,
I am sure there's many soldiers whose thought will be of Thee.[33]

Grand Duchess George took many souvenirs of Harrogate to the little flat in Rome where she lived with her second husband Admiral Pericles Ioannides, whom she married in 1922. 'In a small room in a charming but unpretentious flat in Rome, there is a kind of shrine dedicated to Harrogate,' wrote Miss Eva Barrett, who was invited to visit the grand duchess. 'The walls are entirely covered from top to bottom with the photographs of groups of soldiers, nurses, hospitals, all framed in very simple oak frames. This room belongs to … a Royal lady whose name will always be linked with Harrogate in the last war.'[34]

In 1940, as the Second World War raged, Miss Barrett received a card from the grand duchess: 'Dear old Harrogate! It all reminds me so much of the other horrible war. I hope all my wounded Tommies are too old to take part in this one. Alas, I am not in London. I wish I were.'[35] Grand Duchess George died in Greece on 14 December 1940, just before the Germans invaded the country.

Notes

1. Fuhrmann, *Complete Wartime Correspondence*, p.434.
2. Grand Duchess George of Russua, *A Romanov Diary* (Atlantic International Publications, 1988), p.57.
3. Grand Duchess George, *Romanov Diary*, p.159.
4. Baroness de Stoeckl, *Not all Vanity* (John Murray, 1950), p.149.
5. *Politiken*, 21 July 1914.

6. www.kvinfo.dk/side/597/bio/1589.
7. *The Times*, Saturday 5 September 1914; *Politiken*, 9 August 1959.
8. *Søndags-BT*, 24 December 1965.
9. 'Harrogate Shrine in Rome,' *Harrogate Herald*, 28 August 1940.
10. Grand Duchess George, *Romanov Diary*, p.160.
11. Ibid.
12. Ibid.
13. Marion Wynn, 'Another Royal Visitor to Harrogate: Grand Duchess George of Russia', *Royalty Digest*, Volume 11, no. 3. (2001), p.80.
14. Baroness de Stoeckl, *My Dear Marquis* (John Murray, 1952), pp.166–7.
15. Neesam, Malcolm, 'Bygone Harrogate', *Harrogate Advertiser*, 6 November 2006.
16. de Stoeckl, *Not All Vanity*, p.151.
17. Prince of Hohenzollern-Veringen Radu, *Anne of Romania: A War, An Exile, A Life* (Humanitas, Bucharest, second edition, 2006), p.23.
18. *Søndags-BT*, 24 December 1965.
19. 'Harrogate Shrine in Rome', *Harrogate Herald*, 28 August 1940.
20. de Stoeckl, *My Dear Marquis*, p.168.
21. The brooch is now on display in the Royal Pump Room Museum, to whom it was presented in 1976 by someone who had worked with Christina Macrae. With thanks to Nicola Dyke, the Royal Pump Room Museum, Harrogate, for this information.
22. Grand Duchess George, *Romanov Diary*, p.160.
23. 'Harrogate Shrine in Rome', *Harrogate Herald*, 28 August 1940.
24. de Stoeckl, *My Dear Marquis*, p.167.
25. *Harrogate Herald*, 5 September 1917.
26. *Harrogate Herald*, 15 August 1917.
27. *Harrogate Herald*, 2 January 1918.
28. Grand Duchess George, *Romanov Diary*, p.162.
29. Wynn, in Royalty Digest p.82.
30. Grand Duchess George, p.169.
31. Tyne and Wear Archives, Heatherdene Convalescent Home Minute Book. HO.HEA/1/1.
32. *The Harrogate Herald*, 14 May 1919.
33. Grand Duchess George, *Romanov Diary*, p.163.
34. 'Harrogate Shrine in Rome', *Harrogate Herald*, 28 August 1940.
35. 'Harrogate Shrine in Rome', *Harrogate Herald*, 28 August 1940.

9

'Is She a Real Princess?'

By 1917, King George V's advisors were anxious to advertise the wartime activities of the sovereigns as much as possible. Suddenly accounts of troop reviews, naval inspections, investitures and tours of munitions factories or hospitals began to appear in the press. What better way to stress the fact that the royal family identified with their struggling people than to allow the king's daughter Princess Mary to achieve her wish to become a nurse?

Mary had taken an interest in nursing since childhood and had often said that, given the choice, she would love to be a nurse. Her ambition may have been heightened between 1915 and 1917 when she attended gymnastics classes in London with Princesses Nina and Xenia of Russia, the daughters of Grand Duchess George, from whom she would doubtless have heard stories about their mother's hospitals in Harrogate. When Princess Mary reached her twenty-first birthday in 1918 her wish was finally granted.

Princess Mary was born at York Cottage, Sandringham, on 25 April 1897. Blonde, blue-eyed Mary was everyone's idea of an English rose. Madame Poincaré, wife of the French President, called her '*la belle rose anglaise*'.[1] She rode well, spoke excellent French and German (her German maid was sent quietly home as war broke out) and received a sound education from her tutors and governesses. Yet although Princess Mary was gentle and kind, she was also painfully shy.

When war broke out her elder brothers the Prince of Wales and Prince Albert (later King George VI) reported for active service – the former in France on the staff of Field Marshall Sir John French; the latter in the Royal Navy. Wanting to do her bit, in October 1914, 17-year-old Mary launched an appeal on behalf of Princess Mary's Sailors' and Soldiers' Fund to provide a Christmas gift for men serving overseas. The embossed brass boxes, with

Princess Mary's portrait on the lid, were packed with pipe tobacco and cigarettes, a pipe and a lighter. A card inside from Princess Mary and 'friends at home' wished the men 'A Happy Christmas and a Victorious New Year'.[2] This established the princess as a popular royal figure.

From 1916 she served meals at a munitions factory canteen and in the municipal kitchen in Hammersmith, as well as dutifully visiting hospitals with Queen Mary. Yet she still wanted to be a nurse. After consultation with Queen Mary, in 1917 a new Voluntary Aid Detachment (VAD) unit was formed at Buckingham Palace by Lady Ampthill, chairman of the Women's VAD Committee of the British Red Cross and Order of St John. The princess became commandant of this new detachment, Lady Grey was assistant commandant and about thirty of Princess Mary's friends were the members. They met at the palace on Mondays and Thursdays to go through a course of nursing and first-aid lectures under Sir James Cantlie, senior lecturer of the VAD training courses, who in 1911 had written the Red Cross first aid, nursing and training manuals. The princess passed her Red Cross first aid examinations with honours and later passed the advanced home nursing course, gaining high marks in both practical work and theory.

Every day Princess Mary walked across Green Park to the headquarters of the VAD at Devonshire House, Piccadilly, where she worked in each department in turn. Having gained a complete knowledge of how the organisation operated, she began work in the allocation section of the Naval and Military Department dealing with Movement Orders for nurses, motorists and General Service VADs posted abroad.

In April 1918, the princess celebrated her 21st birthday with a quiet lunch at Windsor Castle, attended by her grandmother Queen Alexandra and her aunt Princess Victoria. When the king asked what she would like as a birthday present, the princess unhesitatingly replied that she would like 'permission to work as a probationer at the Great Ormond Street Children's Hospital'.[3]

The Hospital for Sick Children at Great Ormond Street, Bloomsbury, was founded by Dr Charles West in 1852 as a special hospital whose medical and surgical staff would dedicate themselves exclusively to curing children. Queen Victoria, at the time a young mother with a growing family, was the hospital's first patron, and the current president was Mary's brother, the Prince of Wales.[4]

Queen Mary brushed aside objections that the princess could catch an infectious disease from the children, and in June Mary, wearing her red cotton VAD dress (which denoted her rank as commandant of a detachment), white apron with the Red Cross, and nursing cap, started work as a probationer on two days every week, usually Tuesdays and Fridays. To save petrol she drove to the hospital in a one-horse palace Brougham.

The matron, Miss Gertrude Payne, had been at the hospital since 1898. Together with the resident medical superintendent Dr George Robinson Pirie (a prominent children's doctor born in Canada), Miss Payne had carefully drawn up a special curriculum for an intensive course of training in the care of sick children for Princess Mary. When the Miss Payne asked the queen what special action should be taken to protect the princess during the frequent air raids, she was told that Mary was to be treated exactly the same as the other nurses.

During the war VADs usually devoted more time to actual treatment than more routine duties, for early in their career those old enough were sent to France to relieve the pressure on nurses in the busy base hospitals. Mary worked at first in Alexandra Ward, the medical ward named after her grandmother Queen Alexandra. It had originally been called Alice Ward, after Queen Victoria's daughter. Then, when Victoria's daughter-in-law Alexandra, the Princess of Wales, took a keen interest in the hospital it became Alice and Alexandra Ward, until finally the 'Alice' was dropped.[5]

Alexandra Ward was a long, well-lit room with twenty-six beds, polished floors and walls of glazed brick, with a large rocking horse standing at one end. In the days before the creation of the National Health Service wealthy benefactors endowed individual cots and beds. Cot No. 21, which stood in the large bay window, was given by Queen Alexandra in 1902 with money presented to her by the members of the London Stock Exchange at the Imperial Coronation Bazaar; at the opposite end was one endowed in May 1903 by Mr J.S. Wood, editor of *The Gentlewoman*, on behalf of Princess Mary herself. Above it hung a charming pastel of the princess as a child.

Miss Hughes, known as Sister Alexandra, was the sister-in-charge of Alexandra Ward. She later recalled that the day and time of the princess's arrival soon became known to the children and those who were well enough would go to the windows at 9.45 a.m. to see her carriage arrive at the entrance. When she entered the ward to start her duties at 10 a.m., little girls would stand at the door to greet her with a curtsy and she always shook hands with them all.[6] Mary was soon making beds, washing and feeding the babies and, when she had acquired enough knowledge, doing the rounds with the physician but, unlike most new probationers, she was not required to scrub and polish. The princess quickly became efficient at vapour and hot-air baths, nasal feeding, keeping charts and giving poultices. When a sister tried to prevent her from emptying a chamber pot Mary gave her a warning look and carried on.

The children, who were mostly from the poorer areas of London, loved this capable, smiling nurse, regarding her as a real 'fairy princess', and chatting to her 'without reservations or nervousness'. One curly headed boy called her 'Princess Mary Darling', while another always asked for 'her in the red dress' to tend to his needs,[7] but to the others she was 'nurse' or 'my princess'. Some of them asked, 'Is she a real princess?' One little boy, ill with pneumonia, insisted that the princess wash him herself and then asked her where 'the prince' was and if he was coming today.[8]

Princess Mary also undertook many official duties, including a visit to France to tour the Queen Mary's Army Auxiliary Corps and VAD camps. With time now more limited, her clerical work at Devonshire House gave way to hospital duties. The question of transferring to a surgical ward was put to Queen Mary, who raised no objections. So after a spell on the medical ward Princess Mary transferred to Helena Ward, named after Helena, Princess Christian. Here she helped with dressings, was taught to give injections and assisted at some operations. On the first occasion the operation was particularly unpleasant and difficult and after a while the princess became rather white. The theatre sister whispered that perhaps she would like to slip outside. 'Oh, no!' she replied, shaking her head, refusing the proffered chair and remained until the operation was finished. After a few weeks, Mary was cheerfully assisting at five consecutive operations, 'just clearing up'.[9]

As well as undertaking all the usual nursing duties she often helped serve dinners in the ward's kitchen. Queen Mary was astonished at her daughter's transformation. 'This morning I went to the Great Ormond St Hospital to see Mary working in her ward,' she wrote to King George on 10 August 1918:

> Both Dr and Matron are much pleased with her work which she does very nicely and thoroughly. She has nice light hands for the work and takes a great deal of trouble over the children's cases. She dressed a wound of one child; removed a needle with saline out of a baby's side, & made small incisions on another child's arm, a test to ascertain whether the child is tubercular or not – of course to me who knows little or nothing of such things it was a great surprise to find my daughter doing all this in the quietest most composed manner! I must say it was awfully interesting spending an hour in the ward, just with the ordinary work going on and absolutely no-one to fuss one. I gave one little boy his dinner, fed him with a spoon, which was rather amusing! I believe he thought I was the Sister doing her usual work.[10]

According to *The Times*, the queen fed this delicate little 2-year-old with 'carefully minced food, potatoes and cabbage', and after Princess Mary had finished her duty, 'the royal nurse, still in her VAD uniform, drove back with her mother to Buckingham Palace'.[11]

On Armistice Day in November the princess telephoned Devonshire House to ask the VAD staff to march to Buckingham Palace and form up in the courtyard. 'They marched, headed by Lady Ampthill, from Devonshire

House to the forecourt of the palace and formed up near the King's Guard'. At eleven o'clock King George and Queen Mary appeared on the balcony, the Armistice was proclaimed and the band struck up the National Anthem.

'It was an incredible honour to be with the Guard when the King came out,' recalled Lady (later Dame Beryl) Oliver.[12] On 20 November 1918, Mary travelled to France and Belgium with Lady Ampthill to see the work of the VADs and other women's organisations in the hospitals and visit the troops. In Ypres, still in her VAD commandant's uniform, she witnessed the march past of the Royal Scots (of which she had been appointed Colonel-in-Chief in August 1918) in the marketplace. At the end of her visit she was presented with a gold identity disc inscribed: 'Her Royal Highness Princess Mary, VAD.'

★★★

In January 1919, Lady Louise Mountbatten had a typhoid inoculation in preparation for her return to France. There was little need for nurses now, but Louise had learnt that she and Ida Wheatley could probably work at an Anglo-French canteen in Dunkirk which was due to open at the end of the month. She wanted, and needed, to work abroad and hoped that once in France other opportunities might present themselves. Unfortunately Louise developed a spot on her lung and was unable to travel as planned. By mid-February she was hoping to go to Rouen but did not recover in time.

The wish to return to France may have been connected with the end of her romance. At the end of 1918, Louise was forced to break off her engagement with Alexander Stuart-Hill after she was informed that 'Shakespeare' was homosexual. He was not, said her parents, a decent man. Louise was very unhappy but understood that such a marriage would never work.

Finally, in early March she set off from Southampton. Once again her father took care of the travel arrangements, instructing Louise to write to Mr Wilkinson of the French Red Cross asking him to send her passport and *Ordre de Mission*. Travelling alone, she stayed at the Red Cross hostel in Le Havre and then caught the train to Paris, where she was met by a Miss Hardie who organised the next stage of the journey.

Louise's destination was the Hôpital Militaire No. 1 at Palavas-les-Flots, a coastal resort about 5 miles south of Montpellier, where they treated tuberculosis of the bones. Louise and Miss Wheatley joined the staff of the Hospital for Infectious Diseases, a 150-bed institution established in the former Grand Hotel. Florence Carver had been matron since September 1918 and some of the nurses were Australian.

Louise and Ida's stay in Palavas-les-Flots was short. In June the hospital closed and that was the end of Louise's nursing career, which she later regarded as the happiest days of her life. 'For a long time afterwards grateful patients continued to write to her and the letters nearly always began "Chère Sisteur" – a wonderful mixture of English and French,' wrote her Swedish biographer.[13]

Louise was commended for her hard work. She was awarded the War Medal of Great Britain 1914–18; the British Red Cross Medal; the *Médaille de la Reconnaissance Française*; and the Italian Red Cross Medal. In April 1919 the *London Gazette* noted Lady Louise Mountbatten's award of the Royal Red Cross Medal by King George V for her work at the Princess Club Hospital, Bermondsey.[14]

At the age of almost 34, in 1923, Lady Louise married Crown Prince Gustav Adolf of Sweden, a widower with five children. Although from this time onwards Louise was unable to do any practical hospital work, she continued to work closely with nursing projects in Sweden. Realising that 'the regulations concerning nurses' lives were extremely severe and old-fashioned', she modernised the old rules, which prohibited bobbed hair and skirts shorter than ankle length and forbade them from wearing ordinary dress outside of working hours unless they were on leave. She also fought to raise their wages, which in Sweden 'were based on the theory that nursing was a vocation and not a profession'. Louise's own experience had taught her that it was essential that nurses have good working conditions and reasonable working hours if they were to do their best work, so she insisted that 'they have a say in any question which might affect them.'[15] She became president of the Sophia Hospital Board, supported Crown Princess Louise's Hospital for Children and the Eugenia Home for Disabled or Incurable Children. Louise found it frustrating to be a hospital patron. She preferred to get on with the work, something that was impossible for her to do as crown princess.

During the Second World War she 'played a leading role organising the Swedish Red Cross and Sweden's Women's Army Auxiliary Force', personally broadcasting appeals for money and clothing for the troops.[16] Her husband succeeded to the throne as King Gustav VI Adolf in 1950. Queen Louise became patron of many large hospitals and continued to work with the Red Cross until she died in 1965.

★★★

As the First World War ended the king's niece Princess Arthur of Connaught took a short training course at Queen Charlotte's Maternity Hospital in Marylebone Road, working in the general wards, the labour ward and the theatre. Under supervision she delivered six babies and was present during twenty other births, some of which were abnormal, and even learnt what she described as the tricky job of bathing slippery newborn babies. However, she preferred the bustle of ordinary hospital work, finding the waiting about in the maternity wards monotonous.

In 1919, her paper on eclampsia earned first prize on the course and she qualified as a state-registered nurse, becoming the first member of the royal family to register with the General Nursing Council. The princess's Christmas card that year – 'With best wishes from Alexandra (Princess Arthur)' – proudly showed a photograph of her in nurse's uniform.[17]

Princess Arthur then went to the Samaritan Free Hospital for Women, where she worked most of the time in the operating theatre and obtained a certificate for gynaecology. In November 1920, Prince Arthur was appointed Governor General of South Africa and the princess took a break from nursing to accompany him. She missed hospital work and found official duties hard to get accustomed to, although she enjoyed big-game hunting in Rhodesia and took some excellent photographs.

★★★

With the wholesale collapse of the mighty German, Austro-Hungarian and Russian monarchies as well as the stripping of power from the reigning princes, grand dukes and dukes of Germany, King George V was anxious to consolidate the position of the British Crown. It was therefore decided that for the time being Princess Mary would continue nursing.

Her work as a probationer at Great Ormond Street had made children's nursing more respectable, giving it a much needed boost, and she was said to be popular with the other nurses. Princess Mary grew attached to the children. So much so that when one infant, in whom she had taken a special interest, died during the night when she was not present, the sister told her that the child had gone home. Only later did Mary learn the truth.

Early in 1919, Liza Terry was admitted to Great Ormond Street 'suffering from a very acute form of blood-poisoning, which had affected the bone of the leg and spread right up the tibia. She was very ill indeed, and an immediate operation was necessary to save her life.'[18] The princess nursed 10-year-old Liza devotedly, often bringing in presents for the little girl and proving to be a skilful surgical nurse.

Princess Mary's favourite task was bathing the babies, 'sitting on a low chair by the fire, with a basin of water at her side, and a tiny baby lying on her knee', carefully washing and tending the child. Mothers coming to fetch their babies always asked eagerly, 'Did the princess bath my baby?' If the answer was yes they took the little one home with a feeling of immense pride.[19] For some time she had charge of a baby so small that it slept in a bassinet. She did everything herself for this tiny mite.

One morning, a woman came into the dimly lit entrance hall and was greeted by the hospital porter in his usual cheery manner. 'Well, mother, what is it?', he enquired. 'Ssh!' said the woman, with a conspiratorial smile on her face. It was Queen Alexandra, paying an informal visit to see her granddaughter at work. Shen was delighted at this unceremonious greeting and continued on her way upstairs to Alexandra Ward where she expected to find Mary. However, she discovered that the princess was in the operating theatre assisting the surgeon. 'After a few minutes Princess Mary discarded her mask and operating-gown, and came downstairs; but she soon had to say good-bye, and go back to her duty, while the Queen continued her tour of the wards.'[20]

Another time some members of the royal family appeared when the princess was about to give an injection. '"Are you sure she can do it?" the sister was anxiously asked. "Can she do it without hurting? I've just been having injections, and I know!" But the sister assured the royal speaker that Princess Mary was fully accustomed to her job.'[21]

The princess was generous in providing gifts to staff and patients. The nurses received chocolates, while signed photographs were given to the doctors, sisters and the medical registrar. At Easter every child received a chocolate egg or chicken, and at Christmas there were toys for the children in Alexandra and Helena wards. 'She spent the whole afternoon there, and had tea with the nurses, after her usual distribution of presents and the Christmas tree.' The children treasured these gifts, which were often held out for visitors to see with the proud remark, 'My Princess Mary gave me this!'[22]

One little girl received a storybook from the princess and wanted to ask her to autograph it. She confided in the sister, who suggested she ask Princess Mary the next time she came round. Unfortunately the little girl was too shy and could only blurt out 'what's your name?' when the princess appeared. Rather surprised, the princess answered, 'My name's Mary; what's yours?' but the little girl never managed to ask her to sign the book.[23] One day the sister indicated a little dark-eyed Italian boy, who lay sad and silent. Nobody could speak to him in Italian. 'You can talk Italian, Princess,' urged the lady-in-waiting, but Princess Mary was too shy. The next day she sent him a book of Italian fairytales, with a dedication in his own language – 'for the little Italian boy'.[24]

When Dr Pirie returned to Canada in 1919, the princess commissioned a watercolour of herself in uniform as a parting gift, which he hung it proudly in his Toronto home. When Miss Payne left in February 1920 after twenty-five years at Great Ormond Street, Princess Mary gave her a gold and enamel trinket box. To Princess Mary's great regret, in April 1920 her time at the hospital came to an end too. One of her last acts was to take a bunch of violets to a little child dying of a heart disease who loved the smell of flowers. The princess often said that she had found her vocation in nursing.

When her engagement to Viscount Lascelles was announced at the end of 1921 some 50,000 VADs throughout the Empire subscribed to give her a present. The VAD tiara was described by *The Times* as 'a beautiful tiara in which a large central emerald is surrounded by diamonds, the whole surmounted by a second emerald of a beautiful colour'. The two small side sections were detachable so that part of it could be worn as a brooch.[25] 'I am especially pleased at receiving this gift from the hands of the Matron of Great Ormond Street Hospital for Children, in which I was privileged to share in the work of the nurses, and in which I learned to appreciate the wonderful service that they render to the community,' the princess told a deputation headed by the matron Miss Tisdale.[26] Trained nurses and nurses in training presented a gold-mounted tortoiseshell writing set. When *The Times* published a wedding supplement on 28 February 1922 there was an appeal on the front cover for Great Ormond Street Hospital, which was in debt to the tune of £30,000.

Princess Mary's interest in the hospital never waned and she continued to send presents to the wards. She became vice patron of Great Ormond Street Hospital in 1923 and president in 1936. Her portrait in VAD uniform still hangs in the hospital boardroom, bearing the inscription: 'Presented by H.R.H. The Princess Mary, who was trained as a nurse in the Hospital, 1918–1920.' On Alexandra Rose Day 1921 the princess came all the way to Great Ormond Street to purchase her rose.

In 1928 on a visit to Cardiff, Princess Mary met Sister Alexandra, now the wife of Dr Dan Thomas JP of Bargoed. The *Merthyr Express* reported that 'the Princess showed much pleasure in meeting her old friend and the greeting was an affectionate one'.[27]

★★★

Prince and Princess Arthur of Connaught returned to London in January 1924. Princess Christian had died the previous year and Princess Arthur was invited to succeed her as president of the Royal British Nurses' Association. She accepted with pleasure and the following month paid her first visit to their headquarters at Queen's Gate, London.

She also resumed her nursing career. Using her previous pseudonym of Nurse Marjorie, Princess Arthur worked as an 'extra nurse' in the Casualty and Outpatients Department at University College Hospital where the matron was her old friend Ruth Darbyshire. When necessary, the princess helped in other departments, taking cases to the theatre, assisting at operations and performing some minor surgery. She took charge in casualty and the fracture clinic and helped in the X-ray department and the wards. Later she was put in charge of casualty in the mornings, enjoying being on her own when the staff nurse had time off. She also enjoyed teaching medical students. Princess Arthur became interested in psychology and for several years attended outpatients' clinics for adults and children suffering from mental illness. She had a genuine interest in people and a real desire to help. In 1925, she was awarded the Royal Red Cross.

After some years Princess Arthur transferred to Charing Cross Hospital, working in casualty and the theatre. It was a densely populated area but the casualty department was small, although well equipped. She felt there was 'a distinctly chilly atmosphere in the department'[28] and never really settled in, so she moved to casualty at St Thomas's near Waterloo Station. 'Here, too, I was the only nurse from outside, and as nobody knew anything about me it did not make things too easy, and I never got accustomed to working there,'[29] she recalled.

She found a welcome change in outpatients', working in the dental and psychological departments. In the latter she was on duty in the afternoons and in charge when the other nurse was off. There were three doctors. Princess Arthur sat at a desk, collected the notes, waited for the doctor to ring and ushered the patients to the correct room. One day, having put all the notes in order, she was called away. When she returned the next man was missing. 'That's all right, nurse,' said one of the others, 'he's gone in and taken his notes with him!' She was left hoping that this particular psychological patient had not read his notes first.[30]

Princess Arthur was forced to leave St Thomas's after three months when she was rushed into hospital for a major emergency operation. Recovery kept her away from nursing for some time, although she never regained her former health. Once recovered, the princess decided to go back to University College Hospital where she had formerly been so happy.

Then, on 12 September 1938, Prince Arthur of Connaught died of throat cancer. He had been ill for some time but his death was a terrible blow. Ten days later the princess's only son Alastair left for Palestine with the Royal Scots Greys. It was four years before she saw him again. Left alone, she sold the house in Belgrave Square and moved to a smaller property in St John's Wood.

When Princess Arthur returned to work at University College Hospital she discovered that the personnel had altered. She now felt a change was inevitable. 'All I knew was that I wanted a complete change, a job where I had responsibility, a job of my own, in fact; but I could not see it materialising. It must be hospital work, but what?'[31]

In June 1939, she bought a small nursing home at 23 Bentinck Street. All that summer in between her hospital duties she trudged round the shops armed with a long list of requirements. She planned to establish and re-equip it as The Fife Nursing Home. A new chapter in Princess Arthur's life was about to begin.

Notes

1. Mabel C. Carey, *Princess Mary* (Nisbet & Co., 1922), p.14.
2. Helen Cathcart, *Anne, The Princess Royal*, (W.H. Allen, 1988), p.120; Jeremy Archer, *A Royal Christmas* (Elliot & Thompson, 2012), p.155.
3. Cathcart, *Anne*, p.121.
4. Carey, *Princess Mary*, p.99. In 1929 the writer J.M. Barrie donated all the rights to *Peter Pan* to the hospital.
5. Information from Nicholas Baldwin, archivist at Great Ormond Street Hospital (GOSH).
6. GOSH/14/243.*Merthyr Express*, 21 January 1922.
7. GOSH/14/243.*Merthyr Express* 21 January 1922.
8. Carey, *Princess Mary*, p.113.
9. Carey, *Princess Mary*, p.104; Cathcart, *Anne*, p.122.
10. RA QM/PRIV/CC08/219, 10 August 1918.
11. *The Times*, 12 August 1918.
12. Oliver, *British Red Cross*, p.244; Cathcart, *Anne*, p.122 .
13. Fjellman, *Louise Mountbatten*, p.92.
14. With thanks to Sue Light for this information.
15. Fjellman, *Louise Mountbatten*, p.116–17.
16. Miller, 'A True Queen of Hearts.'
17. Ian Shapiro collection.
18. Carey, *Princess Mary*, p.105.
19. Carey, *Princess Mary*, pp.107, 109
20. Carey, *Princess Mary*, p.110.
21. Carey, *Princess Mary*, p.111.
22. *The Times*, 12 & 27 December 1918 & 20 December 1920; Carey, *Princess Mary*, pp.114, 117.
23. Carey, *Princess Mary*, p.114.
24. Carey, *Princess Mary*, p.117.
25. *The Times*, 11 February 1922. The tiara was sold at auction in 1966 after the princess's death. My thanks to Harold Brown for this information.
26. *The British Journal of Nursing*, 25 February 1922.
27. 7 July 1928. GOSH/14/43.
28. Alexandra, *A Nurse's Story*, p.86.
29. Alexandra, *A Nurse's Story*, p.87.
30. Alexandra, *A Nurse's Story*, pp.88–9.
31. Alexandra, *A Nurse's Story*, p.92.

10

From Italy to Ethiopia

The end of the First World War was not the end of Elisabeth of Belgium's concern for the sick and needy. The Queen Elisabeth Medal was given for valuable service to the military and civilian population in hospitals during the war and showed the queen's head on one side and a seated nurse holding an oil lamp on the reverse. Elisabeth founded the National Defence League Against Tuberculosis, a league for the prevention of venereal disease and, in 1925, the Fondation Médicale Reine Elisabeth, a vast institution for medical research. She also concerned herself with cancer research and work for the indigenous peoples of the Belgian Congo; many homes, crèches, orphanages, preventative institutions, laboratories and research centres were inaugurated through her efforts. Eventually these leagues and foundations were known under the collective name of the 'Front Blanc de la Santé'. In 1922, Pope Benedict XV awarded her the prestigious Golden Rose.

She also inspired a love of nursing in her daughter Marie-José. Born on 4 August 1906, Marie-José was 8 when Belgium was invaded by the Germans. During holidays from school in England she visited the wounded at the Hôpital de l'Océan, where Elisabeth allowed her to wear an overall and veil like a 'real' nurse. 'At the time of the great offensive in 1918,' Marie-José recalled, 'I was proud to be able to make myself useful preparing bandages for the operating room.' Her daughter Marie-Gabrielle later explained: 'In the beginning she was afraid, all that blood startled her. But she had to come. My mother was still a child, but gradually got used to coming with them. It was her [Elisabeth's] way to discipline her daughter.'[1]

Marie-José greatly admired her father, who shared the privations of the Belgian troops, and her mother, who nursed the wounded. For the young princess it was a valuable lesson in sincerity and devotion to duty.

In 1930 she married Umberto of Savoy, Prince of Piedmont, the son of King Victor Emmanuel III and Queen Elena of Italy. The marriage had been planned for some years and, in preparation, Marie-José had studied Italian in Florence.

The queen of Italy was another great influence on the young Belgian princess. Elena, born a princess of Montenegro, was a trained nurse who had studied medicine and gained a *laurea honoris causa*. She was the founder of Italy's first nursing school and in her efforts to fight disease promoted the training of doctors and supported research into poliomyelitis, Parkinson's disease and cancer. In December 1908, when a massive earthquake struck the town of Messina, the queen had rushed to the scene, immediately sensing that the distressed people gained comfort from the mere fact of her presence. She nursed the injured on board the ship *Vittorio Emanuele* and also worked devotedly in the field hospital. 'I am the Queen of Italy and I tell you that you need have no fear,' she told the casualties.[2]

During the First World War, Elena turned the Quirinal Palace into a hospital and worked there as a nurse. With help from the British Red Cross, who sent a donation of £10,000, she established a hospital for artificial limbs along the lines of Queen Mary's Hospital in Roehampton. There was a great deal of difficulty in securing the release of the necessary materials but in the spring of 1917 an expert artificial limb maker was sent to Italy, along with the equipment. A factory was established and the man remained for six months, until the scheme was up and running and disabled soldiers themselves had been trained in the manufacturing process.[3]

By the time Marie-José arrived in Italy, Victor Emmanuel III clung to only an illusion of power. This was the fascist era, with Benito Mussolini as prime minister and, effectively, dictator. Other political parties were banned, civil liberties abolished and the anti-fascist press was censored. In this atmosphere Umberto and Marie-José settled into the Royal Palace of Turin. The court was increasingly infiltrated by fascists, and while Marie-José was unable to voice her disapproval publicly, she increasingly asserted her independence. The princess's lively intelligence, interest in politics and concern for social issues made her ahead of her time in conservative Italy and was not appreciated by the regime.

Marie-José had joined the International Red Cross in 1927, and now she decided to follow the courses to become a Red Cross nurse. Banned by Umberto from visiting the hospice, she went quietly on foot to visit the poorest people in the town. She became president of the Opera Nazionale Maternità e Infanzia (OMNI), founded in 1925 to assist mothers and children under 3 years old. She also befriended Count Umberto Zanotti Bianco who created asylums, kindergartens and schools for poor children under the name

of the National Association for the Interests of the South of Italy. In 1939, to
save the association from suppression by the Fascist party, Marie-José took
it under her wing as the Opera Principessa di Piemonte. She never ignored
appeals for help.

At the end of 1931, Umberto was promoted to general and the couple
moved to Naples, where Marie-José worked as a voluntary nurse in the
Hospital for Incurables. The place was dilapidated and lacked equipment;
the patients' families often came in to help look after them and many things
went missing from the wards. Nevertheless Marie-José happily made the beds,
prepared injections and changed dressings. She was encouraged by Princess
Hélène, the Dowager Duchess of Aosta, daughter of the Count of Paris. In
1890, Hélène had hoped to marry Prince Albert Victor, Duke of Clarence,
eldest son of the future Edward VII, but the plan foundered because her
father forbade her to renounce Catholicism. Five years later Hélène married
Emmanuel Filiberto, 2nd Duke of Aosta, cousin of King Victor Emmanuel.

During the Libyan War of 1911–12, when Italy won a vast swathe of North
Africa from the decaying Ottoman Empire, the duchess created the Army
and Navy Nursing Service, remaining at its head and serving as Inspector
General of Red Cross Nurses from 1911 to 1921. Despite her delicate health
(she suffered from tuberculosis) the duchess was tireless in her work for the
wounded, often putting the other nurses to shame and making them feel they
were not doing enough. She earned a reputation for severity, especially when
vital Red Cross supplies failed to arrive and her demands were not met. It
was, as she pointed out, a matter of life and death; however, the war took its
toll on Hélène's health. 'The war has killed my spirit,' she wrote in her diary.
'I am but a shadow, four years of war has destroyed everything vital in me.
Forced to see people suffer and die, a part of me has broken … how many
young people I have seen in death's grip …'[4]

The Duchess of Aosta had been awarded the Silver Medal for valour. Now,
critical of the training Marie-José had received in Turin, she encouraged the
princess to recommence her nursing training in Naples. 'I have the impression
that … you were treated as a Royal Highness more than as a nurse,' Hélène
remarked.[5] She advised Marie-José to follow a course at the hospital for
Incurables and to insist on having no privileges.

★★★

In October 1935, 'using a clash over waterholes on a disputed frontier as a
pretext', Italy invaded Ethiopia.[6] As western democracies shunned the invader,
Princess Marie-José immediately sprang into action. Having cut all wastage
of food and light in her palace, she set up an establishment to feed every day

100 children of poor soldiers serving in Africa. She and Queen Elena donated their wedding rings to help the cause.[7]

Using the name Sister Maria di Piemonte she then travelled around Italy visiting hospitals, beginning health initiatives and becoming interested in broader sanitary issues. She worked from sunrise to sunset without a break, to the despair of her lady-in-waiting and, like her mother, was not afraid to give instruments to the surgeon in the operating theatre. Finding that this was not enough, Marie-José decided to volunteer as a nurse. The superintendent of Red Cross nurses, the Marchesa Irene di Targiani Giunti, had decreed that all nurses going to Africa must take a course in tropical nursing at the Hospital for Tropical Diseases in Rome. In February 1936, Marie-José therefore attended the course run by Professor Aldo Castellani, physician to King Victor Emmanuel III and an expert on hygiene and tropical medicine. 'It seemed to me that I was back at school,' she said in an interview many years later, recalling the packed class of students.[8] At the end of March she passed the examination with excellent marks and it was announced that she would inspect the tropical diseases section of the Army Medical Corps which was being co-ordinated by Professor Castellani.

By the spring of 1936 the Italians had over-run most of Ethiopia and were preparing to conquer the capital, Addis Ababa. On 26 March, the 29-year-old princess embarked on the Red Cross hospital ship *Cesarea* to join the 384 nurses serving on board hospital ships or in base hospitals. Cheers rose from the huge crowd at the quayside in Naples as the princess emerged from her car wearing the dark blue and white Red Cross uniform. Queen Elena came from Rome to see her off and, together with Prince Umberto, was received at the Beverello dock by the Duchess of Aosta and a civic delegation. 'After bidding farewell to the Princess on board,' reported *The Times*, 'the Royal party returned to the quay and stood in a heavy downpour of rain waving to her.'[9] More cheers broke out as the ship left the quayside while bands played the Royal March and *Giovinezza*, the official hymn of the Italian fascist party and the unofficial national anthem of Italy. A squadron of seaplanes circled overhead as Marie-José stood on deck holding a bouquet of flowers, acknowledging the crowd with a fascist salute. The *Cesarea*, said the *New York Times*, was 'the finest hospital ship of its kind in the world'. On board, Marie-José shared the life of the other nurses, following courses and doing practical training exercises in the surgical room of the ship.

On 3 April the *Cesarea* arrived in Massaua on the coast of East Africa, the largest deep-water port on the Red Sea. In what one author described as 'a much publicised propaganda tour',[10] Marie-José worked first in the military hospital at Asmara, capital of Eritrea, the coastal base of the Italian Army in Northern Ethiopia. The princess, reported the *British Journal of Nursing*, 'gave a fine example. She served as an ordinary nurse, without enjoying or accepting any privileges whatever.'[11]

She then moved on to Keren and Äkurdat, travelling with the soldiers to even the most isolated places, where she visited hospitals full of wounded Italian pilots. In Bender Kassin she dealt with malaria; at the infirmary of Otumulo she found a newborn baby whose mother had leprosy. Famine was widespread.

On 13 April she arrived in Chisimaio south-west of Mogadishu, Italy's most distant port, where she met up with Professor Castellani and visited the hospitals. One man was suffering from a tropical fever. Marie-José put her hand on his forehead and, as Professor Castellani recalled, his delirium ceased abruptly and the fever disappeared within hours. The princess was credited with having healing hands and venerated almost as a saint by the local population.[12]

Marie-José then worked as a nurse at the military hospital in the port of Mogadishu in Italian Somaliland. Emperor Haile Selassie fled into exile on 2 May and three days later Addis Ababa fell to the Italians. Italy annexed Ethiopia, merged Eritrea, Ethiopia and Somaliland into a single state known as Italian East Africa and proclaimed Victor Emmanuel Emperor of Ethiopia. On 3 May, Marie-José learned that the road to the capital was open to General Badoglio's army. The following day, after hearing Mussolini's speech on the radio amidst the cheers of her fellow nurses, a telegram was despatched to him:

> I am proud to have been able to listen to your glorious message. I will never forget this great emotion. Thank you. Very affectionately, Cousin Maria, Princess of Piedmont.

In fact, the telegram was not sent by Marie-José. It was dictated by the ship's telegraph officer on the recommendation of the Minister of the Royal Court. It was later used by her detractors as proof that she supported the fascist regime.[13]

On 10 May she sailed proudly for Italy, arriving the following day aboard the *Cesarea*, which also brought wounded soldiers back from Ethiopia. The following year Marie-José had to take an examination in order to exercise her role in the Red Cross. Before being able to do so she had to produce her party card. However, she was not a member of the fascist party. The princess was angry at being thus forced to become a party member and she became more resolutely anti-fascist.

On 1 September 1939, Marie-José was appointed National Inspector of the Italian Red Cross Voluntary Nurses.[14] At the installation she walked through a line of Red Cross nurses (all giving the fascist salute), was greeted by Hélène d'Aosta and made a speech. The following year she began to reorganise the mobilisation of the nurses.

During the Second World War she had several run-ins with Edda Ciano, Mussolini's favourite child, also a volunteer nurse. During one heated exchange, which Marie-José recorded in her diary, she was informed by Edda that 'as a mere volunteer nurse she [Edda] could see the administration of the hospitals much better than myself in my visits. "You are like my father, they don't show anything to you!" I asked myself if I should be flattered by this comparison,' the princess added.[15]

Marie-José continued her work for the Red Cross until the Italian monarchy was abolished in 1946. Known as the May Queen because her husband reigned for only a month, Marie-José died in Geneva in 2001.

★★★

There is a poignant footnote to this story. As Marie-José was returning from Ethiopia in 1936 an Ethiopian princess was on her way to London, where she would also become a nurse. Princess Tsahai, born in 1919, was the youngest daughter of Emperor Haile Selassie and Empress Menen and traced her ancestry back to the legendary Queen of Sheba. In 1927, she came to England to attend school, but for health reasons was forced to continue her education in Switzerland. By the age of 17 she was already president of the Ethiopian Women's Work Association and a volunteer worker for the first field ambulance unit of the Ethiopian Army.

In March 1936, as the Italians bombed Ethiopia, Princess Tsahai transmitted an urgent request to the Women's Advisory Council of the League of Nations Union in London, 'urging them to do their utmost to put an end to this barbarism'.[16] The Italians were using mustard gas, an action that was widely censured by the Red Cross. Chemical and bacteriological warfare had been 'solemnly condemned' by the Protocol of Geneva on 17 June 1925, but now people were dying like flies in Ethiopia, without help.[17]

A week later the princess sent a telegram to the British government:

> For seven days without break [the] enemy have been bombing [the] armies and people of my country including women and children with terrible gases. Our soldiers are brave men and know they must take [the] consequences of war. Against this cruel gas we have no protection, no gas masks, nothing. This suffering and torture is beyond description, hundreds of countrymen screaming and moaning with pain. Many of them are unrecognisable since the skin has burned off their faces.[18]

Desperate to help her countrymen the princess began cutting out gas masks in the workrooms of the Women's Work Association, helped by local tailors. Meanwhile, the Ethiopian Red Cross sent an urgent appeal to the Red Cross in Geneva for gas masks.

At the end of April, as Italian planes dropped leaflets calling on the people to surrender, Princess Tsahai summoned the foreign press correspondents to the palace and, in fluent English, made a desperate appeal for help. 'If mankind lets armies and gas destroy my country and people, civilization will be destroyed too,' she told them. 'We have a common cause … Italian aggression and gas have set humanity a test. If you fail to help us now, we shall all die.'[19]

A week later Italian troops advanced on Addis Ababa and the royal family was forced to flee. Princess Tsahai left with her father on a British cruiser, eventually reaching London on 3 June. By this time the extensive press coverage of her appeal had turned the teenaged princess into a well-known figure and during the next few months she spoke at many public meetings, attended receptions and opened a Christmas bazaar in aid of refugees. She also did something more positive. Always interested in the work of hospitals, the princess decided to train as a nurse so that she could be of use when the family returned to Ethiopia. On 17 August, *The Times* announced that Princess Tsahai was to train at the Hospital for Sick Children in Great Ormond Street.

The princess's family was currently living in Bath, so she stayed with Lady Barton (whose husband Sir Sidney was on leave from his post as British Minister in Addis Ababa) in South Kensington. The records show that she entered the hospital as a probationer in August 1936 and her father's occupation was 'late Emperor of Abyssinia'. 'Her training was hard,' said Matron Dorothy Lane, a woman who was held in awe and affection by the nurses, 'and she found it difficult, but she was blessed with the qualities that make a good sick children's nurse – patience, loyalty, courage, gentleness, tolerance and self-control' In those less politically correct times the young patients called her 'the brown nurse' and she proved extremely popular with them as well as with the staff. Her sister tutor gave her a glowing testimonial, writing in the nurse register: 'Made a very conscientious reliable nurse – careful in details. Most kind and gentle with the patients. Took her place with her colleagues and was popular with them.'[20]

On the outbreak of war in September 1939, the infant patients were transferred to Stanmore and Princess Tsahai went with them. After three years' training, she passed her final examination with high marks and in December achieved her ambition of becoming a state-registered sick children's nurse. Princess Tsahai now wanted to continue with general nurse training, so in 1940 she left Great Ormond Street. 'One day I shall open a children's hospital: you must come and see it,' she told Dorothy Lane.[21]

The princess transferred to Guy's Hospital and while working there she became a friend of Sylvia Pankhurst. When bombs began raining down on London, Princess Tsahai showed qualities of great courage and leadership. When the hospital was evacuated to Kent the matron of Guy's Hospital, Emily MacManus, recalled that although some of the nurses were comfortably housed others, including Nurse Tsahai, were in the Public Assistance quarters. Facilities there were basic – a set of round holes in a slate slab formed basins in the common washroom and the only toilet was outside. Miss MacManus discussed the possibility of moving Tsahai to better quarters but the princess refused to be treated differently.[22]

Princess Tsahai had not completed her general training when Ethiopia was liberated in 1941. Returning home, the princess took with her 'a band of nurses to help establish a network of medical centres'. She set up two welfare clinics and an orphanage for children whose parents were killed in the war, and was also planning a new hospital.[23]

In 1942, the 22-year-old princess married General Abiye Abebe, who was appointed governor of Welega Province in western Ethiopia. Four months later, on 17 August 1942, she died in remote Lekempti after suffering a haemorrhage. On 9 September a Memorial Service was held in St Christopher's Chapel at the Hospital for Sick Children in Great Ormond Street. Queen Elizabeth sent white carnations from Windsor to decorate the chapel and among the congregation were many nurses who had trained with Princess Tsahai. During the service Dorothy Lane paid tribute to her.

A memorial fund was established to build a hospital in her memory. Silvia Pankhurst (who had a lifelong interest in Ethiopia) was at the forefront of the fundraising and Queen Elizabeth sent a donation. The Princess Tsahai Memorial Hospital opened in Addis Ababa in 1951 in memory of the princess who died for want of the very medical care she was trying to bring to the people. It was staffed by British nurses, many of them from Great Ormond Street.

Notes

1. Marguerite Coppens (ed.), *La Princesse Marie-José: Entre Belgique et Italie* (Éditions Lannoo, Belgium. 2012), p.86; Princess Marie-Gabrielle of Savoy, quoted in de Jonge, p.115.
2. Aronson, *Crowns*, p.44.
3. Oliver, *British Red Cross*, p.248.
4. Sabrina Pollock, 'A Mere Duchess', in *The European Royal History Journal*, February 2000.
5. Luciano Regolo, *Marie-José de Savoie: La Reine de Mai* (Racine, Belgium, 2001), p.125.
6. Moorehead, *Dunant's Dream*, p.302.
7. *Pittsburgh Post Gazette*, 27 April 1936.
8. www.reumberto.it/mjose84-3.htm. Interview with Giorgio Lazzarini.

9. *The Times*, 27 March 1936; also the *New York Times* of the same date.
10. Baudendistel, p.32.
11. *The British Journal of Nursing*, April 1938, p.107.
12. Regolo, *Marie-José de Savoie*, p 141 & information from Luciano Regolo.
13. Regolo, *Marie-José de Savoie*, p 140 & information from Luciano Regolo. Mussolini, as a member of the Order of Annunziata, was considered as a 'cousin', a member of the House of Savoy.
14. *Revue Internationale de la Croix-Rouge et Bulletin Internationale de Societies de la Croix-Rouge*. Vol. 21, September 1939, pp.784–5.
15. 7 June 1943. Arrigo, Petacco, *Regina: La via e i segreti di Maria José* (Mondadori, 1998 pp.190–1.
16. *The Times*, 23 March 1936.
17. Oliver, *British Red Cross*, p 318; Moorehead, *Dunant's Dream*, p.310.
18. Telegram from Princess Tsahai, printed in *The Times*, 30 March 1936.
19. *The Times*, 28 April 1936.
20. Andrea Tanner, 'A Princess on the Wards', GOSH archives. I am grateful to Nicholas Baldwin, archivist at Great Ormond Street Hospital, for bringing this to my attention.
21. Tanner, *Princess on the Wards*.
22. Emily MacManus, *Matron of Guy's* (Andrew Melrose, 1956), p.175.
23. Tanner, *Princess on the Wards*.

11

Ladies of Spain

In June 1905, 19-year-old King Alfonso XIII of Spain visited England in search of a bride. Several candidates had been suggested, but it was King Edward VII's niece, 17-year-old Princess Victoria Eugenie Julie Ena of Battenberg, with her striking blue eyes, blonde hair and fair complexion, who captured Alfonso's heart.

The princess was born at Balmoral on 24 October 1887. Her parents Princess Beatrice and Prince Henry of Battenberg lived with Queen Victoria, so her first years were spent at Windsor Castle, Osborne, Balmoral and Buckingham Palace. In 1896 Prince Henry died from a fever while serving in the Ashanti Expedition and 'Princess Ena', as the public called her, grew close to her widowed mother.

Ena's engagement provoked controversy but despite some outraged letters in the British press the princess quietly converted to Catholicism and renounced her rights to the British throne. The wedding was scheduled for May 1906.

Few people have had such a dramatic start to married life as Ena and Alfonso. As they drove back from the church through the narrow streets of Madrid a bomb was thrown towards their carriage. Ena's wedding dress was spattered with blood, and dead and wounded lay everywhere. It was not a good omen.

Queen Ena's life in Spain was difficult from the start. Shy and immature, she found the sixteenth-century Spanish etiquette and the presence of her austere mother-in-law, Queen Maria Cristina, inhibiting. Her youth, beauty and vitality were resented by the elderly ladies-in-waiting, she knew little Spanish (she conversed with Alfonso in French) and hated bullfights. Worse was to come.

Like her mother, Ena proved to be a carrier of haemophilia. Of her four sons, two (including Alfonso, the heir) were haemophiliacs; another was left deaf and dumb at the age of 4 after an operation for mastoiditis; and only Juan, born in 1913, was healthy. It remained to be seen whether her daughters Beatriz and Maria Cristina would be carriers.

It was vital that the succession be assured and the king, devastated by the fact that Ena had brought haemophilia into the Spanish royal family, began to turn against his wife. He took mistresses who gave him several illegitimate children and his private life became a source of gossip. 'He tires of everything,' the queen once said prophetically. 'Some day he will tire even of me.'¹ To compensate for the failings in her marriage warm-hearted Ena turned to philanthropic work.

During the Moroccan War of 1909 she collected 80,000 pesetas, medical supplies, clothing and other comforts, which were sent to the sick and wounded. Relatives of those killed were summoned to the royal palace, where the queen personally gave them gifts and money. Her most important contribution, however, was the reorganisation of the Spanish Red Cross.²

When Ena arrived in Spain the hospitals were still fairly basic. This was not due to lack of good doctors but mainly because the specialists confined themselves to the royal palace or the important Madrid hospitals where they could charge huge fees. They were therefore of little help to the ordinary working man. Furthermore, there were no trained nurses, as it was not regarded as a serious profession and itt was not considered decent for a woman to become a nurse. This duty was confined to nuns, who ran the hospitals as part of their charity work. There was a saying that 'a woman without a nun's veil is a lost woman if she goes near a man in bed.'³ The queen was determined to change this and create a Red Cross department in every town to provide health care for the poor. At first her activities were treated with suspicion and she had to work slowly.

The Spanish Red Cross was created on 6 July 1864 by Royal Decree of Queen Isabel II. Many important ladies were involved in it before the First World War but the organisation kept a low profile. By another Royal Decree of 16 January 1916 Isabel's grandson Alfonso XIII proclaimed himself Supreme Head of the Spanish Red Cross, although in time of war or other necessity he could delegate this authority to the queen. For Spanish affairs the Red Cross was subject to the Ministry of War; for international affairs, to the Ministry of State. As president of the *Sección de Señoras* (Women's Section), by a Royal Decree of February 1917, Queen Ena created a body of professional nurses and one of voluntary nurses. A curriculum was approved and shortly afterwards an insignia for the Lady Nurses was designed.

During the First World War, Spain was neutral and the Spanish Red Cross became a vital link in international relief. Working in the hospitals, wearing her Red Cross uniform, helped Queen Ena to forget worries over her brothers Alexander and Maurice, who were fighting in the British Army. Queen Maria Cristina (by birth an Austrian archduchess) made no secret of her support for the Central Powers for whom her brother was fighting. When Maurice was killed in action Ena struggled to hide her feelings; the German sympathisers at Court made no attempt to do the same.

The queen worked hard to modernise the Red Cross in line with the methods of other European countries, and as her right-hand man she chose the lawyer Domingo Salazar. Her first problem was how to finance the building of new hospitals and the training of nurses without the aid of government funds. However, the government did agree to organise and back a lottery with tickets at various prices. Queen Ena persuaded many people at court to buy the more expensive tickets and the results were announced annually on 23 December, the queen's Saint's Day.

Thanks to the queen's personal efforts donations poured in and this enabled the building of the first Red Cross hospital in Madrid. The Hospital de San José y Santa Adela was officially created by a Royal Order dated 22 January 1918 and built on land later donated to the Red Cross. It was inaugurated on 16 December 1918 with seventy-two beds. Its first director was Dr Victor Manuel Nogueras, who was also in charge of training at the nurses' school established at the same time. Within a few years fully trained nurses were working around the clock in Spanish hospitals.

Every year Queen Ena also paid for a contingent of Spanish nurses to be trained in England. Several of the young ladies who trained in Madrid under Dr Nogueras and Drs Luque and Serrada were from the nobility, including the queen's daughters Beatriz (who received her nursing diploma in June 1928) and Maria Cristina. Infanta Beatriz recalled:

We used to go to work at the Red Cross hospital [in Madrid] which Mama had founded, and there we talked much to the sick and ailing people. We only spoke to them about their ailments but could not give them money because it was all very well organised and they were given a paper which they had to take to the pharmacy located in Cuatro Caminos, which was not far from the Hospital of Santa Adela. There they would have to pay very little money to obtain their drugs. In 1929 I had to take care of a worker who had a terrible wound in his knee. When I gave him the paper he said: 'I don't think that I will be able to pay for my drugs because I'm trying to save money because of the strike that will take place next week'. In my simplicity I asked him: 'Why do you have to join the strike if you don't want to?' And he replied: 'Because I'm afraid of what might happen to me if I don't join the strikers. Look at my knee after the beating I received during the previous strike. They might kill me next time.' That impressed me terribly.[4]

The queen made great efforts to organise fundraising events in aid of this hospital, to which she always attached enormous importance. There were high society balls at the Ritz Hotel in Madrid and various other cities for the benefit of the Red Cross, and also popular parties (known then as 'kermesses') which Queen Ena and her daughters attended with Queen Maria Cristina, her sister-in-law the Duchess of Talavera de la Reina and the king's aunt the Infanta Isabel. In 1917, she even attended a bullfight in aid of the Red Cross, being careful to ensure that her opera glasses were out of focus when she raised them to her eyes as the spectacle reached its savage climax. She also founded leagues against cancer and tuberculosis. One of the main achievements of her Anti-Tuberculosis League was a 'Victoria Eugenia Dispensary' in Madrid, which was followed by similar dispensaries in other towns.

★★★

Since 1909, Spain had been bogged down in Morocco, occupying the area around Melilla in the north-east and fighting the Moors. The cost in both men and money was enormous and the subject of mounting criticism in Spain. The king needed a great victory. Instead, in July 1921, the Spanish suffered a disaster of the first magnitude.

General Silvestre, a dashing old war veteran, determined to give the king the success the country needed, marched 10,000 men to a place called Annual, where the entire army was surrounded and obliterated in a narrow ravine. By the end of that year, Spain had lost all the territory gained since 1909. The bulk of Spain's army was annihilated and the king was blamed for this shocking waste of life.

Thousands of wounded soldiers began to arrive in Spain but thanks to the queen an important network of hospitals was already in place. The wounded were looked after by Queen Ena's Red Cross nurses, who played a significant central role, while her temporary hospitals and highly trained Lady Nurses became a byword for cleanliness and efficiency.

As it was impossible for the queen to go to Morocco herself she opened public subscriptions all over the country to raise money for the wounded. When news of the uprising of the Bedouin tribes arrived in 1921, Queen Ena sent her close friend Carmen Angoloti, the Duchess de la Victoria, to North Africa with a team of Lady Nurses. The duchess, who trained as a nurse just after the First World War, had worked in the Madrid hospital and collaborated with the queen in the foundation of the Red Cross hospitals and nursing schools. She did a tremendous amount of good work tending the wounded in Morocco.

In 1921, the queen spent several days travelling widely through southern Spain, accompanied by the Inspector General of Hospitals and her lady-in-waiting the Marchioness of La Mina. She visited twenty-five small local 'blood hospitals' (campaign hospitals set up during time of war and partly funded by the Red Cross) such as the Hospital del Corazón de Jesús in Córdoba. By the time she returned to Madrid, Queen Ena had visited over 1,500 sick and wounded in Córdoba and Granada.

Ena was also busy raising funds for hospital trains. They were set up by government authorities but partly financed by the Red Cross, whose nurses tended the sick and wounded upon arrival at the different stations. Gradually the ladies of the court became involved in Red Cross work and the nobility were proud to be involved in an initiative created by the queen. Ena opened Red Cross hospitals in Barcelona and, in 1923, Seville – both with their own training school for nurses. The queen's sister-in-law the Infanta Luisa (maternal grandmother of King Juan Carlos and sister of Hélène Duchess of Aosta) was created Honorary President of the Seville branch of the Red Cross and did much good work there, helped by other noble ladies. Until her marriage and move to Spain in 1907, Luisa had spent part of her youth at Stowe House, Buckinghamshire, and then at Wood Norton Hall, near Evesham (her father the Count of Paris was banished from France in 1886). She was doubtless influenced by the nursing services in England.

Queen Ena maintained a close relationship with the Count de Campo de Alange, Inspector General in the province of Asturias; Doña Dolores Blanco, honorary president of the Red Cross in Galicia; and Doña Jesusa Vega Ortiz, who was president of the First Assembly of the Red Cross. The queen was nominated Honorary President of the Red Cross in the Canary Islands and earned the Silver Cross of the Red Cross of Caracas, Venezuela. She also received the Italian Red Cross Medal from Queen Elena of Italy. A draft of Ena's letter of thanks survives in the Madrid archives:

> It is with the deepest gratitude that I received, accompanied by the charming letter from Your Majesty the brevit of the *Croix au Merite*, created by the Italian Red Cross under Your Majesty's high patronage. I do not know how to express to Your Majesty how sensitive I have been to such a delicate attention and it gives me pleasure to tell you, that I have received this distinction as a precious witness to the sentiments of affection and friendship with which I wholeheartedly correspond.
>
> Your Majesty may be assured of the sincere part with which I took the plight of the Italian prisoners of war, and the keen interest with which I followed the steps taken by the king in favour of these unfortunates.
>
> I seize with pleasure this opportunity to reiterate to Your Majesty the assurance of my sentiments of devoted friendship.[5]

In 1923, Pope Pius XI gave Queen Ena the Golden Rose of Christianity, the highest honour given to a Catholic lady by the church. She was the first British-born royal lady to be awarded this prestigious order since 1555. When the queen was awarded the Spanish Red Cross Order of Merit (First Class) her jewelled breast star was paid for by a subscription raised by the Corps of Lady Nurses of the Spanish Red Cross. The Spanish Red Cross Star was also awarded to her during a presentation by Queen Maria Cristina at the Palacio del Oriente, Madrid's royal palace.

★★★

In January 1931, a large society ball was held in Barcelona in aid of the Red Cross. The event, patronised by the queen, was Ena's swansong. Three months later years of political unrest finally came to a head. In the April elections there was a large swing towards the republicans, especially in the towns and cities, although the rural districts remained predominately royalist. When the army withdrew its support King Alfonso decided to leave his divided country for a while to avoid the risk of civil war. On 14 April he went into exile.

That night, alone with her children in the palace, Queen Ena could hear the howling of the mob outside. Early the next day, as she prepared to leave Spain, Ena was informed that the revolution had begun; the morning's papers were already singing the praises of the republic and the hasty departure of the king. Later that day the queen and her children crossed the border into France in a plain railway carriage.

The exiled queen eventually made her home in Lausanne. In July 1936, as Spain spiralled into civil war, Ena urged the British Red Cross to intercede with their counterparts in Spain for the lives of the Duchess de la Victoria and the Marquis de Hoyos, former president and vice president of the Spanish Red Cross, who were in prison under sentence of death. Both were released due to the queen's intervention.[6]

Later, Ena was able to pay one last visit to her Madrid hospital. In February 1968, she was permitted to return to Spain for the christening of her great-grandson Prince Felipe, son and heir of Prince Juan Carlos and his wife the former Princess Sofia of Greece. While in Madrid, Ena visited the hospital de San José y Santa Adela, where she was welcomed by members of the Supreme Assembly. Nurses, students, volunteer rescue workers and bands stood at the hospital's entrance to greet the woman who had done so much for the Spanish Red Cross. Queen Ena was overcome by emotion. She died in Lausanne the following April.

In 1929, a statue of the queen in nurse's uniform was erected in Barcelona. Although it has since been destroyed, the Red Cross hospital in Madrid still bears Queen Victoria Eugenie's name.

★★★

When the monarchy fell in 1931 another granddaughter of Queen Victoria was also living in Spain. Queen Ena's cousin Infanta Beatrice of Orleans, the youngest sister of Queen Marie of Romania, stayed behind to care for her husband's elderly aunt the Infanta Isabel, who was recovering from a stroke and unable to leave her room. She later said that General Franco's brother threatened to burn down the house if the women refused to depart. Courageously, Isabel elected to go into exile rather than accept the 'hospitality' of the new regime and the women finally left Madrid on 20 April. Although Isabel died in France shortly afterwards such care and compassion was typical of Infanta Beatrice.

The Infanta, born Princess Beatrice of Edinburgh on 20 April 1884 at Eastwell Park, Kent, was one of the four beautiful daughters of Queen Victoria's son Alfred. She spent her early life between England, Malta and Coburg, where her father succeeded to the dukedom in 1893. At Ena's wedding in 1906 she met the Infante Alfonso (later 5th Duke of Galliera), called 'Ali' to distinguish him from his cousin King Alfonso XIII. Ali's mother was the king's unconventional aunt Infanta Eulalia; his father Antonio was the son of the very wealthy Duke of Montpensier, youngest son of King Louis Philippe of France. Ali proposed to Beatrice almost immediately but it was a while before they could marry.

Despite opposition from the Spanish government, because Beatrice refused to become a Catholic, the couple finally married quietly in Coburg in July 1909. When the news reached King Alfonso he had no choice but to strip Ali of his military rank and royal title and banish the couple from Spain. Their eldest son Alvaro was born in Coburg in 1910.

For the next two years, Beatrice and Ali lived mainly in Zurich, where Beatrice trained as a nurse, something she had wanted to do in her youth. In 1905, she had spent a good deal of her time helping at the Klinik in Coburg but did not enrol as a trainee because of opposition from her mother. Now she seized the opportunity.

The king restored Ali's titles in 1912 and the couple returned to Spain. Beatrice became a Catholic and two more sons, Alonso (1912) and Ataulfo (1913), were born in Madrid, but at various times between 1916 and 1923 King Alfonso again banished them from the country.

When the monarchy fell Ali accompanied the king into exile. Their properties confiscated, Ali and Beatrice moved to Zurich and later London, where her cousin George V lent them the King's Cottage, a substantial grace and favour home on Kew Green.

In 1936 civil war broke out in Spain between the republican government and the nationalists under General Francisco Franco. Ali was working for the Ford Motor Company in America; Beatrice was at Kew. Their sons joined the nationalists but in November, 24-year-old Alonso, a qualified pilot, was killed when his plane crashed. Ali then bombarded Franco with requests for an active role and in 1937 returned to command part of the Nationalist Air Force. Beatrice, who had raised considerable sums for the monarchist cause already, decided to become a Red Cross nurse and left England on 21 September 1937 in a chauffeur-driven limousine. With her went Pip Scott-Ellis, 21-year-old daughter of Ali's old friend Margot, Lady Howard de Walden. Pip had taken a crash course in Spanish and was desperate to go and help, so Beatrice told Margot that she needed a secretary to assist with her work among the poor. Brushing aside objections, the Infanta promised to look after Pip as if she were her own daughter.

They travelled via Paris and Biarritz to San Sebastián. After spending several days collecting medicines and foodstuffs, they went on to Burgos, Valladolid and Salamanca. While Pip stayed with the Duchess of Montemar and took a nursing course in Jerez, Beatrice moved into the Palacio de Ventósilla at Aranda de Duero to spend Christmas with her husband and sons who were stationed there.

In the New Year, Beatrice joined La Delegación Nacional de Asistencia a Frentes y Hospitales, a welfare organisation founded by Maria Rosa Urraca Pastor. It was run largely by monarchists who followed the army into recently conquered towns to provide welfare to women, children and the aged. They wore a white uniform with the emblem of a half red and half yellow cross (the colours of the Spanish flag) surrounded by a laurel wreath.

In the bitterly cold winter of 1937–38, as the nationalist air force regrouped at Castejón aerodrome north-west of Zaragoza, Beatrice followed to set up a home for Ali as the battle for Teruel continued. The city fell on 22 February and as the infanta entered the battered remains of the city she found it almost destroyed; most of the inhabitants had fled.

Following the Nationalist advance, in April she reached Lerida, where the Relief Fund established its headquarters in an asylum in the town centre. Beatrice had around 400 old people to look after, with no doctors or help of any sort except for her co-workers from Frentes y Hospitales. The building was full of corpses, as the republicans had shot many people before leaving and they were still lying, or sitting, where they died. The old people who remained had been left completely alone for ten days without getting up. Beatrice's first job was to clear up the consequent mess in the beds. She then 'had to act as doctor and do whatever she thought best with the few things she happened to have with her, and no light, no water and everything filthy'.[7] To make matters worse, the republicans were only 50 yards away and were shooting explosive bullets along all the streets. Beatrice finished her work at Lerida tired but pleased with the job done, which had given her valuable experience for the future.

Beatrice moved to Épila, south-west of Zaragoza, to be near Ali. They lived near the aerodrome in the Palacio de Hijar, which had been requisitioned from the Duke of Alba and was reputed to be haunted. Using Epila as a base, occasionally staying in another town when needed, the Infanta worked in canteens, nursed in hospitals at Cintruénigo and by the end of May was almost in a state of collapse looking after her daughter-in-law Carla, who was laid up at Épila with paratyphoid. In the summer Beatrice was sent to the recently taken air base at Castellón as head of the canteen 'Beneficiencia de Guerra'. She also wanted to organise a kind of flying *equipo* (casualty clearing station) which could go quickly to wherever it was needed when wounded soldiers came in, so that they could lend temporary help to the hospitals and the ordinary clearing stations.

The nationalists captured Tarragona and Reus in January 1939, so Beatrice and Ali moved north-west to Monzón. She had been joined by Pip Scott-Ellis and Consuelo Osorio de Moscoso (daughter of the Duchess of Montemar, a distant relative of Ali), both of whom had been nursing at the front. Beatrice and Pip left on an inspection tour of the front. Taking the road from Reus to Tarragona they were only a couple of days behind Franco's advancing forces, catching up with the troops marching towards Barcelona. At one *equipo* they changed into uniform and watched some operations before helping the staff move the hospital to Reus. Franco had appointed Mercedes Milá as head of the Nationalist Nursing Services, the Jefatura General de Servicios Femeninos de Hospitales. Although Mercedes was an efficient organiser, there were few wounded and, Pip recalled, 'the Infanta is driven just as mad as I am by not having any real work'.[8] By the time they followed the army into Barcelona, Beatrice and Mercedes were having a good old-fashioned row. Beatrice wanted permission for Consuelo to continue working with Pip at the *equipo*. Mercedes refused and Beatrice was livid. 'Milá was being extremely rude, bellowing like God knows what and shouting the Infanta down,' Pip recorded. 'I don't know how the Infanta did not get up and smite her.'[9] In Barcelona, Beatrice took Pip and Consuelo to visit the English Hospital, later going with the diplomatic corps to visit the Checas (communist torture chambers), from where she returned 'quite faint and ill with disgust'.[10] The infanta and Consuelo then went to work in the huge Civil Hospital, where they found all the wounded lying on the filthy floor. Beatrice was in charge of a pavilion with over 200 wounded and was soon rushing around taking temperatures and giving intravenous injections. Later she was called to a man thought to be having an epileptic fit. By March she was working in the local hospitals as well as in the canteen of Barajas, the Madrid airfield.

The war was almost over. On 28 March, while Beatrice was at Leganes organising supplies of food and blankets, news came that Madrid had fallen.

Despite the fact that the main nationalist forces had not entered the city, she immediately returned to Barajas, picked up an aviation car and set off loaded with 'food, condensed milk, Bovril, biscuits, chocolate, tinned meat, etc' and no luggage. Behind her followed Pip in her own car, driving with Consuelo amongst a convoy of aviation lorries. In a suburb of Madrid the road was barred to traffic but finally, after a long wait, they were allowed to pass.[11]

Madrid had been besieged for two-and-a-half years. As they drove through the ruins their convoy was surrounded by people begging for 'food, cigarettes, anything'. Children uttered shrieks of joy as Beatrice threw out chocolates, telling her they had lived on lentils for so long that they had forgotten how anything else tasted. 'The enthusiasm was unbelievable, a thing I shall never forget in my life,' Pip wrote.[12] Finding her Madrid house virtually destroyed inside, the infanta lodged with the Romanian minister before moving into the magnificent former Turkish legation. She then began the task of finding blankets and foodstuffs for the beleaguered residents. 'Here now in Madrid we found the population in a deplorable condition, sights like an Indian famine,' she told Margot. 'We had to visit separately as there was so much work.'[13] Shocked by the gaunt state of the inhabitants in the cold weather, Beatrice and Pip started on an endless round of visits to hospitals, canteens and emergency clearing stations. Family lore says that Beatrice used money from the sale of her personal jewels to buy ambulances. When Lady Howard de Walden complained that Beatrice had helped Pip to go to the front as a nurse, where she was experiencing dreadful horrors, the infanta replied, 'I promised you, dear Margot, that I would look after her as my own daughter; and if I had a daughter she would surely be at the front!'[14]

Despite the fact that she was now tired and unwell, Beatrice continued working, making sandwiches for the canteen at Barajas aerodrome where Ali was stationed, taking a lorry to Leganes to collect stores, arranging food, cigarettes and medicines for the population and sorting blankets for the hospitals. At Valdemoro she organised the loading of a lorry with sacks of sugar, cases of tinned meat and condensed milk. They dropped the milk off at the emergency station store where Beatrice 'to her disgust … was presented with a paper informing her that she had been elected President of the Emergency Stations, which means still more work' and endless committee meetings.[15] She was badly in need of a break. 'I wish she could finish her work here so that we could all go to Sanlúcar for a rest,' Pip lamented. 'But she can't disentangle herself.'[16] Beatrice also worked closely with the exiled Queen Ena to negotiate the exchange of prisoners on both sides. For her good deeds during the civil war Beatrice was awarded the Red Cross Medal and the Cruz de Beneficencia de Guerra.

In April, the republican army surrendered to General Franco and at the end of May Frentes y Hospitales was disbanded. Franco had returned Ali's estates during the civil war, so Beatrice and Ali moved to the Palacio Orleans in Sanlúcar de Barrameda,[17] three buildings combined into a pseudo-Moorish palace by his grandfather. One visitor described its 'crazy mixture of styles' as 'hideously ugly but fascinating'.[18] Much of the family fortune had been squandered by Ali's late father on his mistresses but Ali also owned El Botanico, a large garden with two houses on the outskirts of the village, and Torre Breva, a vineyard at Sanlúcar. During the civil war they had stayed at Sanlúcar several times and found the trees at El Botanico 'growing splendidly, the tennis court has been redone a seductive pink and there is a gorgeous chicken farm with 250 Leghorns all numbered and tabulated',[19] but Torre Breva had been neglected for many years and the grape harvest produced very little money. Short of funds, they both worked hard to restore their fortune while donating money to various local charities, much of it raised by holding the 'Bailes de la Infanta' at the Palacio Orleans, popular balls at which local women could wear flamenco dresses to avoid the necessity of spending money on a new dress.

Their British residence remained the King's Cottage but in 1940 King George VI terminated the lease. As Ali and his sons had flown with German and Italian aviators during the civil war, King George believed they were pro-German and would not let them into Britain. He also believed, without any real grounds, that Beatrice's son Ataulfo was responsible for the bombing of Buckingham Palace.[20]

King Alfonso died in Rome in 1941 but General Franco was equivocal about restoring the monarchy. The king's heir was his third son Don Juan, the exiled Count of Barcelona. From 1943–45 Ali acted as the count's representative in Spain, and that earned him the ill-will of Franco, who in 1945 banished Ali to his estate in Sanlúcar under house arrest. Beatrice spent her time travelling between Sanlúcar and their Madrid house, which had been restored but was sold shortly afterwards.

The infanta had seen the poverty-stricken conditions in which people lived in the area around Sanlúcar. Spain was poor and the women had to work long hours in the cornfields to avoid starvation. Many pregnant women waited until the last moment to stop working, or gave birth in the fields; most had never been checked by a gynaecologist in their lives. Beatrice decided to establish a charity institution to provide help and support for pregnant women and single mothers.

In 1941, she bought a house in the village of Sanlúcar de Barrameda. Still short of money herself but determined to help others, her family believe that she sold some of her jewels to Queen Mary to raise money to buy the house.[21] The Casa de Maternidad de San Ildefonso provided a place where the women could give birth in hygienic conditions. Under the same roof was the paediatric clinic La Gota de Leche ('a drop of milk'), which worked through various different clinics and hospitals in Spain. The idea had originated with Dr Leon Dufour in France in 1894 in an effort to decrease the high child mortality rates. It had been copied in Madrid in 1904 and later spread to other cities. Beatrice had visited La Gota de Leche in Madrid to see the work done there and decided to implement the scheme at Sanlúcar. Poor, pregnant women were fed at La Gota de Leche for two months before their baby was due, they then gave birth at the Casa de Maternidad and were looked after until they and their babies were well enough to leave. La Gota de Leche then fed them for six months after the birth.

Beatrice not only provided the maternity home but she also worked hard there herself. She and her assistants Consuelo Osorio de Moscoso (who was effectively Beatrice's right hand), her mother the Dowager Duchess of Montemar, and Beatrice's niece Princess Alexandra (Dolly) of Hohenlohe-Langenburg, who spent long periods with her in Spain, wore overalls and caps to protect themselves against lice. They received the women who came in, gave them a proper wash to avoid infections and then took care of them. Still, many of them waited as long as possible before coming to the home. When Beatrice asked them why they waited until so late in their pregnancy to stop working they replied in one word – 'hunger'. If they did not work, the women said, they would starve.

For twenty-five years the Casa de Maternidad de San Ildefonso received her total support and commitment. After 1959, Beatrice rarely travelled outside Spain, devoting herself to the maternity home (they founded the Bodega Los Infantes and sold brandy, sherry and wine produced at Torre Breva to raise funds) and enjoying visits from her grandchildren and other relatives. Her niece Princess Dolly also spent long periods living in Sanlúcar.

In 1955, unable to afford the upkeep of the Palacio Orleans, Beatrice and Ali moved to their more modest estate of El Bótanico half a mile away, and it was here that she died on 13 July 1966, leaving the Casa de Maternidad to the Spanish Red Cross. Ali survived her by nine years.

Infanta Beatrice was praised by the local population for her good work. She is still remembered in the area and her memory is also kept alive in the names of many local streets such as Calle Infanta Beatriz and Calzada de la Infanta. In August 2008, a bust of Beatrice in her nurse's uniform was erected in Sanlúcar de Barrameda near the former Casa de Maternidad.

Notes

1. Aronson, *Grandmama*, p.258.
2. Unless otherwise stated, all information about Queen Ena's work for the Spanish nursing services comes from Ricardo Mateos Sainz de Medrano, to whom I am greatly indebted for his help with this chapter.
3. Gerard Noel, *Ena: Spain's English Queen* (Constable, 1984), p.151.
4. Interview with Infanta Beatriz by Javier González de Vega. My thanks to Javier González de Vega for permission to quote this extract.
5. Draft letter. Archivo General de Palacio, Palacio Real, Madrid.
6. Oliver, *British Red Cross*, p.336.
7. Priscilla Scott-Ellis, *The Chances of Death: Diary of the Spanish Civil War*, ed. Raymond Carr (Michael Russell Publishing Ltd., 1995), p.78.
8. Scott-Ellis, *Chances of Death*, p.179.
9. Scott-Ellis, *Chances of Death*, pp.185–6.
10. Scott-Ellis, *Chances of Death*, p.188.
11. Scott-Ellis, *Chances of Death*, p.206.
12. Scott-Ellis, *Chances of Death*, p.207.
13. Margherita Howard de Walden, *Pages From my Life* (Sigwick & Jackson, 1965), p.242.
14. Howard de Walden, *Pages*, p.242.
15. Scott-Ellis, *Chances of Death*, p.221.
16. Scott-Ellis, *Chances of Death*, p.217.
17. Information from Ricardo Mateos Sainz de Medrano.
18. Paul Preston, *Doves of War* (Harper Collins, 2010), p.38.
19. Scott-Ellis, *Chances of Death*, p.107.
20. Preston, *Doves*, p.93; Sarah Bradford, *George VI* (Weidenfeld & Nicolson, 1989), p.429. Ataulfo had been serving with the German Condor Legion. He and his surviving brother were nowhere near London.
21. I am indebted to Ricardo Mateos Sainz de Medrano for much of the information on the work of Infanta Beatrice at the Casa de Maternidad.

12

The World at War Again

When Hitler invaded Poland on 1 September 1939, Princess Arthur of Connaught was on holiday in Scotland. She had intended to return to London to open The Fife Nursing Home but decided to postpone the opening until the European situation became clearer. Three days later, after Hitler failed to reply to an Anglo-French ultimatum, Britain and Germany were once again at war. Princess Arthur abandoned her plan for the nursing home and applied to the Ministry of Health for a full-time job.

After turning down a position as matron in a hospital in the country, she was appointed sister-in-charge of the Casualty Clearing Station at the 2nd London General Hospital at University College Hospital. The matron was Mrs E.O. Jackson.

The Casualty Clearing Station (CCS) was situated in the confined space of the ground floor and basement of the hospital's private patients' wing. In the basement wards there was no daylight, no fresh air and few electric lights; the ground floor wards, operating theatres, X-ray department, consulting rooms, kitchens and offices were slightly less gloomy. Sandbags blocked the windows and there was an occasional blue bulb to light the way. Patients were constantly being admitted, many for emergency operations, while others were evacuated to hospitals in the country. Princess Arthur was in charge of five surgical wards, with another sister in charge of the medical wards. When the medical sister was off she took charge of both, writing reports, attending the doctors on their rounds and supervising the nurses, many of whom were still in training.

As the Blitz began in earnest casualties came flooding in. They had no idea that their nurse was a member of the royal family; to them she was just the sister-in-charge. One evening the father of a young casualty pressed a coin into the princess's hand as they left. 'Ere you are Miss, get yourself a cup of tea or a packet of fags,' he insisted. That sixpence, she later said, became one of her most treasured possessions.[1]

Eventually the long hours and cramped conditions took a toll on Princess Arthur's health, which had never been good, and she collapsed from strain and was forced to take to her bed. Once recovered, she decided to concentrate on her nursing home.

The Fife Nursing Home opened in May 1940 with the princess as matron. The furnishings were simple, solid and unpretentious. The patients' rooms had cream walls, specially made light wood furniture, electric fires and basins with running water; the lofty waiting room was furnished with comfortable sofas and armchairs, with old prints on the walls and a French clock on the mantelpiece; the nurses' dining and sitting room had everything for their comfort; while her own office had a large desk and bookcases with chair seats of *gros-point* needlework sewn herself. As surgery was her particular interest, the most up-to-date equipment (luckily purchased before the outbreak of war) was installed in the theatre. Rooms for the domestic help were in the somewhat gloomy basement where, due to wartime regulations, the windows were blacked out like the rest of the property. The nurses each looked after two patients but, as none of them liked theatre work, the princess and the sister-in-charge took it in turns to attend or assist at operations. Princess Arthur also carried out all the administrative duties. Fees were the same as those charged for a private room in a hospital but half fees were charged to members of the medical profession and their relatives. After just a few years the home was self-supporting.

Soon a routine was established. Princess Arthur read reports and dealt with the administration before discussing the day's work with the sister-in-charge. Every day she visited the patients to make sure they were comfortable, especially those about to have surgery and those returning from the operating theatre. In the evenings she enjoyed cooking and often only returned home in the early hours of the morning. Out of some 3,000 patients admitted during the home's existence, deaths only averaged two a year.

One evening in December 1940 her car left the nursing home during an air raid, but at the end of her road in St John's Wood they were stopped by an air-raid warden, who said there was a bomb crater in the middle of the road and they could go no further. The princess insisted that she must get to her home at No. 64 and the wardens guided her to it. 'The windows at the front were all hanging out of their frames, while the remainder of the wood and glass was scattered over the road below. The front door had been blasted inwards, tearing it away and taking the lock with it,' she recalled. Inside, moving by torchlight because of blackout regulations (many of the blinds were in tatters and much of the house was exposed to the sky) she was surprised to find that most of the pictures and much of the furniture had somehow remained undamaged and the servants' quarters were intact. The wardens said the house was safe to spend the night in and the following day Princess Arthur made arrangements for it to be patched up.[2]

Soon there was no respite from the daily bombings, but The Fife Nursing Home remained open throughout the war, apart from one week in 1941 when an unexploded bomb was discovered at the back of the building and Princess Arthur was ordered to evacuate the home immediately. There was no time to remove anything apart from the patients. With the home closed, temporary accommodation had to be found for the staff. Despite this setback the princess was determined to continue with her work.

When the home reopened new personnel had to be found, as many of the previous staff refused to return because of the constant air raids. Finding and training new staff to her methods meant more hard work for the princess.

The Fife Nursing Home was soon up and running smoothly again but the air raids were causing problems to the business. Incendiary bombs dropped nightly and when one started a fire on the house next door several patients left because of the regularity of the heavy raids. The princess often spent the night in her office so that she was 'on call' in case of wartime emergency.

Her always fragile health was now showing even more signs of strain and long hours of standing in the theatre necessitated the amputation of one of her toes. When the sister-in-charge left, Princess Arthur took over herself until a replacement arrived, but she found it impossible to rest or relax, needing always to be ready in case of a crisis. Then, as the new sister arrived, the princess broke her ankle. Confined to bed, she was unable to show her round the building and had to instruct her from memory. After about a month Princess Arthur returned to light duties, but her troubles were not over. Having bought a smaller car to save petrol she injured her back trying to get into the vehicle with her broken foot. This time she had to be put in a plaster jacket and spent two months as a patient in her own nursing home, once again trying to run the business from her bed.

★★★

Meanwhile, another member of the British royal family was nursing at University College Hospital. The elegant Princess Marina of Greece had married King George V's youngest surviving son Prince George, Duke of Kent, in 1934. When she arrived in England for her wedding the *soigné* Princess Marina took the country by storm. 'Her beauty, dress sense, talents and charm dominated the newspapers.' Women wore the Marina pillbox after the princess was seen wearing a small fez-like hat with a feather quill; the particular shade of blue she wore was christened Marina blue and dominated the season, while Marina cocktails and Marina perfumes were everywhere.[3]

At the outbreak of war, the popular Duchess of Kent was Lady Superintendent-in-Chief of the St John Ambulance Brigade and Commandant of the Women's Royal Naval Service. Initially she helped make bandages, swabs and surgical splints for the British Army at Iver and Denham Cottage Hospital, which lay near the couple's country house Coppins, but she wanted to do more.

Marina contacted Sister Mary Winifred Addison, sister tutor to the Nurses' Training Centre in Oxford, with a view to training as a VAD. Miss Addison, whose father had been a member of Tyneside Council and a Magistrate, agreed to come and teach the duchess. On 20 June 1940, Marina's lady-in-waiting Lady Mary Herbert wrote a short note to Miss Addison, saying that 'Her Royal Highness would be very pleased if you would go to Buckingham Palace at 6 p.m. on Tuesday, June 25th. Would you write a line to the Duchess at Buckingham Palace to confirm the arrangement.'[4] Miss Addison duly replied, telling Marina that she would 'be most pleased to give you all the assistance I can in your study'.[5]

For the next month Miss Addison came to Buckingham Palace to teach first aid and everything else the duchess would need to know to become a VAD. Marina enjoyed the lectures and appreciated her tutor's 'infinite patience and helpfulness'.[6] Then on 23 July came the examination, which Marina dreaded. The following day, thanking Miss Addison for a thoughtful gift of flowers, Marina told her what happened:

I felt quite confident until the examiner, a Miss Powell, arrived in uniform, followed by another lady in uniform who she introduced as 'our patient' and whom ... I subsequently bandaged! Miss Powell ... asked me first of all how I would make a bed for a patient suffering from rheumatism!! I nearly fainted with horror – not having in the least expected that question! I'm afraid I lost my head completely and admitted having no idea what I should do. I even had the audacity to add that I didn't think my little book said anything about it! She looked at me as if I was a little crazy and promptly found me the passage – it was a horrible moment!! Not a very good beginning was it? ... However the other questions went off alright – temperature ... sterilizing of instruments and infectious diseases. Then I was asked how to relieve pain ... We laughed a lot afterwards – but I did not feel very satisfied with my hopeless stupidity as you can imagine! Next week I hope to start my 50 hours [training] probably at University College in London (that is to say if I pass).[7]

The duchess became a fully qualified nursing auxiliary doing regular voluntary duty two days a week. Miss J. M. Bond, the sister of Ward 16 which dealt mainly with women-air raid casualties, was informed by matron that the duchess would be working in her ward under the pseudonym of 'Nurse Kay'. Only the registrar and the senior surgeon were in on the closely guarded secret.

Mrs Jackson, who had been matron when Princess Arthur was at the CCS, was still in charge. She was 'a woman of immense charm, very efficient, extremely likeable and quite unlike the dragon-like character of the usual matron'. She escorted Princess Marina up to the ward on her first day. Nurse Kay was 'neat and smart in a plain, well-cut white coat. Not the ordinary uniform – blue coats – worn by the auxiliaries, nor the striped dress and white apron worn by student nurses,' recalled Sister Bond.[8]

Marina's training at University College Hospital lasted for three months, working when she liked – as much as her royal duties permitted – although she did not sleep or eat at the hospital. During her off-duty spells the duchess regularly travelled down to Gloucestershire in overcrowded trains to snatch a day or two with her young children Prince Edward and Princess Alexandra, who were staying at Badminton House with Queen Mary while their parents were involved in war work.

First thing every morning Marina had coffee with Mrs Jackson, with whom she became firm friends. Then the matron telephoned the ward sister to say they were on their way up. Sister Bond did not always know when the duchess would be coming on duty. One morning Marina arrived to find the sister looking exceptionally tired. She had given the staff nurse a half day off but had then been up for most of the night. Now her plan of catching up on some sleep mid-morning seemed about to be ruined. Princess Marina immediately saw the situation and begged her to go and get some sleep, which Sister Bond gratefully took as a royal command.

The duchess 'took part in all routine activities in the ward,' recalled Sister Bond. She did duty in the Casualty Clearing Station and also helped prepare patients for surgery, although the sister never recalled her assisting at any operations. 'She saw them onto the table and the removal of tubes after the operation was also part of her job.' Marina was hard working, willing and capable. Her personality, said Sister Bond, was 'charming'. She would always find something to do if she was without a specific job for a few minutes and seemed more interested in the care of the sick rather than 'in the medical aspect of the medicine itself'.[9]

Sending Miss Addison a cheque for 17s 3d for expenses incurred, Lady Mary Herbert said that the duchess 'is liking it very much. None of the patients recognise her, partly, I should say, because of the cap, which changes people very much.'[10]

University College Hospital was very vulnerable to attacks. The building's vast amount of glass gave the impression of light and space but also exposed it to great danger from bombs. Nevertheless, when air raids came neither Marina nor any of the other nurses bothered to go to the shelter, they were all too busy. The hospital was extremely short-staffed and the ward always had emergency cases. Turnover was very quick and Marina nursed many bomb victims. Later, after the secret came out, some of her colleagues remembered that 'the Duchess of Kent had to run about the wards like themselves, taking scoldings from the ward sisters and doing the hard and dirty work as well as handing round meals and arranging flowers in vases'.[11]

One day, as Marina was about to go off duty, many wounded Canadians and Australians were brought in after a servicemen's hostel received a direct hit. 'Most were badly burned and some had little time to live,' recalled Sister Bond. Marina immediately asked what she could do to help. Mrs Jackson suggested that, although medically there was little anybody could do, a royal visit to men who were far from home would cheer them up, so she told Marina to change into her outdoor clothes and visit the men as a member of the royal family. 'Tell them you came because you heard about them,' she urged. 'It'll be perfectly true.' Marina immediately changed and went down to casualty, where she remained talking to the men for more than an hour.[12]

Occasionally a visitor remarked that one of the nurses 'looks the image of the Duchess of Kent', but the news was slow to leak out. So slow, in fact, that when the Duke of Kent, the hospital's president, made an official visit, Nurse Kay was presented to him with the other nurses. The duke acknowledged his wife's polished curtsey without the flicker of an eyelid. Then he was shown round the ward, with the duchess following matron and sister like any other obscure nurse.

A patient who worked as a dressmaker's assistant finally recognised the elegant duchess from pictures in the fashion magazines and exposed the secret. The story was published in *The Times* on 16 October 1940 and greatly added to the family's popularity.

In July 1942, the duchess gave birth to a son, Prince Michael of Kent. Six weeks later the Duke of Kent was killed in a plane crash while on active service. The duchess was devastated. 'I feel so stunned – it's all so unbelievable,' she wrote to a friend, 'yet day follows day and one goes on doing, mechanically, the same things.'[13] Conscious of her royal obligations, by early November Princess Marina was once more carrying out public engagements, although she never returned to nursing.

★★★

Princess Marina's cousin had a very different experience of nursing. Princess Katherine of Greece was born on 4 May 1913, the seventh child of

King Constantine of Greece and Queen Sophie, who as crown princess had done so much good during the Greco-Turkish War. In 1934, Katherine had been a bridesmaid at Princess Marina's wedding (their fathers were brothers). Another of the bridesmaids, 8-year-old Princess Elizabeth of York, would later marry Katherine and Marina's cousin Philip.

The Greek royal family had been in and out of exile since 1917 but when war broke out in 1939, Katherine's childless brother King George II was on the throne. The 26-year-old princess, who had already done social and welfare work in Greece, joined the Red Cross voluntary nurses as a VAD, doing did the same work as other qualified nurses, including working in the operating theatre. She was popular in Greece and described by colleagues as 'open, vivacious, unaffected'.[14]

From 1940 the head of the hospital was Henry Alford Moffat (a great-nephew of Dr Livingstone), who had previously been a surgeon in the Greek Army and soon gained the respect of staff and patients. Many wounded RAF officers were sent to the hospital and the princess sometimes found herself looking after people she had known socially before the war. 'When one of the patients she had nursed back to health was later killed in action she would be so distressed we could not speak to her for days,' recalled Katherine's sister-in-law Crown Princess Frederica.[15]

One day, accompanied by her lady-in-waiting Mary Athenogenes, Katherine went to the lounge of the King George Hotel where she had arranged to meet an RAF officer for tea. He never arrived. Later the princess learnt that he had been killed in action while she was waiting for him.

In April 1941, the Germans attacked Greece and the British decided to evacuate the royal family. Crown Princess Frederica and her children Constantine and Sofia, along with the king's uncle Prince George of Greece and his wife Marie, Princesses Katherine, Aspasia (widow of King Alexander) and her daughter Alexandra (who had been helping in the hospitals) were taken by Sunderland flying boat to Crete, where they were joined by King George and his brother Crown Prince Paul. A few days later German troops entered Athens.

As Crete proved vulnerable to attack, the women were moved to Egypt and then South Africa, arriving in Cape Town on 8 July. For two months they lived in a wing of the governor-general's residence. After part of the house caught fire at the end of October 1941 they moved temporarily to the official residence of Field-Marshal Smuts, and then into a five-room bungalow belonging to a country hotel at Summerset West, on the Western Cape. The place was infested with rats, the food was abominable and the service terrible. After each meal Katherine and her companions resorted to opening tins of food and cooking it themselves.

On Christmas Eve, Katherine and Mary Athenogenes took presents to the soldiers in the hospital and on Christmas Day the royal ladies cooked their own celebratory meal. Early in 1942 they moved to Claremont, a suburb 6 miles south of Cape Town, where, on 11 May, Frederica gave birth to her daughter Irene. Katherine was a godmother and attended the christening.

Katherine then worked for six months at the military hospital in the suburb of Wynberg under the name of 'Sister Katherine', nursing and tending Greek sailors on their way through the Cape. Also working there was her cousin Princess Eugenie of Greece (daughter of Prince George and Princess Marie), who nursed under the name of 'Sister Eugenie'. She and her husband Prince Dominic Radziwill had arrived in Durban with their young daughter Tatiana in 1940. Crown Princess Frederica and her family moved to Pretoria, where Field-Marshal Smuts offered them a home. Katherine was given hospitality at Villa Pythagoras in Johannesburg.

Later the royal family moved back to Cape Town and Katherine returned to nursing. In 1942, St Dunstan's Home for the Blind opened a preliminary training centre for troops blinded in the Middle East. As their route home took them past the Cape of Good Hope the obvious place for the centre was South Africa, where they could be trained while awaiting a place on a hospital ship bound for Britain. Norman Kennedy lent them his house 'Tembani' (an African word meaning to hope and go on hoping), set in 3 acres of gardens on the side of the mountain at Wynberg, about 7 miles from Cape Town. Approached via a long, winding drive leading to the 'stoop', a sort of long verandah, the main body of the house contained the lounge, dining room and office. At one end was a two-storey wing containing the kitchen and housekeeper's quarters; the corresponding wing became matron's office and two dormitories which could sleep up to eight people. At first the number of men was small and huts were erected in the grounds for classrooms and workshops where they learnt Braille and basketwork.

Tembani House officially opened on 18 February 1942 with Miss Hester Pease as matron. Katherine was among the volunteers working as a VAD, none of whom had worked with blind people before. Wearing a dark blue uniform, white apron with a red cross and a starched veil, 'Sister Katherine' spent two-and-a-half years providing nursing care and helping men become accustomed to blindness. Some of them also had other handicaps so massage and physiotherapy were called for, but all were taught to become independent. The staff 'never fussed us,' recalled former patient Max Ash. 'They never pestered to want to take us or worry whether we could find our way around the building and the grounds.'[16]

Princess Eugenie was not a trained VAD but she came along to help. 'I used to know when she was on duty,' recalled Joan Clement, 'because I'd be at the bottom of the drive coming up and you could hear her laugh. She had a very loud laugh. She was a very good-hearted person.'[17]

As the numbers increased, an annexe was built on the tennis court for dormitories and training facilities. One room was used to teach typing, another to do basketwork and there was even a small telephone exchange which men could learn how to operate. Eventually Tembani overflowed to a wing of the neighbouring property, where the men could also use the swimming pool.

Arthur Simpson remembered the Greek princesses as 'two of the best people I ever knew'. He enjoyed their company. 'At Tembani they would serve us tea, make the beds, take us for walks or to the pictures,' he recalled many years later. 'I remember going with them and Harry Petty to the seaside and we all took off our shoes and paddled!' The royal family lived in Wynberg and Katherine and Eugenie sometimes invited men from Tembani back to their bungalow for tea or an informal dinner. Eugenie was regularly asked to speak at meetings of the Greek Red Cross and, before she went, 'she would practise on us,' Arthur Simpson recalled. 'She was the easiest person to meet of anyone I have ever met.'[18]

With the end of the war in the Far East, Tembani House closed on 30 September 1945. The following year Princess Katherine sailed for England aboard the Cunard steamer SS *Ascania*. On board she met Major Richard Brandram of the Royal Artillery. The couple became engaged three weeks after the ship docked in Liverpool and married in Athens in April 1947. Among the good wishes the princess received on her engagement was a letter from Hester Pease, who as matron had been like a mother to the VADs. She replied:

> It was so kind of you to have thought of me. I so often look back at those nice days at Tembani and all the 'boys' and how happy you all made them. When I *do* come to England with my husband, I shall let you know, as I would so much like to see you again, and also, if possible, see some of the 'boys' with you.[19]

With the permission of King George VI, Princess Katherine gave up her royal title to become Lady Katherine Brandram and retire to a quiet life in England.

Princess Eugenie, however, continued her interest in the welfare of blinded soldiers after the war. In 1949 she travelled to London to visit Sir Ian Fraser, chairman of St Dunstan's, to seek advice about the care of the 150 blind Greek ex-servicemen for whom little had been done. Sir Ian provided the best advice he could give and the princess left with a sample of the Braille machine used by St Dunstan's, as well as a quarter-hour striking watch for Greek craftsmen to copy. Eugenie later spent several hours visiting the training centre at Ovingdean, Brighton, having suggested to Sir Ian that perhaps one of the war-blinded Greek officers could be trained there.[20]

As a result of her intervention, Sir Ian wrote to the Foreign Secretary Ernest Bevin:

> I have now had a telephone conversation with Princess Eugenie ... and in view of the reports and her strong wish, ... St Dunstan's is glad to issue an invitation to Major Alexopoulos to come to us for a period of training ... he will be the guest of St Dunstan's ... and neither his accommodation, nor his training, nor his books etc will cost him anything.

It was agreed that he would arrive in mid-September for three months' probation to assess his abilities.

Major Alexopolous received six months' special training at Ovingdean before returning home in April to organise a school teaching Braille and typing to his countrymen in Greece.[21] Princess Eugenie was delighted. 'I must also thank you for all you have done for Alexopoulos – and for the opportunity you gave him of learning all there is to know about blind welfare,' the princess wrote. 'I am sure that thanks to you we shall be able to accomplish something for our blinded, who, like me, will remain deeply grateful to you and to St Dunstan's.'[22]

In April, Sir Ian Fraser wrote to the princess to inform her that Air Commodore Dacre, a past commandant of the training centre, was currently visiting Greece. 'I hope he may be able to see something of work for the blind in your country, and I am sure your people will find a talk with him helpful.'[23] Princess Eugenie of Greece died in 1989; Lady Katherine Brandram died in 2007, the last great-granddaughter of Queen Victoria.

★★★

In between her long hours at The Fife Nursing Home, Princess Arthur was often called upon in an official capacity. As the royal family's only qualified, state-registered nurse she regularly inspected many of the Casualty Clearing Stations and during King George VI's absences abroad in 1939, 1943, and 1944 served as a Counsellor of State. From 1939 she was colonel-in-chief of the Royal Army Pay Corps and later became patron of the Plaistow Maternity Hospital.

In July 1943, the princess was asked to become Patroness of the Royal British Nurses' Association. Accepting Isobel Macdonald's invitation, the princess asked her to 'kindly inform your Council that it will give me great pleasure to become Patroness of the RBNA', and she wished 'the Association every success in the future'.[24]

Despite the pilotless 'doodle bugs' which continued to drop bombs in the area the nursing home suffered very little damage, although in December 1944 the large window in the theatre was completely smashed during a near miss. Little other damage occurred and no one was injured. The home was extremely busy but none of the patients wanted to leave and there were bookings well into the future. Then a burglary occurred and Princess Arthur saw the disappearance of a clock from the hall as a bad omen. She was feeling ill and in constant pain but somehow managed to carry on the administrative work of the home.

Finally, on 8 May 1945 the war in Europe ended. Nurses, patients and domestic staff joined the princess to drink to the king's health and listen to his speech on the radio. For Princess Arthur, the jubilation was short lived. In December, her sister Maud, the Countess of Southesk, died. Princess Arthur's health now completely broke down and she took to her bed with chronic rheumatoid arthritis. In 1949, The Fife Nursing Home was sold. During her years in charge Princess Arthur was able to boast 'a Prime Minister, several actors and members of the royal family as patients'.[25]

Although she played no further part in public life, Princess Arthur kept in touch with Miss Macdonald, who in 1953 enclosed a draft of her book *Queens in Nursing History*, asking permission to dedicate it to the princess. This was granted and, said the private secretary, 'Her Royal Highness ... sends her best wishes for its success,' adding, 'the dedication note has been slightly altered to conform to Her Royal Highness's wishes.'[26] Three years later the princess wrote to congratulate Miss Macdonald on 'the decoration conferred on you in the Queen's birthday honours [the MBE]. The nurses I am sure will be very pleased about this and I feel the award is most richly deserved.'[27]

Princess Arthur of Connaught died at her London home on 26 February 1959. After the death of their patroness, Miss Macdonald wrote to the Duchess of Kent, asking whether she would consider assuming the position. The duchess reluctantly declined. Princess Marina 'has naturally given most careful consideration to this kind invitation, which Her Royal Highness has much appreciated,' replied her private secretary. 'But I am sorry to have to tell you that Her Royal Highness has reluctantly decided that it will not be possible to accept this office.' The duchess, it was explained, was already connected with a large number of organisations and has consequently felt obliged to curtail her activities. 'Her Royal Highness accordingly feels that she cannot now make further additions to her patronage list ...'[28]

Notes

1. Obituary of Princess Arthur, *The Times*, 27 February 1959.
2. Alexandra, *A Nurse's Story*, p.133.
3. Cathcart, *Alexandra*, pp.39, 37.
4. King's College London Archives, KH/NL/PP1. Lady Mary Herbert to Miss Addison, 20 June 1940.
5. King's College London Archives, KH/NL/PP1. Miss Addison to the Duchess of Kent, 21 June 1940.
6. King's College London Archives, KH/NL/PP1. The Duchess of Kent to Miss Addison, 24 July 1940.
7. King's College London Archives, KH/NL/PP1. The Duchess of Kent to Miss Addison, 24 July 1940.
8. James Wentworth Day, *HRH Princess Marina, Duchess of Kent* (Robert Hale, 1962), p.118.
9. Wentworth Day, *HRH Princess Marina*, pp.118–19.
10. King's College London Archives, KH/NL/PP1. Lady Mary Herbert to Miss Addison, 14 September 1940.
11. Arturo Beéche, *Dear Ellen* (Kensington House Books, 2012), p.76.
12. Wentworth Day, *HRH Princess Marina*, p.119.
13. Theo Aronson, *The Royal Family at War* (John Murray, 1993), p.90.
14. Obituary, *The Times*, 4 October 2007.
15. Frederica, Queen of Greece, *A Measure of Understanding* (Macmillan, 1971), p.28.
16. *St Dunstan's Review*, April 1990, p.9.
17. *St Dunstan's Review*, April 1990, p.10.
18. *St Dunstan's Review*, May 1989, p.3.
19. *St Dunstan's Review*, April 1947, p.2.
20. *St Dunstan's Review*, February 1949, p.5.
21. Blind Veterans UK archives. Sir Ian Fraser to Ernest Bevin, 25 May 1949; *St Dunstan's Review*, April 1950, p.8.
22. Blind Veterans UK archives. Memo from Sir Ian Fraser's secretary Miss Goole to L. Fawcett, Commandant of St Dunstan's, 20 March 1950, quoting Princess Eugenie's letter.
23. Blind Veterans UK archives. Sir Ian Fraser to Princess Eugenie, 4 April 1950.
24. King's College London Archives, RBNA8/RL6. Princess Arthur to Miss Isobel Macdonald, 29 July 1943.
25. Robert Golden, *Relatively Royal* (Resvall Royal Books, 2000), p.64.
26. King's College London Archives, RBNA8/RL11. J Blunden to Miss Macdonald, 12 October 1953.
27. King's College London Archives, RBNA8/RL12. Princess Arthur to Miss Macdonald, 1 June 1956.
28. King's College London Archives, RBNA8/RL13. The Duchess of Kent's Private Secretary to Miss Macdonald, 2 August 1960

13

The Hospital of the Queen's Heart

By 1942, Princess Ileana of Romania was living in Austria amid wartime fuel restrictions, rationing and the mobilisation of men. Although she had no formal nursing qualifications, the princess already had wide experience of tending the sick in their homes. Concerned for her Romanian countrymen who had been wounded while fighting for Germany, she now took another short intensive nursing course and studied textbooks with a view to opening her own hospital.

Ileana's interest in nursing began when she helped her mother Queen Marie during the First World War. In 1925, while attending the prestigious Heathfield School in Ascot, Ileana joined the Girl Guides. Part of the training included home nursing and first aid. She not only absorbed everything but was eager to know more. The following year her father King Ferdinand died and (Crown Prince Carol having renounced his rights) was succeeded by his young grandson Michael, Ileana's nephew. Ileana returned home and continued her nursing training with the Romanian Red Cross in between her schooling, which now took place in the palace with a tutor. During the next few years she became more involved with the Red Cross and helped to establish the Girl Guides in Romania.

In 1931, she married Archduke Anton of Austria-Tuscany, a great-nephew of Emperor Franz Joseph. Three years later they bought Sonnberg Castle near Hollabrunn, 35 miles from Vienna and just a short drive from the Czech border. Ileana described it perfectly: 'In the centre there is a well; around the well stands the castle; around the castle is an island; around the island is a moat; around the moat is a park; and around the park runs a river.'[1] With its whitewashed walls, stone staircases and antique furniture the 400-year-old castle was a perfect family home.

By now Ileana was the mother of four children – Stefan, Maria-Ileana ('Minola'), Alexandra ('Sandi') and Dominic ('Niki'). Together with the castle nurse she started a small dispensary which opened once a week in Sonnberg village, just outside the castle walls. When treatment had to be followed up in people's homes Ileana made this her responsibility and if a trained nurse was required the princess took on that duty for as long as necessary. In the winter she started a canteen for thirty poor schoolchildren, hiring an old woman from the village to do the cooking.

Then in 1938 came the Anschluss. As German troops annexed Austria, fifty armed soldiers from the SA (the Stormtroopers) were billeted in the castle. Although they left after a week, searches now became a regular occurrence. The following year the first of thirteen medical detachments was billeted at Sonnberg and in March the Germans invaded Czechoslovakia. It was now clear that a European war was likely. Anton was conscripted, but in order to achieve his ambition of serving in the Luftwaffe he first had to undergo six months of basic training as a private soldier. The couple also had to prove that for four generations their ancestors were Christians. Ileana found it amusing to be obliged to write to the royal archives at Windsor asking for proof that her great-grandmother Queen Victoria had been baptised in a Christian church.

In October 1939, Ileana gave birth to her fifth child Maria Magdalena ('Magi'). Soon afterwards she decided to finish the Red Cross training she had started in England and Romania. The Austrian Red Cross was incorporated into the German Red Cross in March 1938. The president was her mother's cousin Charles Edward, Duke of Saxe-Coburg, a grandson of Queen Victoria, but by now his position was purely nominal. From 29 November 1938, the German Red Cross lost its independence, becoming directly responsible to the German government. It was absorbed into the Nazi Party and run on National Socialist principles. Joining the Red Cross would therefore mean swearing loyalty to Hitler, which Ileana felt unable to do, so she never received a nursing certificate. However, the extra training added a great deal to her knowledge of theory and practice and was to prove of enormous value both in Austria and Romania.

Romania's military dictator Marshal Ion Antonescu had allied the country with Nazi Germany. After the birth of her last child Elizabeth ('Herzi') on 15 January 1942, Ileana began tracking down and visiting wounded Romanians in the Vienna hospitals. She distributed food and other necessities and wrote letters for those unable to do so. That summer she decided to expand this work.

With help from the military attaché in Berlin, approval was obtained from both Bucharest and the German authorities for a thirty-bed hospital in five rooms of Sonnberg Castle. This helped wounded Romanian soldiers stranded in a foreign country waiting for operations and prevented troops being unexpectedly billeted at the castle. A military bureau was arranged at the Vienna consulate under Dr Gligore to keep the records and reports of the wounded, and young people from the Romanian Students' Club ran errands, made translations, wrote letters and generally helped in the Vienna hospitals. During the spring and summer of 1943, Ileana divided her time between Sonnberg and Vienna, running Sonnberg hospital with the help of an orderly.

Some men were awaiting painful plastic surgery on badly wounded faces, others were blinded or amputees. Ileana provided beds and equipment, while bedding, bandages and drugs were sent by the army. There was no resident nurse or doctor but the doctor from Hollabrunn called regularly and came over in an emergency. Ileana's servants willingly did the cleaning but she hired extra women to do the hospital's laundry, and all able-bodied men made their own beds and took care of themselves, some even helping to cook or lay the table. The men had to keep their (more appetising) army rations separate, as food shortages were a problem, but soon suet, ham, bacon, sugar, cheese and other foodstuffs unavailable in Austria arrived from Romanian friends. When the washerwomen went on strike demanding extra rations (which was against the law) Ileana summoned her staff to help her finish the job – by hand.

By far the greatest number of men suffered from frostbite, after lying unattended on battlefields or in improvised dressing stations, or being transported in unheated trains from the Russian front. Ileana started occupational therapy courses to exercise weak limbs or frozen fingers. She felt a great sense of triumph when a soldier learned to walk again, to lift a sandbag with a previously limp arm, or use a knife and fork with fingers saved after the others had dropped off from frostbite. She also bathed and fed those who were incapable, changed bandages and dispensed drugs. Having learned massage from a Swedish friend some years back she was able to do this as well.

In September 1943, Ileana took her children to Romania, leaving the three eldest behind with friends so that they could attend day schools in Brasov. She brought back a letter from Antonescu, naming her as 'the delegate of the country to visit all hospitals in Germany and Austria, where Romanian wounded soldiers were nursed'. Moreover, the Romanian High General Staff named Princess Ileana 'the president of the delegation for the co-ordination of the works of the Romanian Red Cross for entire Germany, including the Protectorate and the Polish Government, for nursing Romanian wounded soldiers'.[2] A resident doctor and nurse were now installed at Sonnberg. Meanwhile, Ileana made many trips to seek out wounded Romanians, travelling with hand luggage that could be easily managed if she was caught in a bombing raid.

At Christmas, trees were set up in the hospital and packages from relatives in Romania (often brought back by Ileana on one of her many trips) were distributed, together with the parcels made up by her children. The able bodied were also invited to share Ileana's large tree in the castle. There were carols and presents, Ileana wore her mother's sapphire and diamond diadem and everyone put on their best clothes. This was Ileana's last Christmas in Austria.

★★★

The death of her mother in 1938 had made Ileana long more and more for her native land. As 1944 dawned she yearned to be where adoring Romanians greeted her as a princess, rather than in Austria where there were places she was forbidden to go. Above all she disliked the Nazi doctrine. Romanian girls could petition to keep their citizenship if they married foreigners and Ileana had availed herself of this privilege when she married Anton.

From her mother, Ileana had inherited the Castle of Bran on a rocky promontory above a narrow mountain village in the Transylvanian Alps, on the former frontier between Romania and Austria-Hungary. Built in the twelfth century by the Teutonic knights it had been restored as a summer residence by Queen Marie after the First World War. Conditions in the castle were fairly basic; although there was electricity and plumbing there was no heating, the water froze in winter and the castle was habitable for only four months of the year.

In March, Ileana took Niki, Magi and Herzi to Bran with Gretl, the former maid from Sonnberg who was now the children's nurse, and left them all at the medieval custom house. This was two single-storey houses, with thick walls, low ceilings and whitewashed interiors, joined together by a large passage which served as a dining room. Ileana intended to return to Austria, but in March 1944 the Germans occupied Hungary, making travel between Sonnberg and Bran almost impossible. The Russians were entering Moldova, refugees crowded into southern Romania and all civilian journeys through Hungary were forbidden when the Hungarian border closed. Ileana, who had as usual brought only hand luggage, was stranded at Bran.

Ileana turned over the administration of Sonnberg to Dr Gligore and made arrangements for her other work there to continue. She then went into Brasov and volunteered her services at the railway station's Red Cross canteen. The early shift began at eight o'clock in the morning – Ileana and her colleagues served bread, smoked ham, bacon, apples, cheese, tea and, in needy cases, rum to the troops and refugees passing through. Milk was provided for the children. One day Ileana helped the young duty doctor to deliver a baby girl to one of the refugees and then acted as godmother at the hastily organised christening. When time permitted between trains she went to the rest house and bathed the children, using a portable bathtub donated by a local factory worker. When they were short of volunteers she brought Stefan, Minola and Sandi to help after school.

One day an old friend, General Tătăranu, recognised the princess at Brasov station and asked her to organise a dispensary there, working with the head of the military hospital in Brasov. Ileana now spent three mornings a week at the military hospital updating her previous courses of nursing, four mornings at the station canteen, and afternoons helping with the organisation of the Red Cross hospital. Sometimes in the evenings she returned to help at the railway station. Her four months at the Red Cross hospital were an invaluable experience and taught her a lot about the administration of a hospital in wartime.

Air raids were a frequent occurrence. At Easter, Ileana put on Romanian national dress and took eggs and little gifts to the bedridden in the hospital. As she crossed the courtyard a bomb fell nearby, and she just had time to race to a trench before a second explosion occurred. In the aftermath of the bombing Ileana changed quickly into her Red Cross uniform and went to the military hospital where all hands were needed. Confusion reigned everywhere as the wounded from neighbouring villages were brought in, and she later recalled 'the wailing cries, the deep, anguished groans, and the horrible sights where it was impossible to distinguish man from woman, or the living from the dead …' Ileana had a deep-seated horror of blood, and when blood from a small wound in a man's chest 'spurted out and hit me in a warm, sticky stream on my neck, and gushed down my chest' she felt her knees start to give way.[3] The cries of a nearby child helped her to recover.

In May she was able to return briefly to Sonnberg but realised now that she was badly needed in Romania. She was fortunate to obtain permission to return to Bran, this time by train. Ileana still saw her stay in Romania as temporary, she had intended to travel regularly between Sonnberg and Bran but after May 1944 wartime conditions made this impossible and Ileana was forced into a decision.

★★★

The new Red Cross Hospital at Brasov (officially number ZI 161) was opened on 10 May 1944 with a service of blessing. It was established in a high school belonging to the church and came under orders of the army, who provided doctors, orderlies and all the staff except the nurses. These were provided by the Red Cross, who also donated 350 beds, linen and general equipment, while medical supplies came from both sources. Ileana found the head doctor, Dr Dogariu, easy to work with. The head nurse was Mrs Simone Cantacuzino Pascanu, experienced in nursing incurable diseases; her sister Mrs Nadeje Soutzo came from the field units to be her assistant. Yet Ileana was still a member of the royal family and when officials visited she was treated according to her rank.

On 21 May, 200 wounded arrived from the front. An officer took and filed their papers, and their clothes and personal possessions were marked and numbered. After this they were washed, shaved and deloused in the large shower room. Most had to be washed by the nurses, their wounds protected with anything waterproof that could be found. As the men continued to file in, Ileana's cap became soggy from the shower but she found it satisfying to send them off to the dispensary clean and robed, ready for bandaging and treatment, then to bed where they were fed. Ileana learnt through urgency and necessity, proving a thorough and efficient worker. At first she worked in the wards, fetching basins and bedpans with an aching back and sore feet from walking many miles a day, but she had yet to overcome her horror of blood at operations.

The bombardments continued but there was no really safe bomb shelter. When the alarm sounded those who could not be moved were placed together and the staff took turns to sit with them while the men told stories and jokes to while away the terrifying hours. The hospital was ordered to prepare an annexe in an isolated place where some of the more serious cases could be moved for convalescence, but all the large buildings had been requisitioned and nobody would surrender any of the few available places.

Ileana asked the mayor of Bran to allow the Red Cross to use the village hospital, so that they could evacuate soldiers from the danger of the bombing raids in Brasov. His response was a courteous refusal. A priest then offered a schoolhouse belonging to the church of Bran Poarta, situated against the backdrop of the Carpathian Mountains just outside Bran. The little one-storey whitewashed building could take forty beds, and Ileana immediately mustered some help to clean the place. They asked the hospital for any spare beds and mattresses, friends donated cooking utensils, and Noelle, the daughter of a former Court physician, took over the new hospital's organisation. The place was primitive; there was no running water and no facilities for surgery. They had no ambulances for the 50-mile round trip between Brasov and Bran so King Michael's mother, Helen, allowed her private ambulance to transport some of the men to their new quarters. The nurses carried the stretchers themselves, orderlies only arrived after the wounded men had been carried in.

Soon afterwards the railway station shelter suffered three direct hits. Many people were seriously injured and the doctor was killed. Ileana and Nadeje

Soutzo treated the casualties as best they could. Some were put into Ileana's car (complete with royal flag) and driven to the military hospital. Realising how much more was really needed, Ileana decided to build her own hospital. She turned to General Nicolae Tătăranu for help.

The Hospital of the Queen's Heart (Spitalul Inima Reginei) was built on a piece of Ileana's land in Bran and reached from the main road by crossing the river on a bridge which ended in the building's courtyard. It owed its name to the fact that Ileana's mother's heart had been removed from its resting place in Balcic in 1940 when that area was given to Bulgaria and placed in the small wooden church at Bran. (Later she had a special chapel for it carved into the rock on a hill behind the church.) Progress was helped by donations of two almost new wooden barrack buildings from the Rogifer iron factory in Tohan, as well as equipment, instruments for the operating theatre and even glasses and medicine bottles from other local organisations. Pots and pans were purchased at half the factory price. Cotton for sheets was given by the owner of a cotton mill, and these were sewn by Ileana's Viennese friend Ilse Koller, who had come with her from Sonnberg to help with the children.

The blessing of the unfinished building took place on 22 July. The main entrance was in the left wing, with the office, dispensary and operating theatre. In the middle block were six wards with white walls and bright orange curtains, with ten beds in each and bathrooms nearby. The right wing housed the kitchen, washhouse, laundry, a sitting room for the nurses and the staff dining room. Later the complex was enlarged to provide a pharmacy, laboratory, and X-ray and physiotherapy facilities.

Ileana wanted the nurses to have grey cotton uniforms, or even a quiet blue, but there was no such material available. All she could obtain was brick red teamed with white coifs for the graduate nurses, and royal blue with Dutch-style caps for the six student nurses. After two years' service the hospital's badge held the turnover collar in place. The ward maids wore yellow. Yet before the building was even completed the situation in Romania changed dramatically.

On 23 August 1944, in a dramatic *coup d'état*, King Michael turned Romania over to the Allies. An armistice was signed with the United States, Britain and the Soviet Union, who guaranteed Romania's independence. A National Coalition Government was established and Antonescu was arrested. The Germans were given time to leave peacefully but fighting broke out between the Germans and Russians in Brasov and all Germans were arrested. Anton (who had returned to Bran in July after Hitler ordered that members of ruling or former ruling families must surrender their commissions), Ileana's children, Ilse Koller and Gretl were 'arrested' and confined to the castle. Married to an Austrian, Ileana was technically now an enemy in her own country and with the Russians demanding her internment she was in a dangerous position.

As September dawned, the schoolhouse at Bran Poarta had to be evacuated ready for the children's return. On 8 September the first forty wounded were admitted to the Hospital of the Queen's Heart just as Russian troops passed through Bran, taking whatever they wanted at gunpoint from rich and poor alike. It was dangerous to go to Bran Poarta and no woman was safe, but luckily the Russians never crossed the bridge to the hospital.

Ileana maintained contact with the main hospital in Brasov by telephone, but as the summer helpers returned to Bucharest her own hospital was left almost without nurses, even Noelle had gone. Brasov provided one nurse for night duty and a surgeon who visited regularly; by day there was Princess Ileana, Anna (the daughter of the hospital cook), another girl who came from the village every morning, plus a regular student doctor whom Ileana called 'Max' in her memoirs to protect his identity. With only ten critical cases Ileana managed with these two untrained, inexperienced assistants and the army doctors who came on a weekly rotation from the hospital at Brasov. The more able-bodied men helped where they could. Soon people from the village came to the hospital for treatment as well.

When Max was ill Ileana had to assist the visiting surgeon at an amputation but still felt faint and nauseous at the sight of blood. She now concentrated on the operating theatre, slowly overcoming her abhorrence until she was finally able to watch and understand what was being done. 'I read textbooks and made drawings,' she recalled, 'and at last I became a proficient assistant, able to do surgery myself in later emergencies – but this only came about slowly and with the development of the hospital.'[4]

Then Ileana received an urgent telephone call – the Russians had decided to take over Brasov hospital. With only three hours to evacuate 350 patients and all the equipment Ileana had to work quickly. Whatever was left would fall to the Russians. A Hungarian Catholic convent agreed to take the patients and, with time running out, Ileana risked driving to Brasov in her own car to help with the evacuation. The wounded were carried in their beds to the convent garden with all the equipment piled around them. They only had one old ambulance and a truck, but fortunately troops and workers from the local factories came to their aid.

Ileana was now increasingly bound to her hospital at Bran. Simone and Nadeje returned to Bucharest and Dr Dragomir, second surgeon of the Brasov hospital, was assigned as resident doctor at Bran. He and Ileana often spent their afternoons climbing steep hills to treat patients in remote mountain homes. In one isolated village they found a woman bleeding to death after suffering a miscarriage. Working with Ileana's torch, a mirror and the few instruments at their disposal, they gave her some injections and then arranged for her to be admitted to the civilian hospital in Bran. After this experience the princess insisted that they must always have emergency kits ready with instruments and dressings. She also realised that they needed a women's ward in their hospital. Across the river were some cottages built by Queen Marie for summer guests, of which two were empty, and so Ileana installed a temporary children's annexe under the management of Lorie, a trained nurse from the neighbouring village. The princess then began collecting supplies so that in spring she could open a women's ward in the other cottage.

In November when the castle became too cold the family moved to the old custom house at the foot of the hill. Besides the family and their staff, room had to be found for the doctor, the medical student Max and Lorie. Conditions were crowded but they celebrated Christmas as usual and put a tree in the hospital for the men.

★★★

On 6 March 1945, the coalition government was ousted and the Russians forced King Michael to appoint a Communist regime under Petru Groza. All citizens of German origin (men aged 17–45 and women aged 18–30) were to be deported to Germany. Ileana now joined the 'underground', hiding fugitives in the castle until they could be sent off with false papers. This was extremely dangerous, especially when one of the fugitives was found to have a tumour and surgery proved necessary. Ileana and Anton had to smuggle a friendly visiting surgeon, plus operating equipment, into the castle so that the tumour could be removed. She then had to wash the soiled linen, clear away the smell of ether, smuggle the equipment back into the hospital and send the tumour for examination under the name of a legitimate patient, all without being caught. The tumour proved benign.

The Russians did not fraternise with the Romanians and if they wanted something they had no hesitation in taking it. This included cars, which were often stopped along the road and commandeered by Russian soldiers. Nobody protested – they felt fortunate to get away with their lives. Sometimes, on her frequent journeys to Brasov or Bucharest, Ileana was stopped at gunpoint and forced to give a lift to a Russian soldier, often in the opposite direction to where she was heading.

Among the patients in Ileana's hospital were two Russian soldiers hurt in an accident on a perilous mountain road. When they were brought in the officer summoned Ileana and her team to treat them immediately. He then toyed menacingly with his gun while Ileana washed the dirt from the men's faces and cut away their uniforms so that the doctors could see their injuries.

She was left in no doubt as to what would happen if they failed in their task. One of the men was patched up and able to leave fairly quickly but the other had a fractured hip. A Russian-speaking Bessarabian nurse acted as interpreter between the doctors and the officer, who decided that the hip should be set in the Bran hospital. When the man could be moved he would be taken to the Russian hospital in Brasov.

Ileana now 'looked out for someone in power who would protect her and her much loved hospital'.[5] Her choice fell on Emil Bodnaras, described as 'Moscow's most powerful agent in Roumania,'[6] who later became Secretary General of the Presidency. He had come to Bran on a visit of inspection in February 1945 and was so impressed both by the hospital and by Ileana's vision for it that he promised to help when he came to power. Thus began Ileana's connection with the Ministry of Health, which she claimed opened many doors, but which also earned her a nickname as one of the king's 'red aunts' (the other was her sister Elisabeta, who was 'hobnobbing' with the Communists).[7] Ileana soon took up Bodnaras's offer of help.

Ileana travelled to Bucharest to meet Nicolas Malexa, whose men had constructed the hospital. He said he would be happy to have a new women and children's wing built and gave Ileana a donation so that she could buy what was most urgently needed. She then went to the Ministry of Health, who gave her many necessary supplies free of charge, and then to one of the biggest medical supply stores whose owner, an old acquaintance, donated instruments for abdominal surgery and electrotherapy, adding some items not available on the open market. Having obtained all this for nothing, Ileana spent Malexa's money on thick material to make winter gowns for the patients, plus a quartz lamp, a short-wave diathermy set and some rare instruments for kidney surgery. Most shops 'volunteered a contribution of some kind,' she said.[8]

At the Malexa factory, Ileana discovered a second unused barracks. She decided to use this for the maternity and children's wards and utilise one of the old ones given by General Tătăranu as a storeroom. In the end the architect's plans proved too grand and Ileana decided that the barracks they already had at the factory would suffice if divided more efficiently inside.

The new women and children's wing was blessed on 29 October 1945, Queen Marie's birthday, and was ready for use by the following spring. Eventually it had a maternity ward complete with delivery room, nursery and a small children's ward.

The ZI 161 hospital in Brasov was now disbanded and Ileana's hospital came under the authority of the military hospital sponsored by the Ministry of War, which made it easier to obtain both doctors and supplies. Dr Dragomir's military service had ended and he wanted to return to Jassy, so Ileana requested that the experienced Dr Radu Puscariu be sent from the German front to replace him. He gave her more instruction in medical subjects, including anatomy, and trained her to assist the surgeon during operations. Badillo, a young medical student, took the place of Max, who returned to his studies, and another medical student also arrived. Four more nurses were assigned to Bran by the Ministry of War.

The staff now comprised Dr Puscariu and two students, the intern Dr Lazarescu and his wife, who helped him run the laboratory, the apothecary Dr Herman, the head nurse, the night nurse, plus six other nurses, the administrator and his assistant, the head of the linen room and laundry, two orderlies, four servant girls and a gardener. Some of these people were paid by the army or the Ministry of Health; others received salaries from donations given by the patients or from Ileana's own pocket. Equipment was often in short supply. Brushes and thermometers soon became impossible to obtain, so that a single thermometer had to suffice for a whole ward, and they had to make their own liquid soap in the sterilising room. They had discussion groups, lectures, a glee club, sports club, literary club and various other societies for the doctors and nurses.

Ileana arrived at the hospital at seven o'clock every morning, returning home for breakfast and to walk the younger children to school. By nine she was back at the hospital doing the rounds with Dr Puscariu before taking the outpatients' clinic and assisting at operations until one o'clock. After lunch and a short rest she spent the afternoon with her family before going back on duty until seven. She was usually in bed by nine. If there was an emergency she spent all day, and a good part of the night, at the hospital and sometimes arrived unexpectedly for inspections.

On summer afternoons Ileana, her family and the staff congregated around the swimming pool near the Chapel of the Queen's Heart to swim in the icy mountain water and lie in the warm sunshine to relieve the tensions of the working day. As its reputation spread, patients came from far beyond the thirteen villages of the official district. Young women were recruited to help as maids in the hospital and Ileana organised a crèche in the charge of a student nurse so that they could leave their children safely. Ileana tried, with some success, to interest her own children in the hospital's work; one summer, Minola and Sandi ran the children's ward under Gretl's supervision while the regular nurse was on holiday.

★★★

In 1946 a minor typhoid epidemic broke out in Bran. Nearly all the hospital staff contracted it, leaving only Ileana and two duty nurses able to work. Frau

Koller and Gretl helped out, the military hospital sent a doctor and aid also came from the American and Swedish Red Cross associations. Nevertheless, one day Ileana had to help deliver a baby by Caesarean section. As the situation became increaisngly grave Ileana closed the hospital for a month and refused to take new patients until the cause of the epidemic was established. The water in the well and the river was tested, as was the food; the toilets and cesspools were disinfected and the patients were given tests to establish whether any of them was a carrier. Nothing was found and the hospital reopened.

An even worse outbreak occurred in the summer and this time Ileana's son Dominic went down with it. His illness encouraged the local people to be inoculated, on the basis that if the princess's son could catch it nobody was safe. The Ministry of Health put Ileana in charge of administration of the local civilian hospital and subsidised it as a contagious disease annexe under Dr Lazarescu and his wife.

Meanwhile, Ileana and one of the doctors set out to inspect houses in the adjacent villages. Some were so isolated that it was only possible to drive part of the way on the rough, ancient mountain trails and they carried their equipment the rest of the way to the tiny cottages. Sometimes the only method of reaching them was on horseback. Anyone infected was brought back to the hospital, while those uninfected were instructed how to protect themselves against contagion. Ileana carried a DDT spray to disinfect any houses where there was, or had been, an outbreak of typhoid. Finally, she appealed to the Ministry of Health, who sent a high-ranking official on an inspection tour. The response was immediate. The Hospital of the Queen's Heart became the authorised head of a regional organisation in the district's fight against the epidemic. They were empowered to draft doctors, midwives and district nurses throughout the thirteen villages in their area, who then came to Ileana for supplies of serum and DDT so that they could inspect, inoculate, instruct, nurse and disinfect. As diphtheria, scarlet fever and typhus appeared that winter even the buses running between the isolated mountain villages had their passengers and interiors sprayed with DDT.

As the Communist regime tightened its grip everyone feared the sudden knock on the door. They never knew when yet another band of Russian soldiers or the NKVD (Communist secret police) would come to arrest someone in the village on a trumped up charge of supposed anti-Communist activities, or even no reason at all. Some were never seen again. One slack afternoon at the hospital Dan Tomascu, tutor to Ileana's son Stefan, dashed inside frightened and breathless, gasping that the police were after him, they had been knocking at his front door as he ran out the back way, and he begged Ileana to hide him. With no time to get him to the castle, where there were plenty of concealed places, Ileana turned to Dr Puscariu and suggested they perform an immediate operation for an internal obstruction. They hurried to the operating theatre and scrubbed up, followed by Sister Heidi, who quickly began sterilising instruments. Badillo donned a gown and grabbed the ether, while Dan undressed and got onto the operating table. Badillo put the ether cone over Dan's face and he went to sleep. Dr Puscariu needed an effect that would produce plenty of blood but minimum upset to the patient, so he decided just to cut through the skin, which he thought should look impressive enough and could be sewn up nicely. He had hardly begun when the police arrived and were met in the waiting room by Dr Lazarescu. Refusing to accept his assurances that the wanted man was not in the building, they insisted on searching the hospital. With no choice now, Dr Puscariu drove his scalpel in deeper and pulled out the patient's intestines. At that moment the door flew open and three policemen appeared. Ileana indignantly ordered them out. 'There is an operation in progress! Do you want to kill the patient?' she yelled.[9] The policemen glared in horrified fascination at the sight before them, then almost apologetically withdrew. None of them thought to look at the face under the ether cone. As soon as they had left Dr Puscariu stuffed Dan's intestine's back inside and, with a sigh of relief, sewed him up. Ileana kept him hidden in a little private room until he was well enough to escape from Bran and go into hiding.

Soon Ileana was convinced that she was being watched. The Communists were waiting for a mistake – any excuse to imprison everyone and take the hospital from her. Ileana trusted her staff implicitly but the smallest mistake would bring the might of the regime down and could cost them their freedom, even their lives. She rigorously counted the drugs, sheets and provisions; she checked the account books carefully and from now on made all the entries herself.

On top of this, Ileana was suffering from crippling back pains caused by lifting heavy bodies, pushing cars and shovelling snow in the harsh winters, but she continued working at the hospital and distributing food and clothing to families of political prisoners for the 'underground', despite the constant risk of discovery. Ileana understood the consequences. 'I carried with me a poison,' she wrote, 'and I saw to it that I had enough for the children in case it should be decided that they were to be taken from me and sent to Russia.'[10]

Ileana also began making plans to start a school of nursing. Some visiting Americans had passed on messages to friends in the USA and they sent some badly needed textbooks. She translated the texts and read them to the nurses, then adapted the charts and diagrams for use in the hospital. Many generous Americans also sent gifts to the hospital. This was just as well, because after Ileana fought and lost a battle to keep the Red Cross of Romania as part of the International Red Cross, many of the foreign relief organisations were forced to withdraw from the country.

★★★

The beginning of 1947 brought drastic financial changes. On 1 January Captain Boeriu was appointed administrative director of the hospital, charged with checking the activities of the staff and co-ordinating the hospital supplies with those of the castle. All statements now had to be verified by Boeriu. Keeping pace with inflation was almost impossible; though they raised the hospital fees it became more and more difficult to make ends meet. Official sources provided food and hospital supplies and more food came from Ileana's farm near Brasov. The American and Swedish Red Cross associations sent further materials for the hospital but Ileana was sometimes forced to sell one of her jewels in order to pay the staff. Lack of money led to petty thieving but the goods stolen were things not always available on the open market. The situation was becoming dangerous.

In early summer the Ministry of Health unexpectedly gave Ileana a large grant of money to build the children's ward and the day nursery which she had so long wanted. She was advised to spend the money quickly and immediately foresaw that something bad was about to happen. She obtained the necessary permits to purchase building materials and then went out and searched for the things herself. By August the plans had been approved and a large pile of bricks, lumber, cement, glass and other necessary things had been assembled ready for use. Then the blow fell.

On 15 August the Communist government devalued the currency. All the now worthless paper money had to be deposited with state representatives in Bran, in exchange for which everyone received a specified small amount of new currency irrespective of the sum they had surrendered. Only gold could be used to purchase more of the new money. This was followed by a heavy new tax which had to be paid in goods.

The Hospital of the Queen's Heart had to surrender its funds to the state. In return, as an institution, it received nothing. The hospital, with its 120 beds, military section, civilian section, maternity wing and a children's ward, plus the annexe for infectious diseases, was penniless. Ileana had no money with which to pay the staff and even less hope of being able to do so in the future. She told them they would be housed and fed but would have to work for nothing. Not one of the staff elected to leave and not one of them claimed back pay when Ileana again received government funds.

Christmas came, they decked the wards with pine and fir branches, and patients and staff decorated the tree with paper chains, ribbon, and gilded apples and nuts on string. Candles, which had been carefully hoarded, sat on the branches waiting to be lit.

On Christmas Eve, Ileana exchanged her familiar nurse's uniform for a silver evening gown with a small train. Then she put on her diamond bracelets, diamond and ruby earrings, and her grandmother's ropes of pearls with their huge diamond cross. On her head she wore Queen Marie's beautiful sapphire and diamond diadem. Then the whole family walked down the snow-covered village street to the hospital.

The party was already in full swing. Sister Lorie's little girl was dressed as a tiny Father Christmas, other little children were angels in white nightgowns with paper wings. After a reading of the Nativity story, gifts were distributed and carols were sung by the glee club under the direction of Dr Puscariu. Ileana and her children moved along the wards of the bedridden patients, whose eyes sparkled when they saw her dressed once more as a princess. Ileana had collected presents of clothing for the staff, while each patient was given an icon, prayer book and sewing kit (donated by the American Junior Red Cross). In return she was presented with a huge bouquet of freesias. Afterwards they had a feast of cakes, *cozonac* (the traditional sweet bread) and wine. The party ended with more carols and dancing to an accordion and fiddle played by two of the soldiers.

On 30 December came the shock radio announcement of King Michael's abdication, forced upon him by the Communist regime. In Bucharest red flags fluttered everywhere and posters proclaimed insults against the royal family.

A few days later the Ministry of Interior sent Ileana 'a curt order to leave the country within three days. ... this was backed up by an equally curt pencilled note from Bodnaras, her close "friend", that she must comply with police orders that he could not see her'.[11] Ileana's properties and land were confiscated, the household was cut off from the hospital and the family portraits which had adorned the wards were replaced by pictures of Stalin.

Ileana gathered the staff in the hospital's dining room and gave her last speech, 'choked by tears', before saying goodbye to all the patients in the wards. 'I gave one last look into the operating room, which seemed in its gleaming whiteness to stand for all the love and service I had given to the hospital,' she recalled.[12] Then, after a final prayer, Ileana said a tearful goodbye to her co-workers and friends. Bran castle was sealed, Ileana's house was placed under guard, doubled by the addition of Communists, and nobody was allowed to enter or leave the grounds. Hurriedly the family began to pack. They were only allowed to take personal belongings – Ileana's American nursing textbooks, clothes, linen, silver for eight people and family jewels not acquired in recent years. Artworks had to be left – they were now the property of the people. A Control Commission ensured that these rules were observed.

Ileana and her family left Bran on 7 January en route for Switzerland. The hospital staff and many of the patients came out to see them depart. In her memoirs, Ileana justified her sometimes controversial conduct:

I was concerned most often with the sick and dying, and they have no political colour, race or faith to distinguish them in a hospital ward. My first concern was to help them, and not to let personal feelings or political opinions overshadow the service I was there to perform. Therefore I made it my business to work with all authorities as long as this did not conflict with my religious convictions.[13]

Princess Ileana settled in America, bringing with her a metal box filled with Romanian soil. She later became a nun. In the early 1950s her daughter Sandi gave up college to attend New England Baptist Nursing School and later worked as a nurse in Austria.

In September 1990, after the overthrow of the dictator Nicolae Ceauşescu, Ileana made one final visit to Romania accompanied by her daughter Sandi and by King Michael's daughters Margarita and Sophie. In Bran 2,000 people turned out to greet her. It was an emotional moment, 'seeing old friends and remembering the hospital she had created and struggled so hard to protect'.[14] Mother Alexandra, Princess Ileana of Romania, died on 21 January 1991.

Notes

1. Ileana, Princess of Romania, *I Live Again* (Victor Gollancz, 1952), p.36.
2. Daniel Tiberiu Apostol, Dr Narcis Dorin Ion & Nicoleta Petcu, *Bran Castle: Museum and Collections* (Bran National Museum, 2008), p.57.
3. Ileana, *I Live Again*, p.137.
4. Ileana, *I Live Again*, p.190.
5. David Horbury, 'The Red Aunts', in *Royalty Digest*, Vol. 8, No. 10 (1999).
6. Ivor Porter, *Michael of Romania* (Sutton Publishing, 2005), p.152.
7. Porter, *Michael*, p.152; Horbury, 'The Red Aunts'.
8. Ileana, *I Live Again*, p.209.
9. Ileana, *The Hospital of the Queen's Heart*, pp.153–4.
10. Ileana, *I Live Again*, p.301.
11. Foreign Office Report, London, 8 January 1948. Quoted in Horbury, 'The Red Aunts'.
12. Ileana, *I Live Again*, p.303.
13. Ileana, *I Live Again*, p.309.
14. Horbury, 'The Red Aunts'.

Post-war Princesses

Although since 1945 there have been no major wars, it has not stopped queens and princesses from enrolling in nursing courses to work in the wards. Princess Alexandra of Kent had long been interested in nursing – her mother Princess Marina nursed during the war and Alexandra was delighted to receive a Red Cross nurse's uniform for her sixth birthday. When her little brother Prince Michael was vaccinated Alexandra insisted on having her dolls immunised as well. The princess, recalled her headmistress at Heathfield School, 'adored helping others'.[1]

In October 1953, Alexandra went to Paris to attend finishing school. She stayed with the head of the descendants of the French royal family, Henri, Count of Paris, at his fifteen-roomed home at Louveciennes near Versailles, the Manoir du Coeur Volant. (Henri's sister Françoise had been the second wife of Princess Marina's uncle, Prince Christopher of Greece). The Count and Countess of Paris had a large family, so Alexandra lived with the younger children and their governess in a pink-washed cottage in the grounds called *Blanche Neige* (Snow White). For the next six months she and the count's daughter Princess Anne, two years her senior, attended the select Mademoiselle Anita's in the Rue de l'Amiral-d'Estaing, learning cooking, dressmaking, current events and appreciation of the arts. She also polished her French.

It was not the finishing school that impressed Alexandra though. Anne's 21-year-old sister Isabelle had trained at the Hôpital Peupliers, a hospital and nurses' training school for the French Red Cross. Part of her apprenticeship was served as a district nurse in the workers' flats at Ivry, sometimes also acting as a home help, or cooking a decent meal for a large, motherless family. Now she was working in casualty at a hospital near the Porte d'Italie in preparation for her final State Nursing examinations. Her graphic accounts of accidents, factory mishaps or failed suicides in the River Seine led the family to call her 'Frankenstein',[2] but Alexandra listened avidly to these candid and often gruesome reports. Sometimes she went to the hospital to meet Isabelle when she came off duty, glimpsing the behind-the-scenes side of hospital life not usually shown to the royal family and smelling the aroma of blood and poverty. Isabelle's tales ignited her interest in becoming a nurse but it was some time before Alexandra could fulfil her wish.

In August 1954, the princess became patron of the Junior Red Cross, receiving the badge of office at a reception at St James's Palace. Earlier that year her elder brother Edward, the Duke of Kent, was taken to hospital with concussion after a car accident. 'Thank God Eddie is making a very good recovery,' a relieved Princess Marina wrote from Coppins, 'and the doctors are very satisfied. It was a horrible shock as you can imagine when I heard the news ...'[3] The incident revived Alexandra's ambition to have some nursing experience but Princess Marina thought her daughter was too young. Alexandra, however, saw no reason why a princess could not combine a career with royal duties.

Shortly before Alexandra's 21st birthday it was finally agreed that she could learn childcare. The obvious place to do so was the Hospital for Sick Children at Great Ormond Street. The matron was 46-year-old Gwen Kirby, an architect's daughter from Kent who had trained at St Thomas's Hospital in London before moving to Great Ormond Street during the Second World War, becoming matron in 1951. One afternoon Princess Alexandra and her lady-in-waiting Lady Moyra Hamilton arrived by appointment to be shown round the hospital. The princess said that if possible she would 'like to gain experience of looking after children so that when she married ... she would not be entirely inexperienced'. Of course, she would probably employ a nanny, but nevertheless 'thought it best to know from experience what the nanny was doing and why'. Miss Kirby took her to the nursery attached to the hospital, where treatment was given to babies and toddlers with sleeping or feeding problems. 'This is where I should like to start,' the princess exclaimed delightedly.[4]

It was decided that she would study child development, as well as learning how to make up artificial feeds and bathe and dress a baby. The princess would work as a part-time trainee nurse on two or three days a week, fitting in around her public engagements. The course was arranged by Mr H.F. Rutherford, house governor of the hospital, in consultation with Miss Kirby and would 'resemble the post-graduate course sponsored by the Institute of Child Health'.[5]

On Monday 28 October 1957, 'Miss Kent' drove herself in an Austin Mini to Mothercraft House, where to her dismay she was welcomed with a bouquet by Miss Kirby 'while students, ward-maids and cameramen crowded the pavement'. After the initial introductions she was shown to the locker room to change into a blue overall and no cap (not into uniform as the press wrongly predicted). Otherwise, she said, 'Mothers might take me for a nurse and ask me questions that I shouldn't be able to answer'. Also at her request she was treated like the other nurses, with no special fuss made. 'This was the first job she had done on her own and clearly she wanted to be left to fend for herself, learning from any little mistakes she might make,' explained Gwen Kirby. She was also anxious that nobody thought she was just 'playing at nurses'.[6]

'Miss Kent' studied textbooks on children's development and growth, and attended lectures and demonstrations. In the evening she drove back through the rush-hour traffic to Princess Marina's Kensington Palace apartment. Media interest was immense. At a press conference Miss Kirby was asked if the princess was going to eat with the nurses. 'Oh yes, I expect she's hungry, she's quite young, of course she will,' matron replied. The headlines next day said 'Matron Says She Will Muck in With the Nurses'. In the canteen she had an especially good rapport with the overseas students, and 'certainly was a promising nurse in simply having no colour bar', one explained.[7] Alexandra quickly overcame the natural doubts of her colleagues as to the capabilities of a royal princess, and she was soon taking temperatures, coping with colic and dealing with all the little problems found in a children's ward. Miss Kirby described her as marvellous, saying that all the nurses loved her. After a while she transferred to the outpatients' department, where mothers concerned about their sick children usually failed to notice the identity of the well-scrubbed nurse attending them. She sat no formal nursing examinations, 'apart from the informal written questions-and-answers of the welfare course', but gained valuable knowledge and experience.[8]

One of her first 'private patients' was the Duke of Kent, who arrived back at Kensington Palace with his face badly scratched by the branches of a tree while riding at full gallop on an army course at Aldershot. Alexandra gave the grazes her professional attention.

In between hospital work Princess Alexandra was also undertaking a full round of public engagements, both daytime and evening. One moment she would be bandaging a baby's foot and the next reviewing a regiment. Once while opening an exhibition a woman nearby tripped and fell over on the pavement, and it was the princess who helped the woman to her feet and ran a professional eye over her injured leg. In a school science laboratory she could deftly handle the microscope, a nd an official visit to a Juvenile Court neatly dovetailed into her studies of child delinquency. On a visit to a Sheffield cutlery manufacturer she was presented with seven pairs of scissors. They soon found their way back to her colleagues at Great Ormond Street.

All was going well until on 8 March 1958 it was announced that Princess Alexandra was confined to bed in Kensington Palace with glandular fever. For the next few weeks her official engagements were cancelled 'but her elders could now advance the persuasive argument of the risks that might be carried into the royal circle' from the wards.[9] So after about six months, Princess Alexandra's nursing career came to its natural end.

★★★

Another royal lady who worked with babies and children was Princess Sofia of Greece. Born in Athens on 2 November 1938, Princess Sofia was the eldest child of Crown Prince (later King) Paul and Princess Frederica and thus a great-great-great granddaughter of Queen Victoria. Sofia's childhood was nomadic, as the royal family were evacuated in the wake of the German invasion, finally returning to Greece in 1946.

The following April, Paul became king on the death of his brother George II. With northern Greece racked by civil war the royal family lived modestly at Tatoi, their villa outside Athens. Sofia had always loved children, especially babies, and after completing her secondary education at Schloss Salem in Germany she decided to train as a children's nurse.

Queen Frederica was not keen on her daughter's choice (although through force of circumstances the queen had briefly done some nursing in Greece during the war) but Sofia was insistent. In 1955, the queen had founded the Mitera School to give assistance to orphans and single mothers (*mitera* means mother in Greek) and it was here that the princess chose to enrol. Unlike the other students, however, she lived at home in Tatoi and not at the school.[10]

On 16 November 1956 the princess began her training in a class of twenty students and after a couple of months began taking care of babies. Sofia loved the work and attended the classes regularly. Part of the curriculum involved child psychology, and when the students were told that even newborn babies have erotic feelings, the princess was heard to murmur, 'I wonder which baby told that story to our teacher?'[11]

After completing her two-year training course in 1958 the princess continued at the Mitera School for another year, during which time she remained very committed to the work.

In 1962 she married Prince Juan Carlos of Spain, grandson of King Alfonso XIII and Queen Ena. After the death of General Franco in 1975 Juan Carlos became king.

Although she has never done any nursing in Spain, Queen Sofia continues to visit the Mitera School (now the Mitera Orphanage). When King Juan Carlos and Queen Sofia paid an official visit to Greece in May 1998 the queen was delighted to have the opportunity to visit Mitera again after so many years and to meet old friends like Joanna Rabani. In September 2005 the queen was visibly moved to find herself among former teachers and classmates. Queen Sofia is also involved in fundraising for the Red Cross.

★★★

Princess Margarita of Baden, another descendant of Queen Victoria, was for several years a dedicated nurse in London. She was born at Schloss Salem on 14 July 1932, the daughter of Prince Berthold, Margrave of Baden and Princess Theodora of Greece (a sister of Prince Philip, the Duke of Edinburgh). With the example of her grandmother Princess Alice of Greece before her, Margarita moved to London to become a nurse.

She trained at St Thomas's Hospital under the name of Nurse von Baden, never standing on ceremony and quite happy to scrub floors like all the other nurses. The princess often stayed with her great-grandmother Princess Victoria, the Dowager Marchioness of Milford Haven, at Kensington Palace. 'The old lady was of a frugal nature, not liking to spend too much on heating her apartment. Margarita would take her text books to the considerably warmer café at Barkers department store nearby.'[12]

In 1954, much to her relief, Margarita passed her final nursing examinations., but shortly after hearing the news she was confined to bed with influenza. She was allowed out on 6 December to receive her certificate and diploma as a qualified nurse from the Duchess of Kent, along with other nurses from St Thomas's Hospital.[13]

From her home at Salem, where she had been sent to recuperate, Margarita poured out her frustration to Grand Duchess Xenia of Russia:

> It is such a bore because I have not been to work since the last days of November. I was in bed for a week and only was allowed out of bed when Aunty [Princess Marina] came to present us with our certificates and diplomas. And then I hung around London for almost a week and then was sent home by the ear nose and throat specialist for a fortnight … Alexander wrote me a rude letter about my exams … [Xenia's grandson was teasing Margarita] And there I was so proud of having passed them all at last. I hardly could believe it when I found that out and the effect proved too much and I retired to bed.[14]

Now a fully qualified nurse, Margarita lived in a student nurses' hostel and worked in the busy outpatients' department of St Thomas's. While working in London she met her future husband Prince Tomislav of Yugoslavia, second son of King Alexander I and Queen Marie ('Mignon', who had nursed in the

Romanian hospitals during the First World War). After their marriage in 1957 Margarita and Tomislav ran a fruit farm in Kirdford, Sussex and the princess devoted herself to various Serbian charities.

The fruit farm failed to prosper and after the births of her two children, Margarita returned to St Thomas's Hospital. In the 1970s she was sister of the Stoma ward, working under the name of Mrs George (the name was chosen because Prince Tomislav was a member of the royal house of Karageorgevitch).

'I knew her as the sister with the unmistakable German accent,' recalled one former student:

> who, within hours of a patient arriving on the ward with a stoma [an artificial exit from the bowel] would appear, white coat flapping (it was a measure of her status that we never did see her in the famous sister's navy and white spots) and issuing firm instructions in the care of that patient to any professional that might be involved in their care regardless of their seniority. Woe betide anybody, be they nurse, intern, registrar or consultant, who did not heed her advice or direction. Patients and their welfare were the focus of our world and she was their passionate advocate and remained so until the day she died. We learned so much from her and she blazed a trail for us to follow.[15]

She was also vice-president of the Friends of the Martha and Mary Convent in Moscow, founded in 1909 by her great-aunt Grand Duchess Elisabeth (Ella), playing a significant part in the convent's restoration. Princess Margarita remained passionately interested in healthcare until her death on 15 January 2013.

★★★

Princess Margriet of the Netherlands, the third daughter of Crown Princess Juliana and Prince Bernhard, was born on 19 January 1943 in Ottawa, where Juliana and her children Beatrix and Irene had been evacuated as the Germans occupied Holland in 1940. The family returned home at the end of the war and in 1948 Juliana became queen. Princess Margriet was educated at Baarn Grammar School and then went on to study law at Leiden University, where she met Pieter van Vollenhoven – they became engaged in March 1965. In those days it was usual for girls to stop working when they married and with her wedding almost two years away, the princess wanted to occupy the time by doing something useful for society. A friend in Germany had done a Red Cross course as a general nursing assistant and when Margriet discovered that this was also possible in the Netherlands she decided to enrol.

With the agreement of her parents, on 18 October 1965 Margriet enrolled on a short course of practical training as a Red Cross Nursing Assistant

First Class in De Lichtenberg Hospital Amersfoort, about 25 miles south-west of Amsterdam. 'The princess wants to get acquainted with as many aspects of nursing as possible,' reported the Netherlands government information service, 'and will be in a group of student nurses receiving initial training.'[16]

De Lichtenberg was a pleasant modern hospital with a full range of specialist services. On arrival the princess was welcomed by the director Baroness van Tuyll van Serooskerken, who had previously worked for the Red Cross in the Dutch East Indies, as well as an army of photographers. 'I just want to take part in the training class,' she told the baroness, 'and I want to be called Sister Margriet'.[17] She then joined the general nurses' training course five days a week, with the difference that she was the only trainee Red Cross Nursing Assistant First Class (a course now obsolete).

Shy by nature, Princess Margriet was happy to be just one of a crowd, although at age 22 she was older than the other girls, most of whom were 18-year-old school leavers. They were a high-spirited bunch, always ready to laugh when a cap fell off onto a bed, or when someone arrived too late with a commode, but equally ready to work. 'You just forget that she is the princess,' said one of the students, 'but she is not haughty'.[18] After preliminary training Margriet followed a modified course in order to meet the requirements of the Red Cross certificate.[19] This involved theory, which her university education enabled her to absorb easier than some of the other students, as well as practical skills in every department of the hospital. She changed beds and bandaged people requiring first aid, although her favourite duty was working in the children's ward. She became familiar with the orthopaedic ward, the laboratory and the surgical department, and received additional private instruction in theory and practical work from the specialist Dr Breske and the surgeon François Insinger. 'Sister Margriet' always had a ready smile for the patients and they were pleased to see this down to earth young woman who showed a genuine interest in her work.

The princess lived in the nurses' home like the other students but found Amersfoort dull after the bustle of university life at Leiden. Many an off-duty hour was spent alone in her room, although she had the advantage of a car and was able to drive to Soestdijk Palace in nearby Baarn to see her parents. Male visitors were prohibited at the nurses' home and the princess had to obtain permission before her fiancé could visit her.

In 1966, having completed a year of training, she took part in the Netherlands National Nursing Competition in the fire brigade barracks in Arnhem. With no nervousness in front of the judges the princess successfully bandaged children as if she had been nursing for years.

On 28 June 1966, Princess Margriet received her certificate and badge as an Assistant First Class from Dr W.H. de Beaufort, vice-president of the Netherlands Red Cross, in the presence of her proud mother Queen Juliana. From that day she was permitted to wear the official uniform of a nurse. Criticism from former nurses who protested that the princess had received her badge after only a year, when they were required to train for four years, was countered by the hospital management as a 'very unfortunate' misunderstanding. They pointed out that the princess was a nursing *assistant*, not a nurse. The princess then joined a local branch of the Netherlands Red Cross as a volunteer, working for five days on the *J Henri Dunant*, a Red Cross hospital ship taking seventy-two disabled people on a much needed holiday.

The following January she married Pieter von Vollenhoven, finding her hospital training especially useful over the next few years when raising their four sons.

Since 1987 she has been vice-president of her Red Cross National Society and in 1996 was elected as chairman of the Standing Commission of the Red Cross, being re-elected for a second term during the International Conference in Geneva in 1999.

★★★

'I want to be a nurse in Africa,' declared Princess Marie-Astrid of Luxembourg on her 21st birthday.[20] This announcement came as a surprise to her family, although the young princess had always been concerned with helping the needy and suffering.

Princess Marie-Astrid was born at Castle Betzdorf on 17 February 1954, the eldest child of the hereditary Grand Duke Jean of Luxembourg and Princess Josephine-Charlotte of Belgium (granddaughter of King Albert and Queen Elisabeth), who had studied paediatrics and child psychology in Geneva and was later president of the Luxembourg Red Cross.

Marie-Astrid studied English and English literature at Cambridge and in the late 1970s was seen by the British tabloid press as a potential bride for Prince Charles – impossible at that time because of her Catholic religion. In 1970, the princess succeeded her mother as president of the youth section of the Luxembourg Red Cross (in 1974 a stamp was issued to mark the event) and the following year she entered the Nurses' Training School in Luxembourg for a three-year course. She studied anatomy, biology, chemistry, physics and psychology and received her State Nursing Diploma as a registered nurse in 1974. The princess then worked in a private clinic. Marie-Astrid completed her training in 1977 at the Prince Leopold Institute in Antwerp (now the Institute of Tropical Medicine), where she passed her examinations with great distinction and was awarded a nursing certificate in tropical diseases.

In 1974 she officially inaugurated a Nurses'Training School financed by the Luxembourg State in Rwamagana in the Republic of Rwanda. The following year, accompanied by her sister Princess Margaretha, she returned to Rwanda. 'It was in connection with the aid given by Luxembourg to developing African countries that Marie-Astrid had the opportunity to fulfil her nursing vocation.'The princesses spent three months nursing in various hospitals and Marie-Astrid later returned to Africa, where 'she was able to realize her wish to alleviate human suffering; there she showed enthusiasm, courage and self-denial.'[21]

Returning home she carried out many duties in connection with the youth section of the Luxembourg Red Cross, gradually overcoming her shyness and showing great energy in devoting herself to others. In December 1979 she travelled to Tunisia to inaugurate the new social and public health centres, also financed by the Luxembourg State.

On 6 February 1982 in Luxembourg Cathedral, the princess married Archduke Carl Christian of Austria, grandson of the last Habsburg rulers of Austria-Hungary Emperor Carl and Empress Zita.

★★★

All these royal women, as well as many more, have contributed in some way towards the relief of human suffering. In her 1882 preface to Professor Esmarch's book Princess Christian wrote:

> The satisfaction of being able to render the needed aid to those in pain, and of possibly being the means of saving a valued life, should more than counterbalance the scruples that some might feel on entering such a study.

The contribution made by royal women towards nurses and nursing from the reign of Queen Victoria onwards cannot be overestimated. It also shows that caring and compassion among queens and princesses is certainly nothing new.

Notes

1. Cathcart, *Alexandra*, p.72.
2. Cathcart, *Alexandra*, p.91.
3. The Duchess of Kent to Grand Duchess Xenia of Russia, 27 June 1954. Copy in author's possession.
4. Gwen Kirby, 'The Mother of Great Ormond Street', in *Woman's Own*, 2 August 1969.
5. *The Times*, 26 October 1957; Cathcart, *Alexandra*, p.120.
6. Kirby, 'The Mother of Great Ormond Street', 2 August 1969.
7. www1.somerset.gov.uk/archives/exmoor/kirbysummary2.htm; Cathcart, *Alexandra*, p.120.

8. Cathcart, *Alexandra*, p.123.

9. Ibid.

10. My thanks to Ricardo Mateos Saintz de Medrano for providing most of the information about Queen Sofia's work at the Mitera School.

11. Frederica, *Measure of Understanding*, p.227.

12. Golden, 'And Finally'. In *Majesty*, March 2013.

13. *The Times*, 7 December 1954.

14. Princess Margarita of Baden to Grand Duchess Xenia of Russia. Salem, 17 December 1954. Copy in author's possession.

15. 'Princess was a highly dedicated nurse', Stella Wiseman. *The Farnham Herald*, 1 February 2013.

16. *Spokesman-Review*, 19 October 1965.

17. Phé Wijnbeek, *Prinses Margriet: Fotoalbum* (N.V. Gebroeders Zomer & Keunings Uitgeversmaatschappij/Wageningen. 1965), p.17.

18. Ibid.

19. Much of the following information about Princess Margriet is taken from an interview given by the princess to the journalist Helma van den Berg in January 2013. I am indebted to Mrs H.G. Eerkes, Private Secretary to Her Royal Highness Princess Margriet, for the text of this interview.

20. Raymond Reuter, *Marie-Astrid* (Éditions Luxnews, Luxembourg, 1982), p.54.

21. Ibid.

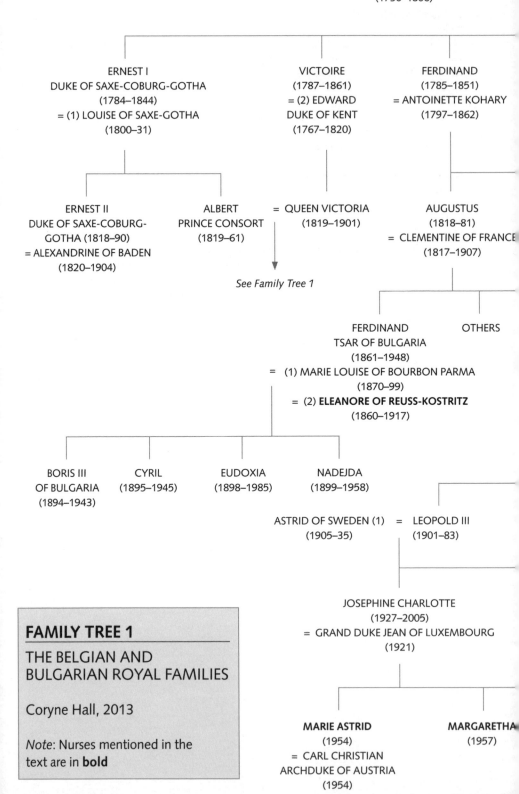

FRANCIS, DUKE OF SAXE-COBURG-SAALFIELD
(1750–1806)

ERNEST I
DUKE OF SAXE-COBURG-GOTHA
(1784–1844)
= (1) LOUISE OF SAXE-GOTHA
(1800–31)

VICTOIRE
(1787–1861)
= (2) EDWARD
DUKE OF KENT
(1767–1820)

FERDINAND
(1785–1851)
= ANTOINETTE KOHARY
(1797–1862)

ERNEST II
DUKE OF SAXE-COBURG-
GOTHA (1818–90)
= ALEXANDRINE OF BADEN
(1820–1904)

ALBERT
PRINCE CONSORT
(1819–61)

= QUEEN VICTORIA
(1819–1901)

See Family Tree 1

AUGUSTUS
(1818–81)
= CLEMENTINE OF FRANCE
(1817–1907)

FERDINAND
TSAR OF BULGARIA
(1861–1948)
= (1) MARIE LOUISE OF BOURBON PARMA
(1870–99)
= (2) **ELEANORE OF REUSS-KOSTRITZ**
(1860–1917)

OTHERS

BORIS III
OF BULGARIA
(1894–1943)

CYRIL
(1895–1945)

EUDOXIA
(1898–1985)

NADEJDA
(1899–1958)

ASTRID OF SWEDEN (1)   =   LEOPOLD III
(1905–35)   (1901–83)

JOSEPHINE CHARLOTTE
(1927–2005)
= GRAND DUKE JEAN OF LUXEMBOURG
(1921)

MARIE ASTRID
(1954)
= CARL CHRISTIAN
ARCHDUKE OF AUSTRIA
(1954)

MARGARETHA
(1957)

FAMILY TREE 1

THE BELGIAN AND
BULGARIAN ROYAL FAMILIES

Coryne Hall, 2013

Note: Nurses mentioned in the
text are in **bold**

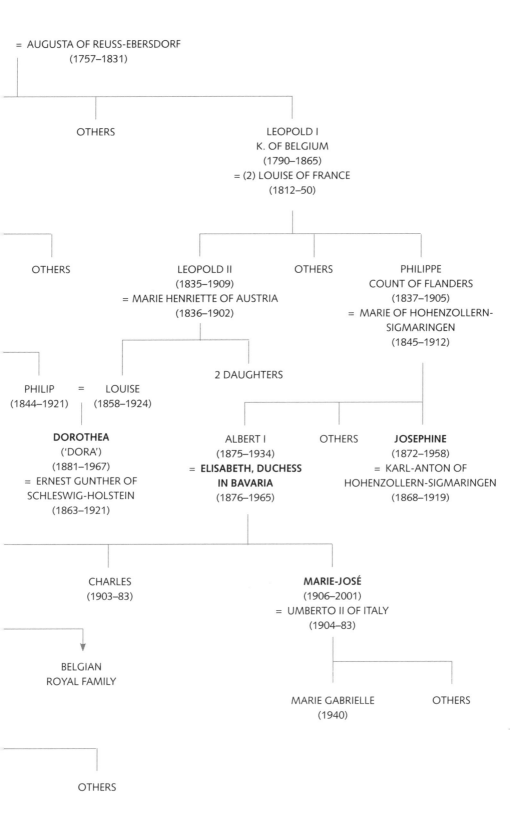

= AUGUSTA OF REUSS-EBERSDORF
(1757–1831)

OTHERS

LEOPOLD I
K. OF BELGIUM
(1790–1865)
= (2) LOUISE OF FRANCE
(1812–50)

OTHERS

LEOPOLD II
(1835–1909)
= MARIE HENRIETTE OF AUSTRIA
(1836–1902)

OTHERS

PHILIPPE
COUNT OF FLANDERS
(1837–1905)
= MARIE OF HOHENZOLLERN-
SIGMARINGEN
(1845–1912)

2 DAUGHTERS

PHILIP   =   LOUISE
(1844–1921)   (1858–1924)

DOROTHEA
('DORA')
(1881–1967)
= ERNEST GUNTHER OF
SCHLESWIG-HOLSTEIN
(1863–1921)

ALBERT I
(1875–1934)
= ELISABETH, DUCHESS
IN BAVARIA
(1876–1965)

OTHERS

JOSEPHINE
(1872–1958)
= KARL-ANTON OF
HOHENZOLLERN-SIGMARINGEN
(1868–1919)

CHARLES
(1903–83)

MARIE-JOSÉ
(1906–2001)
= UMBERTO II OF ITALY
(1904–83)

BELGIAN
ROYAL FAMILY

MARIE GABRIELLE
(1940)

OTHERS

OTHERS

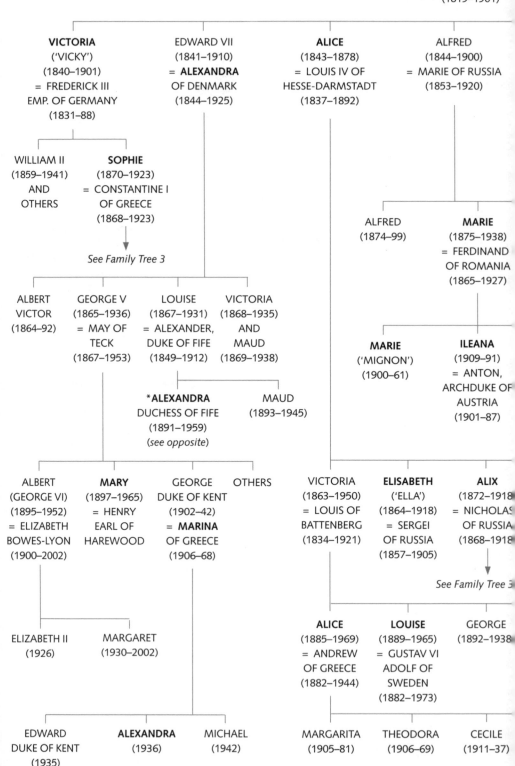

QUEEN VICTORIA
(1819–1901)

VICTORIA
('VICKY')
(1840–1901)
= FREDERICK III
EMP. OF GERMANY
(1831–88)

EDWARD VII
(1841–1910)
= **ALEXANDRA**
OF DENMARK
(1844–1925)

ALICE
(1843–1878)
= LOUIS IV OF
HESSE-DARMSTADT
(1837–1892)

ALFRED
(1844–1900)
= MARIE OF RUSSIA
(1853–1920)

WILLIAM II
(1859–1941)
AND
OTHERS

SOPHIE
(1870–1923)
= CONSTANTINE I
OF GREECE
(1868–1923)

See Family Tree 3

ALFRED
(1874–99)

MARIE
(1875–1938)
= FERDINAND
OF ROMANIA
(1865–1927)

ALBERT
VICTOR
(1864–92)

GEORGE V
(1865–1936)
= MAY OF
TECK
(1867–1953)

LOUISE
(1867–1931)
= ALEXANDER,
DUKE OF FIFE
(1849–1912)

VICTORIA
(1868–1935)
AND
MAUD
(1869–1938)

MARIE
('MIGNON')
(1900–61)

ILEANA
(1909–91)
= ANTON,
ARCHDUKE OF
AUSTRIA
(1901–87)

*ALEXANDRA
DUCHESS OF FIFE
(1891–1959)
(*see opposite*)

MAUD
(1893–1945)

ALBERT
(GEORGE VI)
(1895–1952)
= ELIZABETH
BOWES-LYON
(1900–2002)

MARY
(1897–1965)
= HENRY
EARL OF
HAREWOOD

GEORGE
DUKE OF KENT
(1902–42)
= **MARINA**
OF GREECE
(1906–68)

OTHERS

VICTORIA
(1863–1950)
= LOUIS OF
BATTENBERG
(1834–1921)

ELISABETH
('ELLA')
(1864–1918)
= SERGEI
OF RUSSIA
(1857–1905)

ALIX
(1872–1918)
= NICHOLAS
OF RUSSIA
(1868–1918)

See Family Tree 3

ELIZABETH II
(1926)

MARGARET
(1930–2002)

ALICE
(1885–1969)
= ANDREW
OF GREECE
(1882–1944)

LOUISE
(1889–1965)
= GUSTAV VI
ADOLF OF
SWEDEN
(1882–1973)

GEORGE
(1892–1938)

EDWARD
DUKE OF KENT
(1935)

ALEXANDRA
(1936)

MICHAEL
(1942)

MARGARITA
(1905–81)

THEODORA
(1906–69)

CECILE
(1911–37)

= ALBERT OF SAXE-COBURG-GOTHA
(1819–61)

HELENA
(1846–1923)
= CHRISTIAN OF
SCHLESWIG-HOLSTEIN
(1831–1917)

LOUISE
(1848–1939)
= JOHN, 9TH DUKE
OF ARGYLL
(1845–1914)

ARTHUR
(1850–1942)
= LOUISE
MARGARET
OF PRUSSIA
(1860–1917)

LEOPOLD
(1853–84)
= HELENE
OF WALDECK
AND PYRMONT
(1861–1922)

BEATRICE
(1857–1944)
= HENRY OF
BATTENBERG
(1858–96)

CHRISTIAN
VICTOR
1867–1900)

ALBERT
(1869–1931)

HELENA
VICTORIA
(1870–1948)

MARIE
LOUISE
(1872–1956)

ALICE
(1883–1981)
= ALEXANDER
OF TECK, EARL
OF ATHLONE
(1874–1957)

CHARLES EDWARD
DUKE OF SAXE-
COBURG
(1884–1954)

VICTORIA
MEILITA
('DUCKY')
(1876–1936)
= (2) CYRIL OF
RUSSIA
(1876–1938)

ALEXANDRA
(1878–1942)
= ERNEST OF
HOHENLOHE-
LANGENBURG
(1863–1950)

BEATRICE
(1884–1966)
= ALFONSO
OF BOURBON-
ORLÉANS
(1886–1975)

ARTHUR OF
CONNAUGHT
(1883–1938)
= **ALEXANDRA***
DUCHESS OF FIFE
(1891–1959)

OTHERS

**VICTORIA
EUGENIE**
('ENA')
(1887–1969)
= ALFONSO XIII
OF SPAIN

3 SONS

OTHERS

ALEXANDRA
('DOLLY')
(1901–63)

ALAISTAIR
(1914–43)

ALVARO
(1910–97)

ALONSO
(1912–36)

ATAULFO
(1913–74)

OTHERS

ALFONSO
(1904–38)

BEATRIZ
(1909–2002)

JUAN
(1913–93)
COUNT OF BARCELONA
= MARIA MERCEDES OF
BOURBON TWO SICILIES
(1910–2000)

GONZALO
(1914–34)

JAIME
(1908–75)

**MARIA
CRISTINA**
(1911–96)

JUAN CARLOS I
(1938)
= **SOFIA** OF GREECE
(1938)

OTHERS

LOUIS
('DICKIE')
ARL MOUNTBATTEN
OF BURMA
(1900–1979)

SOPHIE
(1914–2001)

PHILIP
DUKE OF EDINBURGH
(1921)
= ELIZABETH II

FAMILY TREE 2

QUEEN VICTORIA'S FAMILY

Coryne Hall, 2013

Note: Nurses mentioned in the
text are in **bold**

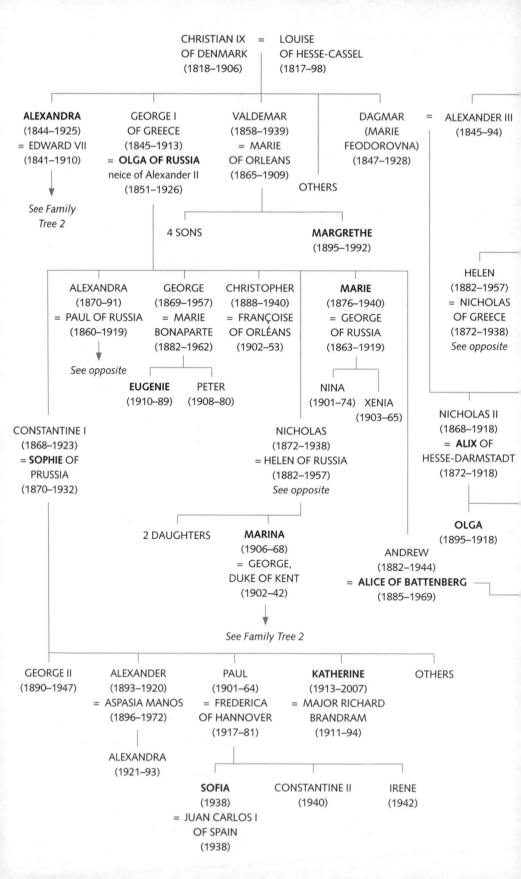

CHRISTIAN IX = LOUISE
OF DENMARK   OF HESSE-CASSEL
(1818–1906)   (1817–98)

ALEXANDRA
(1844–1925)
= EDWARD VII
(1841–1910)

See Family Tree 2

GEORGE I
OF GREECE
(1845–1913)
= **OLGA OF RUSSIA**
neice of Alexander II
(1851–1926)

VALDEMAR
(1858–1939)
= MARIE
OF ORLEANS
(1865–1909)

OTHERS

DAGMAR
(MARIE
FEODOROVNA)
(1847–1928)

= ALEXANDER III
(1845–94)

4 SONS

MARGRETHE
(1895–1992)

HELEN
(1882–1957)
= NICHOLAS
OF GREECE
(1872–1938)
See opposite

ALEXANDRA
(1870–91)
= PAUL OF RUSSIA
(1860–1919)

See opposite

GEORGE
(1869–1957)
= MARIE
BONAPARTE
(1882–1962)

CHRISTOPHER
(1888–1940)
= FRANÇOISE
OF ORLÉANS
(1902–53)

MARIE
(1876–1940)
= GEORGE
OF RUSSIA
(1863–1919)

EUGENIE   PETER
(1910–89)   (1908–80)

NINA
(1901–74)   XENIA
(1903–65)

NICHOLAS II
(1868–1918)
= **ALIX** OF
HESSE-DARMSTADT
(1872–1918)

CONSTANTINE I
(1868–1923)
= **SOPHIE** OF
PRUSSIA
(1870–1932)

NICHOLAS
(1872–1938)
= HELEN OF RUSSIA
(1882–1957)
See opposite

OLGA
(1895–1918)

2 DAUGHTERS

MARINA
(1906–68)
= GEORGE,
DUKE OF KENT
(1902–42)

ANDREW
(1882–1944)
= **ALICE OF BATTENBERG**
(1885–1969)

See Family Tree 2

GEORGE II
(1890–1947)

ALEXANDER
(1893–1920)
= ASPASIA MANOS
(1896–1972)

PAUL
(1901–64)
= FREDERICA
OF HANNOVER
(1917–81)

KATHERINE
(1913–2007)
= MAJOR RICHARD
BRANDRAM
(1911–94)

OTHERS

ALEXANDRA
(1921–93)

SOFIA
(1938)
= JUAN CARLOS I
OF SPAIN
(1938)

CONSTANTINE II
(1940)

IRENE
(1942)

ALEXANDER II = MARIE
OF RUSSIA OF HESSE-DARMSTADT
(1818–81) (1824–80)

VLADIMIR (1847–1909) = MARIE OF MECKLENBURG-SCHWERIN (1845–1920) ('Grand Duchess Vladimir')

SERGEI (1857–1905) = **ELISABETH** OF HESSE ('ELLA') (1864–1918)

PAUL (1860–1919) = (1) ALEXANDRA OF GREECE (1870–91)

MARIE (1853–1920) = ALFRED, DUKE OF EDINBURGH (1844–1900)

OTHERS

MARIE (1890–1958)

DMITRI (1891–1942)

CYRIL (1876–1938) = **VICTORIA MELITA** ('DUCKY') (1876–1936)

OTHERS

MARIE (1875–1938) = FERDINAND I OF ROMANIA (1865–1927)

See Family Tree 2

ALFRED (1874–99)

ALEXANDRA (1878–1942)

↓
See Family Tree 2

BEATRICE (1884–1966)

↓
See Family Tree 2

OTHERS

XENIA (1875–1960) = ALEXANDER OF RUSSIA ('SANDRO') (1866–1933)

OLGA (1882–1960) = (1) PETER OF OLDENBURG (1868–1924) = (2) NICOLAI KULIKOVSKY (1881–1958)

TATIANA (1897–1918)

MARIE (1899–1918)

ANASTASIA (1901–18)

ALEXEI (1904–18)

IRINA (1895–1970) = FELIX YOUSSOUPOV (1887–1967)

6 SONS

MARGARITA (1905–81)

THEODORA (1906–69) = BERTHOLD OF BADEN (1906–63)

CECILE (1911–37)

SOPHIE (1914–2001)

PHILIP DUKE OF EDINBURGH (1921) = ELIZABETH II (1926)

MARGARITA OF BADEN (1932–2013)

2 SONS

FAMILY TREE 3

THE GREEK AND RUSSIAN ROYAL FAMILIES

Coryne Hall, 2013

Note: Nurses mentioned in the text are in **bold**

Bibliography

Books

Alexandra, Duchess of Fife. *A Nurse's Story* (John & Edward Bumpus Ltd, 1955. Printed for private circulation)

Alexandra, Queen of Yugoslavia. *For a King's Love* (Odham's Press, 1956)

Alexandra, Queen of Yugoslavia. *Prince Philip: A Family Portrait* (Hodder & Stoughton, 1960)

Alice, Grand Duchess of Hesse. *Biographical Sketch and Letters*, Foreword by HRH Princess Helena. (John Murray, 1884)

Almedingen, E.M. *An Unbroken Unity* (The Bodley Head, 1964)

Allsebrook, Mary. *Born to Rebel: The Life of Harriet Boyd Hawes* (Oxbow Books, 1992)

Anon. *Russian Court Memoirs 1914–1916* (Herbert Jenkins, 1917)

Anon. *The Fall of the Romanovs* (Herbert Jenkins, 1918)

Apostol, Daniel Tiberiu; Ion, Dr Narcis Dorin & Petcu, Nicoleta. *Bran Castle: Museum and Collections* (Bran National Museum, 2008)

Archer, Jeremy. *A Royal Christmas* (Elliott & Thompson, 2012)

Aronson, Theo. *Crowns in Conflict* (John Murray, 1986)

Aronson, Theo. *Grandmama of Europe* (Cassell, 1973)

Aronson, Theo. *Princess Alice, Countess of Athlone* (Cassell, 1981)

Aronson, Theo. *Royal Vendetta: The Crown of Spain* (Oldbourne, 1966)

Aronson, Theo. *The Coburgs of Belgium* (Cassell, 1969)

Aronson, Theo. *The Royal Family at War* (John Murray, 1993)

Arrigo, Petacco. *Regina: La via e i segreti di Maria José* (Mondadori, 1998)

Barkovets, Alia & Tenikhina, Valentina. *Nicholas II: The Imperial Family* (Abris Publishers, St Petersburg, 1998)

Battiscombe, Georgina. *Queen Alexandra* (Constable, 1969)

Baudendistel, Rainer. *Between Bombs and Good Intentions* (Berghahn Books, 2006)

Beéche, Arturo. *Dear Ellen* (Kensington House Books, California, 2012)

Beéche, Arturo (ed.). *The Other Grand Dukes* (Kensington House Books, 2012)

Belyakov, N.A., & Michaelovich, V.A. (eds). *Sestry Miloserdiya Rossii* (Likki Rossi, St Petersburg, 2005)

Binyon, Laurence. *For Dauntless France* (Hodder & Stoughton, 1918)

Blangstrup, Chr. (1–21); Brøndum-Nielsen, Johs. & Raunkjær, Palle (22–26) (eds). *Salmonsens konversationsleksikon*. Anden Udgave Bind II: Arbejderhaver-Benzol (J.H. Schultz Forlagsboghandel, Copenhagen, 1915–30)

Bokhanov, Alexander N.; Knodt, Dr Manfred; Oustimenko, Vladimir; Peregudova, Zinaida & Tyutyunnik, Lyubov. *The Romanovs: Love, Power & Tragedy* (Leppi Publications, 1993)

Borden, Mary. *The Forbidden Zone* (Hesperus Press Ltd, 1929. Reprinted 2008)

Bradford, Sarah. *George VI* (Weidenfeld & Nicolson, 1989)

Brook-Shepherd, Gordon. *Royal Sunset* (Weidenfeld & Nicolson, 1987)

Buchanan, Meriel. *Petrograd, The City of Trouble 1914–18* (Collins, 1918)

Buchanan, Meriel. *Ambassador's Daughter* (Cassell, 1958)

Buxhoeveden, Baroness Sophie. *The Life and Tragedy of Alexandra Feodorovna, Empress of Russia* (Longmans Green, 1930)

Carey, Mabel C. *Princess Mary* (Nisbet & Co., 1922)

Cathcart, Helen. *Anne, The Princess Royal* (W.H. Allen, 1988)

Cathcart, Helen. *Princess Alexandra* (W.H. Allen, 1967)

Chomet, Seweryn. *Helena: A Princess Reclaimed* (Begell House Books, New York, 2000)

Christopher, Prince of Greece. *Memoirs* (Hurst & Blackett, 1938)

Colin, Gerty. *Les Châtelains de Laeken*, 2 volumes (Éditions Luc Pire, Brussels, 2001)

Constant, Stephen. *Foxy Ferdinand: Tsar of Bulgaria* (Sidgwick & Jackson, 1979)

Cooke, Bev. *Royal Monastic* (Conciliar Press Ministries, California, 2008)

Coppens, Marguerite (ed.). *La Princesse Marie-José: Entre Belgique et Italie* (Éditions Lannoo, Belgium. 2012)

Cowen, Ruth (ed.). *War Diaries: A Nurse at the Front* (Simon & Schuster, 2012)

Cunliffe-Owen, Sidney. *Elisabeth, Queen of the Belgians* (Herbert Jenkins, 1954)

Cyril, Grand Duke of Russia. *My Life in Russia's Service* (Selwyn & Blount, 1939)

de Jonge, Ralf. *Koningin Elisabeth: Zwierige Vorstin in Woelige Tijden* (Standaard Uitgeverij, Antwerp, 2007)

de Stoeckl, Baroness. *Not All Vanity* (John Murray, 1950)

de Stoeckl, Baroness. *My Dear Marquis* (John Murray, 1952)

Defrance, Olivier & Vachaudez, Christophe. *L'Album Royal: De Léopold 1er à Baudouin* (Racine, Belgium, 2011)

Devere-Summers, Anthony. *War and the Royal Houses of Europe* (Arms & Armour Press, 1996)

Dimond, Frances & Taylor, Roger. *Crown & Camera* (Penguin Books, 1987)

Duff, David. *Alexandra, Princess and Queen* (William Collins & Sons, 1980)

Eilers, Marlene. *Queen Victoria's Descendants* (Rosvall Royal Books, Sweden, 1997)

Elsberry, Terence. *Marie of Romania* (Cassell, 1973)

Epton, Nina. *Victoria and Her Daughters* (Weidenfeld & Nicolson, 1971)

Esmarch, Professor Friedrich. *First Aid to the Injured*, 7 editions (Smith, Elder 1882–1907)

Fabergé, Tatiana; Proler, Lynette & Skurlov, Valentin. *The Fabergé Imperial Easter Eggs* (Christie's, 1997)

Farmborough, Florence. *With the Armies of the Tsar* (Stein & Day, New York, 1975)

Fjellman, Margit. *Louise Mountbatten, Queen of Sweden* (George Allen & Unwin, 1968)

Fraser of Lonsdale, Lord. *My Story of St Dunstan's* (Harrap, 1961)

Frederica, Queen of Greece. *A Measure of Understanding* (Macmillan, 1971)

Fulford, Roger. *Dearest Mama* (Evans Brothers, 1968)

Fulford, Roger. *Your Dear Letter* (Evans Brothers, 1971)

Fuhrmann, Joseph T. (ed.). *The Complete Wartime Correspondence of Tsar Nicholas II and the Empress Alexandra* (Greenwood Press, Connecticut, 1999)

Gabriel Constantinovich, Grand Duke of Russia. *Memories in the Marble Palace* (Gilbert's Books, Canada, 2009)

Gerlardi, Julia. *Born To Rule* (St Martin's Press, 2005)

Gerlardi, Julia. *From Splendour to Revolution* (St Martin's Press, 2011)

George, Grand Duchess of Russia. *A Romanov Diary* (Atlantic International Publications New York, 1988)

Golden, Robert. *Relatively Royal* (Rosvall Royal Books, Sweden, 2000)

Gould Lee, Arthur (ed.). *The Empress Frederick Writes to Sophie* (Faber & Faber, 1955)

Gould Lee, Arthur. *The Royal House of Greece* (Ward Lock, 1948)

Grabbe, Paul & Beatrice. *The Private World of the Last Tsar* (Collins, 1985)

Hall, Coryne. *Little Mother of Russia: A Biography of the Empress Marie Feodorovna 1847–1928* (Shepherd-Walwyn, 1999)

Harmer, Michael. *The Forgotten Hospital* (Springwood Books, 1982)

Horn, Pamela. *Ladies of the Manor* (Alan Sutton, 1991)

Hough, Richard. *Louis & Victoria* (Weidenfeld & Nicolson, 1974)

Howard de Walden, Margherita. *Pages From My Life* (Sigwick & Jackson, 1965)

Hudson, Helen. *Cumberland Lodge* (Phillimore, 1989)

Ileana, Princess of Romania. *I Live Again* (Victor Gollancz, 1952)

Ileana, Princess of Romania. *The Hospital of the Queen's Heart* (Rinehart & Co., New York, 1954)

Ion, Narcis Dorin. *Castelul Bran* (Tritonic, Bucharest, 2003)

Kejserinde Dagmar, Empress of Russia. Exhibition catalogue. (Christiansborg Slot, Copenhagen, 1997)

King, Greg & Wilson, Penny. *The Fate of the Romanovs* (John Wiley, 2003)

King, Greg & Wilson, Penny. *The Resurrection of the Romanovs* (John Wiley, 2001)

Kleinmichel, Countess. *Memories of a Shipwrecked World* (Brentano's Ltd., 1923)

Kleinpenning, Petra H. *The Correspondence of the Empress Alexandra of Russia with Ernst Ludwig and Eleonore, Grand Duke and Duchess of Hesse* (Books on Demand, Germany, 2010)

Kozlov, Vladimir A. & Khrustalev, Vladimir M. (ed.). *The Last Diary of Tsaritsa Alexandra* (Yale University Press, 1997)

Kulikovsky, Paul; Roth-Nicholls, Karen & Woolmans, Sue. *25 Chapters of My Life: The Memoirs of Grand Duchess Olga Alexandrovna* (Librario, 2009)

Kurth, Peter. *Tsar: The Lost World of Nicholas and Alexandra* (Little, Brown, 1995)

Laird, Dorothy. *Royal Ascot* (Hodder & Stoughton, 1976)

Longford, Elizabeth. *Victoria R.I.* (Weidenfeld & Nicolson, 1964)

MacManus, Emily. *Matron of Guy's* (Andrew Melrose, 1956)

Maria of Russia, *Education of a Princess* (The Viking Press, New York, 1931)

Marie Gabrielle of Savoy, HRH Princess & Bracalini, Romano. *Casa Savoia: Diario di una Monarchia* (Leonardo Arte, Milan, 1996)

Marie zu Erbach-Schönberg, Princess of Battenberg. *Reminiscences* (The Ipswich Book Company, Suffolk, 1925. Reprinted by Royalty Digest in 1996)

Marie, Queen of Roumania. *The Story of My Life* (Charles Scribner's Sons, 1934)

Marie Louise, Princess. *My Memories of Six Reigns* (Evans Brothers, 1956)

Massie, Robert. *Nicholas and Alexandra* (Victor Gollancz, 1968)

Massie, Robert & Swezey, Marilyn. *The Romanov Family Album: Assembled by Anna Vyrubova* (Allen Lane, 1982)

Michael, Prince of Greece. *Nicholas and Alexandra: The Family Albums* (Taurus Park, 1992)

Mienert, Dr Marion. *Maria Pavlovna: A Romanov Grand Duchess in Russia and in Exile* (Lennart-Bernadotte-Stiftung, Germany, 2004)

Millar, Lubov. *Grand Duchess Elizabeth of Russia: New Martyr of the Communist Yoke* (Nikodemos Orthodox Publication Society, California, 1991)

Miller, Ilana D. *The Four Graces: Queen Victoria's Hessian Granddaughters* (Kensington House Books, California, 2011)

Miller, Ilana D. & Beéche, Arturo. *Royal Gatherings: Who is in the Picture?* (Kensington House Books, California, 2013)

Moorehead, Caroline. *Dunant's Dream* (Harper Collins, 1998)

Morgenthau, Henry. *Ambassador Morgenthau's Story* (Doubleday, Page & Co., New York, 1918)

Narishkin-Kurakin, Elizabeth. *Under Three Tsars* (E.P. Dutton, New York, 1931)

Nicholas, Prince of Greece. *My Political Memoirs, 1914–17* (Hutchinson, 1928)

Noel, Gerard. *Ena: Spain's English Queen* (Constable, 1984)

Noel, Gerard. *Princess Alice: Queen Victoria's Forgotten Daughter* (Constable, 1974)

Oliver, Dame Beryl. *The British Red Cross in Action* (Faber & Faber, 1966)

Pakula, *The Last Romantic: A Biography of Queen Marie of Roumania* (Weidenfeld & Nicolson, 1985)

Pakula, Hannah. *An Uncommon Woman: The Empress Frederick* (Weidenfeld & Nicolson, 1996)

Phenix, Patricia. *Olga Romanov: Russia's Last Grand Duchess* (Viking, 1999)

Ponsonby, Sir Frederick. *Letters of the Empress Frederick* (Macmillan, 1929)

Porter, Ivor. *Michael of Romania* (Sutton Publishing, 2005)

Poore, Judith. *The Memoirs of Emily Loch* (Librario Publishing, 2007)

Preston, Paul. *Doves of War* (Harper Collins, 2010)

Prime, Peter. *The History of the Medical & Hospital Services of the Anglo-Boer War, 1899–1902* (Anglo-Boer War Philatelic Society, 1998)

Radu, Prince of Hohenzollern-Veringen. *Anne of Romania: A War, An Exile, A Life* (Humanitas, Bucharest, second edition, 2006)

Ramm, Agatha (ed.). *Beloved and Darling Child* (Alan Sutton, 1990)

Regolo, Luciano. *Marie-José de Savoie: La Reine de Mai* (Racine, Belgium, 2001)

Reuter, Raymond. *Marie-Astrid* (Éditions Luxnews, Luxembourg, 1982)

Scott-Ellis, Priscilla, *The Chances of Death: Diary of the Spanish Civil War*, ed. Raymond Carr (Michael Russell Publishing, 1995)

Serck-Dewaide, Myriam (ed.). *Dynastie & Photographie* (Institute Royal du Patrimoine Artistique, Brussels, 2005)

Severin, Kid & Dickson, Eva. *Drottningen, en minnesalbum* (Åhlén & Åkerlands Förlags AB, Stockholm, 1965)

Shelayev, Yuri; Shelayeva, Elizabeth & Semenov, Nicholas. *Nicholas Romanov: Life and Death* (Liki Rossi, St Petersburg, 1998)

The Martha-Mary Convent and Rule of St Elizabeth the New Martyr (Moscow, 1914. Reprinted by Holy Trinity Monastery, Jordanville, 1991)

Trevelyan, Raleigh. *Grand Dukes and Diamonds* (Secker & Warburg, 1991)

Tschebotarioff, Gregory P. *Russia, My Native Land* (McGraw-Hill, USA, 1964)

Udaltsov, M. *Belikaya Knignya Olga Aleksandrovna Romanova-Kulikovskaya* (Forum, Moscow, 2011)

Van der Kiste, John. *A Divided Kingdom* (Sutton Publishing, 2007)

Van der Kiste, John. *Kings of the Hellenes* (Alan Sutton, 1994)

Van der Kiste, John. *Princess Victoria Melita* (Alan Sutton, 1991)

Van der Kiste, John. *Queen Victoria's Children* (Alan Sutton, 1986)

Van Schaick, John, Jr. *The Little Corner Never Conquered* (Macmillan, New York, 1922)

Vickers, Hugo. *Alice, Princess Andrew of Greece* (Hamish Hamilton, 2000)

Vorres, Ian. *The Last Grand Duchess* (Hutchinson, 1964)

Vyrubova, Anna. *Memories of the Russian Court* (Macmillan, New York, 1923)

Warwick, Christopher. *Ella, Princess, Saint & Martyr* (John Wiley, 2006)

Warwick, Christopher. *George & Marina* (Weidenfeld & Nicolson, 1988)

Weber, Patrick. *Dix Princesses* (Racine, Brussels. 2002)

Wentworth Day, James. *HRH Princess Marina, Duchess of Kent* (Robert Hale, 1962)

Whiting, Audrey. *The Kents* (Hutchinson, 1985)

Wijnbeek. Phé. *Prinses Margriet: Fotoalbum* (N.V. Gebroeders Zomer & Keunings Uitgeversmaatschappij/Wageningen. 1965)

Zeepvat, Charlotte. *From Cradle to Crown* (Sutton Publishing, 2006)

Zinovieff, Elizabeth. *A Russian Life* (Y.N. Galitzine & J. Ferrand, 1997)

Zvereva, N.K., *Avgusteishie sestry miloserdiia* (Veche, Moscow. 2006)

Zwerdling, Michael, R.N., *Postcards of Nursing* (Providence Hospital, Washington D.C., 2003)

Articles

Holley, T.F. 'Bargoed Lady's Reminiscences: Princess as Nurse', *Merthyr Express* (21 January 1922) (Copy in GOSH/14/243)

Horbury, David. 'The Red Aunts', *Royalty Digest*, Vol. 8, No. 10. (1999)

Hyland, Jeffrey. 'Good Samaritans', *Majesty* (September 2005)

Kirby, Gwen. 'The Mother of Great Ormond Street', *Woman's Own* (26 July, 2 August & 9 August 1969)

Miller, Ilana D. 'A True Queen of Hearts', *The European Royal History Journal* (February 2000)

Pollock, Sabrina. 'A Mere Duchess', *The European Royal History Journal* (February 2005)

Popova, Kristina. 'Between Public Health & Social Work', *Social Work and Society International Online*, Vol. 9, No. 2. (2011.)

Tanner, Andrea. 'A Princess on the Wards', Transcript in GOSH archives, n.d.

Van Hee, Professor Robert MD, PhD. 'Antoine Depage's Relationship with Queen Elisabeth of Belgium', *Acta Chirurgica Belgica*, the official journal of the Royal Belgian Society for Surgery, No. 112 (2012), pp 170–81.

Wimbles, John, 'The Marriage of Baby Bee', *Royalty Digest*, Vol. 13, No. 8. (2004)

Wynn, Marion 'Another Royal Visitor to Harrogate: Grand Duchess George of Russia', *Royalty Digest*, Vol. 11, No. 3 (2001)

Archives

Archivo General de Palacio, Palacio Real, Madrid

Archivo Orleans-Borbón. Fundación Infantes Duques de Montpensier

Blind Veterans UK (formerly St Dunstan's)

Broadlands Archives

Great Ormond Street Hospital (GOSH)

King's College, London:
  Papers of Winifred Addison
  Royal British Nurses' Association:
    Letters of HRH Princess Arthur of Connaught
    Letters of HRH Princess Christian

Leeds Russian Archive

The Royal Archives, Windsor

The University of Southampton:
  The Mountbatten Papers, Hartley Library

Newspapers and Magazines

British Journal of Nursing
Evening Post
Farnham Herald
Harrogate Advertiser
Harrogate Herald
Majesty
Politiken
Søndags-BT
Spokesman-Review
St Dunstan's Review
The New York Times
The Times
Women at Home

Websites

www.1914-18.be
www.alexanderpalace.org
k.finkelshteyn.narod.ru
www.kvinfo.dk
www.pravaya.ru
www.reumberto.it
www.scarletfinders.co.uk
www.somerset.gov.uk
tzarskoe-selo.spb.ru

Index

The main nurses covered in the text appear in **bold** type.

Princesses on the Wards

If you enjoyed this book, you may also be interested in...

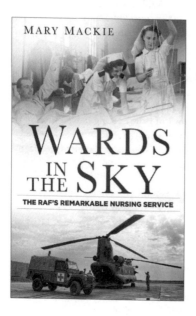

Wards in the Sky: The RAF's Remarkable Nursing Service

MARY MACKIE

978 0 7509 5956 8

This is the eventful story of the nurses who since 1918 have worn the grey-blue uniform of the RAF, from the Great War to D-Day; through the Falklands, in Bosnia and on to Afghanistan. These brave professionals dealt with snakes, malaria, desert dust and Arctic ice. Their main field of expertise is their skill for in-flight nursing, caring for very sick patients while flying back to hospitals in the UK. Over time, the caring, white-veiled 'angels' of fond memory have transformed into multi-skilled technicians, female and male, whose work has helped to advance medical knowledge and practice for all of humankind. Wards in the Sky traces their history and brings to life the drama, romance, hardship and, often, the hilarity, as told in the words of the nurses themselves.

Visit our website and discover thousands of other History Press books.

www.thehistorypress.co.uk

The History Press